Internationalisation and the Student Voice

This groundbreaking volume seeks to take the first steps in analysing the impact of internationalisation initiatives from student perspectives. As programmes are increasingly delivered overseas and we seek to offer domestic students an international experience, how do we know what works for students and what does not? Encompassing the fast-growing global imperative is a significant challenge for higher education and this collection identifies opportunities for enrichment of the learning environment, with all chapters based on direct research with students. The book provides essential reading for anyone engaged in internationalisation and wishing to learn more about the impact on students of a range of initiatives in order to apply the lessons in their own contexts. Chapters include student responses to the following learning contexts:

- 'traditional' international contexts, where students study outside their home country for shorter or longer periods;
- 'transnational' programmes where students study at home or in a neighbouring country and faculty from the awarding university fly in to deliver courses;
- domestic students studying in their home country, with staff seeking to internationalise the curriculum;
- students having transformational international experiences in other countries through service learning/volunteering, or study abroad.

Elspeth Jones is Professor of the Internationalisation of Higher Education and International Dean at Leeds Metropolitan University.

Internationalisation and the Student Voice

Higher Education Perspectives

Edited by Elspeth Jones

Routledge
Taylor & Francis Group

NEW YORK AND LONDON

First published 2010
by Routledge
270 Madison Ave, New York, NY 10016

Simultaneously published in the UK
by Routledge
2 Park Square, Milton Park, Abingdon, Oxon OX14 4RN

Routledge is an imprint of the Taylor & Francis Group, an informa business

© 2010 Taylor & Francis

Typeset in Minion by Book Now Ltd, London
Printed and bound in the United States of America on acid-free paper by
Walsworth Publishing Company, Marceline, MO

Library of Congress Cataloging-in-Publication Data
Internationalisation and the student voice: higher education perspectives /
edited by Elspeth Jones.
    p. cm.
Includes bibliographical references and index.
1. Foreign study. 2. College students—Cross-cultural studies. 3. Education, Higher—
Curricula. 4. Education and globalization. 5. Multiculturalism. I. Jones, Elspeth, 1956–
LB2375.I6 2009
378'.016—dc22
2009021333

ISBN10: 0–415–87127–1 (hbk)
ISBN10: 0–415–87128–X (pbk)
ISBN10: 0–203–86530–8 (ebk)

ISBN13: 978–0–415–87127–3 (hbk)
ISBN13: 978–0–415–87128–0 (pbk)
ISBN13: 978–0–203–86530–9 (ebk)

Contents

Illustrations

Contributors

Christine Allan is Principal Lecturer in Primary Education at Leeds Metropolitan University, with interests in literacy and internationalisation of the curriculum. Christine worked in primary schools for nineteen years as a class teacher and deputy head teacher with leadership and co-ordination roles in English, mathematics, assessment and support for special educational needs, including gifted and talented students. Christine also spent three years as a literacy consultant in a school improvement team working for a local government education authority. Her research includes effective literacy teaching and raising boys' achievement. More recent research with Jon Tan considers students' learning through international experiences.

Michaela Borg is a Research and Development Adviser at Nottingham Trent University where she works in the Centre for Academic Standards and Quality. She began her career teaching English as a Foreign Language, working in Japan, Indonesia and South Korea before returning to the UK to undertake a doctorate at the University of Leeds. Michaela has also worked at the University of Warwick and Northumbria University. Her research interests focus on cultures of learning and teaching and the experiences that people have as they join these cultures.

Douglas Bourn is Director of the Development Education Research Centre at the Institute of Education, University of London. Established in 2006, the Centre acts as the knowledge hub for research and learning about development education and related themes within higher education. Editor of the *International Journal for Development Education and Global Learning*, his most recent publications are: *Creating Global Citizens*, monograph for Plan UK; *Development Education: Debates and Dialogues* (2008). He was formerly Director of the Development Education Association and Chair of the UK Committee for Decade on Education for Sustainable Development.

Viv Caruana is Reader in Internationalisation at Leeds Metropolitan University. During her five years in education development at the University of Salford, UK, she developed research interests in the impact of the global knowledge economy and learning society on UK higher education with particular reference to internationalisation. Viv's role in education development benefited from her prior experience lecturing in Modern Economic and Social History. Her most notable contribution to the field of internationalisation is the Higher Education Academy commissioned report 'The Internationalisation of UK Higher Education: a review of selected material' co-authored with Nicola Spurling in 2007.

Valerie Clifford is Acting Head of the Oxford Centre for Staff and Learning Development at Oxford Brookes University, Director of the Centre for International Curriculum Inquiry and Networking (CICIN) and Editor of the *Brookes electronic Journal of Learning and Teaching* (BeJLT). Formerly Head of the Academic Development Unit at Monash University, Australia, Valerie worked at Monash's Malaysian and South African campuses. Before that she was Director of the Centre for the Enhancement of Learning and Teaching at the University of the South Pacific, Fiji. Her research interests include internationalisation of the curriculum and reflective practice in multi-cultural environments.

Danuta de Grosbois is an Assistant Professor in the Department of Tourism and Environment at Brock University, St Catharines, Canada. She holds two Master degrees received at Warsaw School of Economics, Poland and a Ph.D. in Management from Carleton University, Canada. Before joining Brock University she worked as an Assistant Professor at Warsaw School of Economics, Division of Decision Analysis and Support. Ms de Grosbois' research is in the area of sustainable tourism management, sustainability performance of tourism companies, and tourists' environmental behaviour.

Roberto Di Napoli is Senior Lecturer in Educational Development at Imperial College, London. He obtained his Ph.D. in Higher Education Studies at the Institute of Education, University of London. He is co-editor (with Ron Barnett) of *Changing Identities in Higher Education: Voicing Perspectives* (Routledge, 2008) and (with Loredana Polezzi and Anny King) of *Fuzzy Boundaries? Reflections on Modern Languages and the Humanities* (CILT, 2001). His academic interests include: academic identities; changing nature and scope of doctoral studies; and theory and practice of higher education. He has been a consultant for the University of Barcelona (Spain) and UNESCO, Paris.

Heather Fry is Head of Learning and Teaching for the Higher Education Funding Council for England. After teaching and lecturing in Nigeria she worked at the Institute of Education, London, and the Bart's and Royal London School of Medicine and Dentistry at Queen Mary, University of London, and became founding Head of the Centre for Educational Development at Imperial College London. She teaches, researches and publishes on academic practice in higher education. She is joint-editor of the widely used *Handbook for Teaching and Learning in Higher Education. Enhancing Academic Practice* (with Steve Ketteridge and Stephanie Marshall, third edition, 2008, Routledge).

Neil Harrison is a Senior Research Fellow in the School of Education at the University of the West of England, Bristol. His academic interests include student retention, widening participation, student volunteering and citizenship, and the experiences of international students.

Xiaoli Jiang recently gained her Ph.D. in English Language Teaching and Applied Linguistics after obtaining a Master's degree from the Centre for Applied Linguistics at the University of Warwick in 2004. Previously she worked as a lecturer in English language teaching at Bejing University of Chemical Technology for six years. Her research interests include learner autonomy, language learning strategy, and culture.

Elspeth Jones is Professor of the Internationalisation of Higher Education and International Dean at Leeds Metropolitan University, responsible for leading internationalisation across the university. She has worked for many years with students from different nationalities and cultural backgrounds, including in Japan and Singapore. Her output includes *Internationalising Higher Education* (edited with Sally Brown) (Routledge 2007) and a range of chapters and papers on values-driven internationalisation and world-wide horizons. Elspeth edits Leeds Met's daily *International Reflections* webpage, which she initiated in 2003, and is on the Editorial Advisory Board of the *Journal of Studies in International Education.*

John Kaethler developed an interest in international development and service learning by working with the Canadian University Services Overseas in Nigeria (1974–76) and Papua New Guinea (1978–80). In addition to a BA (honours) in Political Science, Brock University, and a BEd, Ontario Teacher Education College, he has a diploma in Germanistik from the Friedrich-Alexander-Universität, Erlangen, Germany. John has worked for 26 years in the Office of International Services at Brock University as its founder and director. He has developed student exchanges on six continents and has assisted in developing experience learning programs in Peru, Brazil, Ecuador and South Africa.

Betty Leask, Associate Professor, is Dean of Teaching and Learning in the Division of Business at the University of South Australia. She regularly researches, publishes and consults in the area of internationalisation in higher education, including internationalisation of the curriculum and professional development for transnational teaching. She is an elected Board member of the International Education Association of Australia (IEAA), convenor of the Internationalisation of the Curriculum Special Interest Group of the IEAA and is on the Editorial Advisory Board of the Journal of Studies in International Education. Her publications and research interests are available from her home page (http://people.unisa.edu.au/betty.leask).

Rachel Maunder is a Lecturer in Psychology at the University of Northampton, specialising in Educational Psychology. Her doctorate in Psychology from Liverpool John Moores University investigated pupil and staff perceptions of bullying in secondary schools. Rachel previously worked as Learning and

Development Adviser at the University of Warwick supporting the development of learning and teaching of academic staff. Rachel's research interests centre around group belonging, integration and socialisation in educational settings. Her focus is on people's perceptions, thoughts and feelings about their experiences.

Jane Osmond is Senior Research Assistant for the Centre of Excellence for Product and Automotive Design (CEPAD) at Coventry University, England. She was previously research assistant on a number of UK retention and equality projects, including Improving Retention, Supporting Students and Managing Equality & Diversity in Higher Education. Selected publications include Osmond, J. & Turner, A. (2008) 'Measuring the creative baseline in transport design education', in Rust, C. (ed.) *Improving Student Learning For What?*, and Osmond et al. (2007) 'Threshold concepts and spatial awareness in automotive design', in Land, R. & Meyer, J. H. F. (eds) *Threshold Concepts Within the Disciplines.*

Nicola Peacock has been working in international student support for over seven years at Bournemouth University and more recently at the University of Bath. A significant part of her remit is to lead on aspects of 'internationalisation at home', particularly the integration of diverse student groups.

Jannie Roed is Senior Lecturer in Higher Education in the Centre for the Study of Higher Education at Coventry University, England. She is programme leader of the university's Postgraduate Certificate in Higher Education Professional Practice, and coordinator of training programmes for research supervisors. Other roles include developing the university's internationalisation agenda, in particular with regard to internationalisation of the curriculum.

Mark Russell is Professor in Animal Sciences at Purdue University and has made a career designing curricula to develop leadership in others. He was Outstanding Teacher of the Midwest Section, American Society of Animal Sciences; Outstanding Teacher, School of Agriculture; member of the Great Book of Teachers of Purdue University, and Purdue Diversity Fellow. Mark develops travel and service learning courses for students, studying the impact on leadership attributes. He is current President of the Association of Leadership Educators and has travelled internationally with students in Australia, The Czech Republic, China, Ecuador, Hungary, Poland, Romania and Slovakia.

Jacqueline Stevenson is Principal Lecturer in Widening Participation at Leeds Metropolitan University. Much of Jacqueline's work has centred on issues around race, ethnicity and social class in relation to access to higher education and educational achievement. She has researched extensively with refugees and asylum seekers, members of ethnic minority communities, offenders and ex-offenders, young people leaving public care, those who are long-term unemployed, substance misusers and people who are homeless. Her research is primarily qualitative in focus and she has a particular interest in narrative research including story-telling and narrative inquiry.

Jon Tan is Senior Lecturer and Research Co-ordinator in the field of Education at Leeds Metropolitan University. Graduating from the University of York with a D.Phil. in Social Policy, his work draws from a range of disciplines including social welfare, education and critical social theory. His current research in the area of professional learning and critical reflective pedagogies interconnects work both with practitioners in urban educational contexts and with undergraduate and postgraduate teacher education students. In recent years, collaborating with co-author Christine Allan, he has conducted research focusing on student teachers' experiences of school practice placements in international settings.

Viv Thom is the International Student Education Adviser at Sheffield Hallam University. She is responsible for the management and delivery of student support for international students and for collaborative learning projects with faculties. Based in the Learner Support Team, she has longstanding experience developing inclusive and responsive strategies for students making transitions into unfamiliar learning cultures. She has worked throughout South Asia and established an international reputation for innovative approaches to internationalisation, teaching and learning in higher education. She is a member of the Higher Education Academy.

Sheila Trahar is Senior Lecturer at the University of Bristol, with research interests in Cross-Cultural Communication, Learning and Teaching in Higher Education and Methodological Complexities of Researching Across Cultures. She was academic lead on a 2008 UK Higher Education Academy Internationalisation study. Other research projects focus on Widening Participation and experiences of Black and Ethnic Minority postgraduate students. Sheila is Director of the Master of Education (M.Ed.) programme in Hong Kong and teaches on M.Ed. and Doctor of Education programmes and on the M.Phil./Ph.D. research training programme. Sheila is Secretary of the British Association for International and Comparative Education (BAICE).

Linda Vallade is responsible for the overall leadership of the College of Agriculture study abroad at Purdue University, which she has been instrumental in developing into one of the top programs on campus. Linda is a member of NAFSA and Phi Beta Delta (Honor Society for International Scholars). A member of the team awarded the College of Agriculture 2003 Agriculture Team Award, she is also a recipient of the Michael P. Malone Award through NASULGC. She has travelled to many partner institutions to better serve Purdue students and to solidify Purdue's affiliations.

Elaine Walsh is Senior Lecturer within the Graduate Schools at Imperial College, London. Elaine graduated from the University of Cambridge in Engineering Science and has an M.Sc. in Aerospace Engineering from the University of Cincinnati, Ohio. After a career as a Chartered Mechanical Engineer in both industry and academia, she joined Imperial College, firstly as a Careers Adviser. In 2004, she joined the Graduate Schools to develop and deliver many transferable skills courses for research students. Her research interests include the evaluation of transferable skills development courses and the Ph.D. experience of overseas students in the UK.

Gabriele Weber-Bosley is Director of International Programs, and Associate Professor for Foreign Languages at Bellarmine University in Louisville, KY. She designed and implemented Bellarmine's trans-curricular Baccalaureate Foreign Languages and International Studies Degree in 1998, and is founding Chair of the Foreign Language Department and founding Director of Bellarmine's International Programs Office. Gabriele studied at the University of Paderborn, Germany and the University of Louisville. Her research interests include Twentieth Century German Women's Literature, Foreign Language Acquisition, Curriculum Development, and Intercultural Education. Gabriele regularly presents at national and international conferences and serves on numerous boards and committees to international level.

John Willott, following a Ph.D. in Environmental Science, lived and worked for six years in Malaysia and Spain on international research projects, where he also developed courses and supervised undergraduate and postgraduate students. He joined Leeds Metropolitan University in 2002, and is currently Research Manager in the International Faculty, and member of the School of Applied Global Ethics. He helped establish the Access Institute, a focus for research and evaluation projects on widening participation and social inclusion. This included working with refugees, and regional and national support organisations, resulting in changes to university policy in supporting them.

Alexandra Young holds a Bachelor Degree in Tourism Studies (Honours) from Brock University and plans to continue her academic career by completing a Master's degree in tourism. In 2007 she travelled to Namibia through a Solidarity Experiences Abroad program. She has extensive experience working in the hospitality industry, as well as travelling and volunteering with a number of organizations.

Preface

Nurturing the Global Graduate for the Twenty-First Century: Learning from the Student Voice on Internationalisation

ELSPETH JONES AND VIV CARUANA

Contributions from diverse countries and contexts will engage the reader of this volume with the 'student voice' on internationalisation in higher education. The book acknowledges and learns from students' perceptions of internationalisation, and what it means for their learning experience, in order to understand how the experience of internationalisation can be enhanced for future students. Contexts include 'at home' (embracing the multicultural community as well as the multicultural classroom) and 'abroad', in the shape of study abroad, international volunteering and international placement and internship.

Whilst research on internationalisation has been conducted with students in the past, this volume is distinctive in a number of ways. The breadth of views represented includes not only conventional groupings of postgraduate, undergraduate, home and international students, but also other voices less frequently heard, such as the refugee (the 'home' international student) and the 'new' academic as learner in the field of internationalisation. In effect, this volume represents an act of 'boundary crossing' in engaging so many students of different nationalities and ethnic backgrounds in discussing a key curriculum concept designed to produce the graduate for the twenty-first century.

The Editor and principal authors have extensive experience in internationalisation with a particular interest in its impact on students. Collectively they represent a global community of practice, drawing on the diverse experiences of scholars and professionals in a variety of disciplines and fields to interpret the student voice from multiple perspectives. Whether chapters result from serendipity and opportunism or intentional and systematic research design, all are informed by a social reality that embraces complexity and multiple meanings. This produces a richness of data which cannot be adequately captured by quantitative measurement tools, such as the International Student Barometer, Intercultural Development Inventory (IDI), etc., which seem more akin to performance indicators. Having engaged with the complexity of internationalisation in different geographical, pedagogic and participative contexts, there is a surprising consensus on critical issues, the interpretation of experience, the perennial challenges and dilemmas and the key lessons to be learned from the student voice.

Part I: Student Response to Internationalisation of the Curriculum

Chapters in this part show that students see the relevance of the intercultural and global dimensions of their learning for future employability and personal growth, development and wellbeing, although civic duty is likely to be subordinate to career potential. Some authors go so far as to suggest that students regard global citizenship as a potentially elitist concept. Nonetheless, students feel they need to be informed about global issues and value meeting and talking with real people. This provides the opportunity to question, clarify, consider one's own cultural position and find common territory and understanding. Engaging at a personal level provides a welcome respite from the bombardment of potentially biased media coverage.

Another clear message is the need to appreciate that students and staff alike are learners in crossing cultural boundaries and may benefit from sharing experiences and perceptions in order to gain mutual understanding of the complexity of internationalisation and the internationalised curriculum. The key to developing cross-cultural capability at home seems to lie in providing space for reflection and support for students and staff to work together in developing the multicultural classroom as a safe environment to traverse complex cross-cultural terrain (a theme further developed by contributors to Part III). However, whilst institutions espouse the internationalised curriculum, global citizenship, cross-cultural capability and multiple perspectives for *all* students, the key determining factor in interventions remains the discipline. This is perhaps the first boundary which needs to be breached. Acknowledging that cross-cultural capability for *all* transcends the finite needs of disciplinary perspectives will enable students to develop as graduates for the globalised knowledge economy and society of the twenty-first century.

Betty Leask argues that internationalisation of the formal curriculum should be complemented by a range of 'risk free' interventions between hosts and sojourners outside the classroom, with interaction across cultures a normal part of everyday life. Her study found that students in Australia believe an internationalised curriculum should develop communication with cultural others in a global community. However, in group work, the high levels of risk associated with task failure and the limited amount of time available mean that most students will walk past 'the empty chair' next to someone from another culture and work with others more like them.

Douglas Bourn explores the concept of 'students as global citizens' and suggests better dialogue with students on how they see their role and identity in a global society. Some universities link the term 'global citizen' to the ethos of the institution. The outcome of research in two UK universities suggests a high degree of scepticism about the term unless, as is the case with one of these student cohorts, it is part of their studies. It is argued that through 'social networking' students are creating a new form of global citizenship using their own forms of dialogue, learning and action.

Viv Caruana describes research with new academics exploring their attitudes towards internationalisation and the challenge of designing the internationalised curriculum. She suggests that new academics steeped in philosophy of the scholarship of teaching and learning, schooled in reflexive practice and eager to provide the best possible student learning experience see the internationalised curriculum as a distant, objective phenomenon pursued by the institution, but struggle with the concept in the more proximate, subjective territory of their own learning and teaching practice. She recommends collective discussion between academics and students in the spirit of collaboration and insider perspectives characteristic of action research.

Jon Tan and Christine Allan's study has generated a breadth of interesting findings about the experiences of initial teacher education students on bilateral exchange programmes in France and the UK. Focusing particularly on the development of professional awareness, the most noteworthy response is students' perception of personal and professional change following the international placement and their capacity to engage critically with developments in practice. Alongside acquisition of linguistic skills, the international components of the curriculum develop cultural awareness, and provide them with a significantly different and illuminating lens through which they scrutinise and evaluate their own professional practice and culture.

Part II: The Impact of Study Abroad and International Volunteering

The student voice as articulated in Part I implies that universities should recognise students' rights to determine the nature of their individual contribution to global perspectives, and create curricula which develop independence of thought and criticality through open dialogue and debate. It may well be that those institutions willing to facilitate such a personalised student experience are those investing time, effort and resources in developing and embedding short-term international placement and volunteering schemes. The value of such initiatives lies in recognising that intercultural and international learning is transformative, based on empathetic engagement and reflection that disturbs epistemological and ontological positions, rather than supplementing an essentially western-based curriculum with international content.

In a multicultural society, the manner in which we engage with diversity at home will have a lasting impact on our and others' future lives. Chapters in this part show how short-term experiential learning programmes overseas can be as effective as longer-term assignments in developing the skills, attitudes and behaviours characteristic of cross-cultural capability. Research in 'internationalisation abroad' implies consensus and contradiction which anticipates further research with students. It is claimed that when studying at universities overseas students can assume a surface approach to their experience unless explicit and intentional interventions are in place to enable them to identify critical incidents within a framework of experiential learning. This proposition is based on the notion that heightened intentionality of consciousness or orientation of the mind to its object intentionally and consciously deepens the experience itself. Evidence from international volunteering, however, suggests that we need to carefully consider the degree to which we intervene if we are not to undermine the authenticity of experience which seems to be an equally essential component of the cross-cultural dimension of learning. There is apparent consensus in the proposition that international experience will be enhanced by a home campus curriculum catering for guided discussion and providing the space and time to reflect on cultural immersion within familiar surroundings. Authors also tend to agree that the extent of discovery and change resulting from experience abroad depends on attitudes, expectations, previous experiences, maturity and motivation.

Gabriele Weber-Bosley examines the effectiveness of a formative on-line course to aid students in the development of target culture behaviour and transformation during long-term study abroad from an American university. She focuses on student narratives, providing testimony of intercultural adjustment and transformation brought about by the general, everyday experience of cultural immersion, as well as critical, salient events, forcing students into a confrontation with cultural difference. The course which produced these narratives integrates the 'laboratory' of study abroad with the US home-campus curriculum and examines the limitations of an on-campus intercultural course versus this cultural immersion variant.

Danuta de Grosbois, John Kaethler and Alexandra Young examine the personal development of two groups of students in Canada who took part in study abroad and experiential learning programs. They consider student motivations for taking part, experiences gained and personal growth and find that students want new experiences and to see the world. Although international experiences enable students to discover more about themselves, the extent of discovery and change depends on the participant's attitude, expectations, previous experiences and maturity. The findings indicate that volunteers are motivated by a need to help others while study abroad participants seek fun and recreation.

Elspeth Jones considers international volunteering initiatives in a UK university. Students identify personal transformation through these short intensive periods of activity in learning about self, about cultural 'others' and about group empathy. It is suggested that sharing these authentic international experiences in groups could introduce an additional dimension to cross-cultural activity, enhancing internationalisation at home. The study found that, rather than widening the range of students taking part in international opportunities, we may be merely providing more opportunities for those already engaged. It is argued that volunteering programmes can be seen as a viable alternative to long-term academic exchange.

Mark Russell and Linda Vallade report on the outcomes and impacts of short-term international study and service learning at a large American Land Grant university. They argue that since more students are participating in shorter programmes there is a pressing need to determine whether the desired outcomes, such as enhanced global perspectives, are being achieved. Guided reflective journaling elicits the impact of these experiences in the students' own words. The journals illustrate the growing intercultural competence of individuals within a group of students undertaking a service learning experience in Ecuador and on a study tour of agriculture in Central Europe.

Part III: Student Learning in the Cross-Cultural Classroom

The student voice tells us that, almost instinctively, students both home and international gravitate towards like-minded individuals. However, even for students inherently disposed to crossing cultural boundaries, it is embarrassing to approach a group and ask to join in. This seems to be a powerful argument for tutors allocating individuals to multicultural groups rather than asking students to form their own. Furthermore, it seems that students hold tutors responsible for designing teaching and learning strategies which provide sufficient time to build communicative skills and relationships within groups. This need for time to develop group processes across cultural boundaries assumes tremendous significance where group work also includes group assessment. It may well be a significant factor in accounting for dichotomous responses from home and international students. Home students claim that working with international students increases motivation but reduces grade, some regard international students as hard working whilst others see them as poor attendee-contributors. International students say they like working with home students since they can offer peer support in coursework and can make learning more intellectually challenging, yet some international students think home students are lazy. Of course individuals, irrespective of cultural background, may bring their own unique and personal characteristics, experiences and behaviours to group work. However, these dichotomies reflect the tendency for assessed group learning to be driven by the frantic pursuit of product without due consideration of process. This, in itself, undermines the quality of the product in the final analysis. Clearly, group work is challenging for most students and the burden of effort added by the cross-cultural dimension in the context of 'high-stakes' group assessment may result in a negative experience which, for the participant, has little to do with enhancing cultural understanding and employability.

Domestic students generally claim to value 'international perspectives' in their learning, they are eager to 'come out of their comfort zone' and welcome the breadth of opinion and variation encountered in the multicultural classroom. Yet multicultural group work does not generally facilitate lasting friendships which is a particular issue where domestic students live at home, maintain their local friendship networks and may themselves be finding UK academic culture a challenge. Contributions in this part suggest that communication problems colour the perceived value of interaction with international counterparts. Language difficulties are compounded by other communication issues. Domestic students say they are reluctant to engage as a result of discomfort created by 'walking on eggshells', 'mindfulness', fear of 'offence using colloquialisms' and 'communication paralysis'. However, this might be interpreted as a form of 'passive xenophobia' where considerations of language mask much deeper cultural difficulties such as conflicting values.

The real challenge is to design learning strategies enabling students, regardless of ethnicity or race, to ask the 'embarrassing questions', to know they have 'permission to ask' in order to understand why we think differently and to appreciate that 'to err is good' since we all learn from our mistakes. In so much of our work with students we readily acknowledge the value of learning spaces as safe environments in which to prepare for the real world, which may seem unsympathetic, unaccommodating and even hostile. Presentation skills are a case in point, where students can be confident that in casting themselves in the role of performer they can be assured that no member of the audience will seek to gain from their faltering. Teachers provide a learning context that enables students to develop skills in the safe university environment which can then be applied in the workplace. These chapters suggest the need for dogged pursuit of this safe environment, enabling students to develop cross-cultural capability which will serve them well for the rest of their lives. This will not stop us feeling threatened at times by one another or always result in us liking each other, but it is vital that relationships develop despite differences and that tolerance replaces violence and disengagement.

Jane Osmond and Jannie Roed explore domestic and international students' views of group work and the extent to which this promotes cross-cultural understanding. They argue that while working in groups is generally accepted as an important part of students' intellectual development fostering higher-level critical thinking, it also encourages the development of employability skills such as communication and teamwork. Their findings suggest that students see working in mixed-cultural groups as a positive experience which promotes cross-cultural understanding. However, language barriers and a lack of familiarity with group work on the part of some international students can preclude better understanding.

Neil Harrison and Nicola Peacock explore the impact of internationalisation on domestic student experience. They find that many domestic students perceive a high level of risk associated with intercultural communication, combined with a significant amount of effort required to understand, be understood and not offend. Many lack the courage, motivation or skills to communicate successfully across cultures, yet are not averse to the idea in principle and not blind to the associated benefits for personal development and global employability. They also call for creative ways to approach opportunities to explore dissonance, discomfort and discussion around difference, ideally in mixed groups.

Sheila Trahar considers the extent to which academics and students are perpetuating a form of neo-colonialism by not reflecting critically on approaches to learning and teaching when working alongside people from different academic traditions. The chapter illustrates how it is possible to make adjustments to teaching in order to develop strategies that are inclusive of diversity and which are evaluated positively by students. For learning and teaching to be effective for all, the complexities of the constituency need to be considered. It is argued that complexity will not reduce, even if numbers of international students decrease through greater overseas competition.

Viv Thom notes that although international students want more contact with domestic students, most will not choose to go outside their cultural groups and this division reinforces negative perceptions. When mixing occurs, students claim they learn new ways of interacting, perform better and see value in learning from each other, and that intercultural engagement contributes to the breaking down of stereotypes. She notes the rare provision by universities of safe opportunities for genuine engagement with other academic cultures, styles and forms of knowledge and suggests universities can contribute much to this vital development if they begin with simple integrationist initiatives.

Part IV: Transnational Education and Support for International Students

Chapters in this part show how not only international but also home students possess a diverse range of culturally based educational experiences which can enrich academic culture. However, they too may find challenging the process of acculturation into a new way of working and studying. Authors suggest the importance of relationships (peers, tutors, mentors, formal, informal), common identity and shared space in successfully negotiating the dissonance and disturbance of learning in 'other' academic cultures. Represented here are the voices of students studying at the same university but on three different continents. These voices focus on the interpersonal and intercultural. They show how regionally different and seemingly contradictory responses to academic issues may register in different locations and cultural settings, reminding us not to forget the 'local' in pursuit of 'global' ambitions and endeavours.

The voice of the Ph.D. student, often marginalised in internationalisation discourse, sounds a word of caution on teaching and learning strategies which assume familiarity with the host academic culture. Acculturation is a particular challenge for Ph.D. students who, as individuals, may lack the support networks offered by cohort study at Master's level. Finally, in this part we are alerted to the need for us to be aware of our own engagement with the cultural stereotypes of 'home' versus 'international' students. The final contribution in this volume offers an unfamiliar perspective in the field of internationalisation in giving voice to the refugee as the 'home international' student – a community all too often silent amidst more audible voices of international peers who are represented in greater numbers.

Valerie Clifford introduces voices of students studying at the same university but on three different continents. The large Australian university studied has many onshore and offshore points of delivery, and had developed a packaged delivery model which was beginning to be questioned by staff. At the same time international student enrolment in Australia seemed to be declining through increased competition from west and east, prompting the university to reconsider its approach to internationalisation. Interviews with staff and students explore the meaning of an internationalised curriculum to assist the university in moving forward in this area.

Michaela Borg, Rachel Maunder, Xiaoli Jiang, Elaine Walsh, Heather Fry and Roberto Di Napoli explore issues for the increasing number of students studying for a Ph.D. outside their own countries. International students bring a diverse range of expectations and educational experiences, enhancing and enriching the academic culture in which they study. This chapter reports on relationships formed by science and engineering postgraduate research students from China and South America studying in the UK. Of high importance are relationships with supervisors, peers and more experienced others, while relationships and interaction with the wider academic community are seen as considerably less central.

Jacqueline Stevenson and John Willott note that refugees are often educated high achievers in their home countries, yet, on reaching their destination country, find it difficult to access tertiary education, or sustain their studies. Many countries consider refugees to be domestic students so support available to international students may not be routinely offered. Bereavement, trauma, separation and loss, the threat of violence, interrupted education and poverty, along with language difficulties and culture shock may require further support. Others in higher education may have similar needs but refugees often face them all in a country they do not see as home.

Future Challenges and Dilemmas

A continuing challenge for those concerned with internationalisation of the curriculum is *inspiring* and capturing the *imagination* and *curiosity* of the seemingly ethnocentric student, encouraging them to seize the opportunity of international experiences, campus engagement, or innovative pedagogy for the development of cross-cultural capability. In some ways this challenge is the outward manifestation of the paradox we encounter in all our endeavours to internationalise the student experience.

This volume shows that the value to be gained from international experiences depends on prior experience and attitudes (the very qualities which we hope students will develop through such international experiences) including openmindedness, flexibility and adaptability. In multicultural group work designed to develop skills to enable communication across cultural boundaries, students are reluctant to engage because they lack the very skills which are developed by the internationalised curriculum. In the internationalised classroom we seek to foster tolerance, understanding and develop broader global perspectives on cultural 'others', yet crossing those boundaries is time consuming, frustrating and an additional burden which – heightened in intensity by group assessment – can reduce tolerance and perpetuate negative stereotypes. In what is initially an unfamiliar but potentially alien and hostile rather than 'safe' and inviting learning environment, difference of language can become a proxy for unspoken power relationships. Students who feel marginalised by academic discourse seek to assert their superiority in cross-cultural encounters as a mechanism to ease the discomfort of working in a culture which is nationally and ethnically familiar (after all it's home!) and yet intellectually alien and unsympathetic.

We need to engage more with our students from monocultural or lower socio-economic communities who may be more conscious of their institutions' and society's need to evidence 'political correctness' within public encounters, and may lack confidence in using the kind of language which is needed to help them cross cultural boundaries. We have much to learn about internationalising the curriculum from engaging student voices, both domestic and international. There may be a parallel with those who cross cultural boundaries to establish meaningful relations in the virtual world, such as social networking and massively multi-player online role-playing games (MMORPG). Perhaps the digital world offers the potential to capture student imagination and ease the intensity and discomfort of cross-cultural encounters which some may find threatening face-to-face.

This volume also suggests the need to transcend notions of 'internationalisation at home' and 'internationalisation abroad' when designing curriculum in order to explore how what works in one context can be applied in another. For example, in the context of 'internationalisation abroad', assessment generally tends to involve reflective processes with others, yet assignments tend to be individual submissions. In seeking to 'internationalise at home' perhaps we need to rethink the tendency to assess in groups, which may heighten anxiety. Discussion of multiple perspectives through the medium of text can depersonalise interaction and lessen anxiety. Individual assessment may capture the group dynamic as a developmental process moving through progressive stages of traditional reading, through critical reading to critical literacy, with each stage encompassing, for example, greater awareness of the cultural bias of knowledge and acknowledgement of multiple perspectives. In this context we should also consider how those who have found their lives transformed by international experience can share this within peer groups and assist in providing the safe, comfortable environment which can enable cross-cultural terrain to be explored with ease and confidence.

Other challenges are rehearsed in this volume. How to re-create at home the international opportunities which provide significant gains for students, in terms of cross-cultural capability, employability and real-life skills? How to engage more students in international opportunities whilst ensuring that the learning experience of students who do not take part is not compromised? How do we know that the types of experience we offer overseas are not limiting the number of students who wish to be involved?

These issues may find solution in the application of new technologies to learning. However, we need to be aware that technology is no panacea and that the design of curricula enabling students to become global graduates in the twenty-first century will continue to be an iterative process of 'trial and error'. This can only be enhanced by proactively seeking out and listening to the student voice as it is heard in this volume.

Acknowledgements

With thanks to all contributors and, in particular, to the students whose voices are heard in this book. Thank you to Viv Caruana and David Killick for enlightening conversations and to Sally Clayton for detailed and tireless editorial work.

I

Student Response to Internationalisation of the Curriculum

1

'Beside Me Is an Empty Chair'

The Student Experience of Internationalisation

BETTY LEASK

Introduction

Internationalisation is often described as a positive force in higher education by educators and policy makers. It is seen as important in preparing graduates for participation in an increasingly globalised society, the creation of an 'open, tolerant and cosmopolitan university experience' (Kalantzis & Cope, 2000, p. 31) and the development of 'the cultural bridges and understanding necessary for world peace' (Larkins, 2008, p. 25). The internationalisation agenda in higher education is seen as one of international, national, institutional and personal significance based on reciprocal relationships and a 'flow of knowledge and cultures across national boundaries' (Slethaug, 2007, p. 5).

For some years much energy and commitment on the part of international educators the world over have focused on student mobility in the belief that bringing people from different backgrounds and cultures together on campus will result in the development of transformative cross-cultural understandings and friendships which will lead naturally to this flow of knowledge and cultures. Developments in Europe, the United Kingdom and Australia in the 1990s led to a broadening of this traditional, narrow focus on student mobility to include the internationalisation of staff and the curriculum. This was largely driven by the desire to provide the non-mobile majority of 'domestic' or 'home' students with an international education that prepares them for life in a global society. Concurrently, the worldwide movement towards the development of generic skills in universities saw some institutions, including my own, the University of South Australia (UniSA), use graduate attributes as a mechanism to redefine and reshape their approach to internationalisation of the curriculum.

In 1996, UniSA introduced a set of seven Graduate Qualities, one of which related to the development of international perspectives in all students. The intention was to broaden the focus of the internationalisation agenda to all students, utilising the cultural diversity on campus to achieve learning goals for all. However, it soon became evident in both my own and in other institutions that in spite of our best intentions there was little meaningful interaction occurring across cultures in or out of classrooms. That this has remained the case over many years is evidenced in the literature (Hanassab, 2006; Hills & Thom, 2005; Robertson et al., 2000; Volet & Ang, 1998).

Against this background this chapter describes research to investigate international and domestic student experiences of internationalisation and interventions taken to improve these through facilitating interaction between international and domestic students. This is part of a story which is incomplete. The interventions have been implemented over ten years and some are described in more detail in other places. They were implemented from 2000 to 2008 as part of a broader internationalisation strategy, their impact regularly evaluated and adjustments made in response. Much has been learned and the need for further learning has been identified. This chapter shares those that relate to the student experience of internationalisation.

An Institutional Approach

UniSA has a total enrolment of around 33,000 students and one in four on campus is an international student with 95 countries represented. Domestic students are also culturally diverse. A focus on intercultural learning through engagement across cultures as a key component of internationalisation is evident in the university's mission statement, goals and plans, key policies and codes (Leask, 2001). A number of these policy statements' supporting documents focus on student and staff engagement with cultural diversity on campus. For example, Graduate Quality #7 (GQ7), one of the seven graduate attributes introduced in 1996 across all undergraduate programmes, has a specific focus on the development of international perspectives (Leask, 2001). It states that 'graduates of the University of South Australia will demonstrate international perspectives as professionals and as citizens' and nine generic indicators are provided to academic staff as a guide to what this graduate quality means for student capabilities.[1] While the specific skills required in different professions may be quite different, the generic indicators focus not only on the acquisition of skills and knowledge related to professional areas, but also on the development of values and cross-cultural awareness through intercultural learning and engagement. Support materials provided to academic staff responsible for embedding the development of GQ7 into their curricula emphasise strategies to create classroom learning environments that encourage and reward intercultural engagement between international and domestic students in very specific ways. They provide staff with ways to facilitate active engagement with the diversity of cultures existing within their classrooms, recognizing that while cultural diversity within the student body is a valuable resource for internationalisation of the curriculum, much work is needed in order for the benefit to be realized.

From 2000 to 2003 this focus on the concern of internationalisation of the formal curriculum, as much with teaching and learning processes as with content, was complemented by the introduction of a range of interventions to influence the quality and quantity of contact between hosts (domestic students and staff)

Table 1.1 Agreement Rates of International Students for Student Experience Questionnaire 'University Life', 2002 and 2004

	Agreement Rate (%)	
SEQ Item	2002	2004
I am happy with the level of interaction I have with other students	52	62
I feel I am part of the UniSA community	40	51

and sojourners (international students) *outside* the classroom. A framework designed to develop a campus environment and culture which motivated and rewarded interaction across cultures for all students outside as well as inside class was developed in 2000 and a number of strategies to facilitate interaction were introduced in a planned and systematic way from 2000 to 2003 (Leask, 2003). The university community was involved in the development and implementation of strategies within this framework with a goal to improve the quality of the student experience of internationalisation and in particular to improve the levels of interaction and engagement between international and domestic students.

The effectiveness of interventions was evaluated directly and indirectly. Participants in individual activities completed 'end-of-session' questionnaires and facilitators of various activities met regularly to discuss these and other data such as participation levels and observations of student interactions. The entire suite of activities was evaluated using the institution-wide Student Experience Questionnaire (SEQ) (University of South Australia, 2006). There was some encouraging movement in these items from international students across the institution from 2002 to 2004 (see Table 1.1).

Given the increase in agreement rates, there was a degree of comfort at an institutional level that we were on the right track, although we would have preferred much higher levels of agreement. We also recognized the difficulty of establishing any direct link between the strategies implemented and the movement in these agreement rates. The need for further research was clear.

In 2004, as part of a doctoral research project, I conducted a number of focus group interviews with a small number of domestic and international students. These explored student expectations and experiences of a business curriculum with a stated aim of developing international perspectives. In total 16 students were involved in the focus group discussions; nine were international students (four of these were based in Hong Kong and five were international students studying in Australia) and seven were domestic students in Australia. The focus groups were small enough to allow in-depth exploration of issues to capture different cultural perspectives, shared and divergent interpretations and subjective views of the lived experience of internationalisation, a complex issue situated within overlapping personal, institutional and cultural situations. Sections of the transcriptions of the interviews were analysed using an approach to critical discourse analysis (CDA) informed by the work of Fairclough (1992, 1995) and Foucault (1972, 1981). This revealed much about the students' lived experience of internationalisation.

The Lived Experience of Internationalisation

In contrast to the SEQ which was administered to the entire onshore student population, the 2004 focus groups were conducted with students from one faculty studying both onshore and offshore. Participants in the research were all actively involved in business programmes taught in Adelaide and Hong Kong. The methodology enabled the exploration of multiple perspectives on the student experience of internationalisation. Focus group and one-to-one interviews were used to capture and investigate the different cultural perspectives, shared and divergent interpretations and subjective views of students working in different cultural and physical environments within a common internationalised curriculum.

The focus groups were conducted eight years after the introduction of the Graduate Qualities and involved students and staff who were actively engaged in courses within a programme with a significant emphasis on the development of Graduate Quality 7.

How Do Students Conceptualise International Perspectives?

Both domestic and international students in this study saw international perspectives as being primarily concerned with understanding and appreciating other cultures and the related ability of communicating effectively with people from other cultures. They thought that people who had international perspectives would have certain mindsets or 'ways of thinking' as well as certain 'ways of doing'. International perspectives were personal in nature but also important for success in the business world. They had a certain instrumental value and relevance for their future life as professionals as well as being important to their personal development and well-being.

Three dominant themes emerged, 'understanding the world out there', 'respect for cultural difference' and 'the ability to work effectively across cultures'.

1. *Understanding the world out there.* The importance of understanding other countries, cultures and people in order to make informed decisions as members of a global community, was a recurring theme. There was a strong sense that the world is getting smaller due to the effects of globalisation and no matter where you live you need to be conscious of and informed about global issues and perspectives. On a professional level this was seen to require an understanding of how business is done differently in different places, but like the policy makers, students also saw it as being important on a much higher level. They too recognised the importance of education in assisting individuals to overcome their fear of culturally different others. However, on a personal level international perspectives were not just about understanding others – they were also about understanding your own culture

better: '[i]t means having an understanding and appreciation of other cultures and your own' (Andrew). A number were concerned that they were not able to gain the knowledge and understanding they needed to develop balanced international perspectives from the media and they therefore saw the exposure to a range of cultural and national perspectives as an important aspect of their university education.

2. *Openness and respect for cultural difference.* The personal, attitudinal aspect of the development of international perspectives was seen as important by all students. Increased self-awareness, resulting in the acceptance of cultural difference at a personal level, the potential to continue to grow and learn throughout life and particular attitudes such as openness to and respect for the views of others emerged as important. These things are closely related and intertwined, intensely personal and concerned with attitudes and ways of thinking as well as ways of doing.

> 'I think it's more about somebody who is willing to look out and receive what opinions others have. Because to make our own ideas or to give our own perspective to something is quite easy, but when we come, when you deal with something international, there's always so many issues involved … I think it depends on the individual … how you feel, how you're going to open up to somebody.'
> (Siva)

Personal growth and being able to learn and develop beyond graduation was identified as an important part of developing international perspectives, what was learned at university being important but just 'the tip of the iceberg'.

3. *Working effectively across cultures.* The ability to communicate across cultures in order to 'do business' and work effectively, knowing what to expect and how to respond appropriately in different situations, was seen as an important aspect of international perspectives, particularly by domestic (Australian) students. They linked internationalisation to globalisation and its impact on the business world with the need for building and maintaining constructive relationships with people from other cultures and nations. They believed internationalisation of the curriculum should provide them with the opportunity to develop those abilities.

These three themes are inter-related rather than separate and disconnected. Understanding the world beyond our own national borders and openness and respect for cultural difference are in large measure enablers of working effectively across cultures. International perspectives are complex and multi-faceted. Their development is a life-long process involving the development of knowledge and understandings, attitudes and values, and ways of thinking and doing that enable effective communication with cultural others in a dynamic global community.

Students believed their university education had an important role to play in this process even though international perspectives were identified as being concerned not only with the development of their 'knowledge of other' but also with the development of their 'knowledge of self' – with their personal feelings, attitudes, values and self awareness. This suggests a level of emotional as well as intellectual engagement with the university experience that is difficult to achieve but an essential element of intercultural learning (De Vita, 2005, p. 76).

The Importance of Experience

There were some interesting contrasts between the views or the different groups of students involved in this study. As indicated earlier, students interviewed were (1) domestic Australian students (DS) studying in Australia, (2) international students (IS) studying business degrees in Hong Kong and (3) students studying business degrees in Australia. This third group were in many ways 'cultural outsiders' far away from home and the personal rather than the professional dimension of international perspectives was the primary concern. Meeting with and learning from people from different cultures was one decision-making factor for them in studying overseas: '[t]hat's why I came here, because international, to mix with different people' (Mei-Li, IS); '[h]ere I can meet with any foreigners, Aussies and the UN from Europe and maybe Americans' (Ting-Hwa, IS).

Their experiences were not all positive though and some, in the same focus group, had obviously found it easier than others: 'Sometimes it is a bit hard for us to mix with the Aussie. Yeah, like they just stick together with their own students' (Mei-Li, IS).

More specifically, in relation to mixing in tutorial classes one student reflects on the empty chair beside her and wonders why Australian students will not sit with her:

'For example, in tutorial class, you know. Like, okay, beside me it's empty chair, but this girl she, I remember, like, I was like smiled at her, then she just walking back and she sit at the back at the end of the class … why didn't you just like sit here.'

(Aziz, IS)

Some speculation on the reasons for these empty chairs followed, with an awareness of various factors likely to impact on cross-cultural engagement in class.

'I feel that is just because there is a communication problem, so sometimes Aussies tend to stick with other Aussies, because it helps them communicate better when they're doing their own assignments and work, because sometimes students are competitive. I find that they are competitive and they want to do work quickly, so they don't want this kind of small problems coming in the way, and they want to get things done quickly. I feel it's normal, because I guess I would do the same if I was back in Malaysia, and I would stick to people whom I can communicate well with, rather than you know, trying to mix around. Unless I want to get to know international students and to understand them better, then I would make an effort.'

(Gupta, IS)

'Maybe … white people, like Aussie, they like to be alone. They prefer to work alone, as compared with Asian cultures, I guess.'

(Aziz, IS)

Domestic students recognised the value of interaction for the development of GQ7 'international perspectives': 'International students who are able to be communicated with provide the best means of developing this graduate quality' (Andrew, DS). However, they were concerned that communication problems could create unnecessary problems, the same student commenting that 'in cases where they (international students) cannot communicate in English it is useless and they can create a burden to team work'. Thus the stakes were just too high when the assessment task could be more easily completed with other domestic students.

Domestic students also highlighted the important role of the tutor in ensuring that international students were heard in class. For example: 'It seems that if tutors don't specifically and continually ask international students to participate in conversations and offer their knowledge it is not shared' (Mariana, DS).

The complexities of working across cultures in class, a number of barriers to it happening and the effort required to overcome these barriers, emerged from this data. Barriers included perceptions of the English language competence of international students, high levels of risk associated with task failure, the limited amount of time available in class to build the communicative skills required to produce a high-quality outcome and the substantial effort required to work across cultural and linguistic borders. Collectively these things result in domestic students, when given the choice, walking past the empty chair next to someone from another culture and moving on to work with those who are more like them.

The international perspectives described by these students as the outcomes of an international education require meaningful, deep levels of intercultural communication and engagement. This puts the student experience at the heart of an international education that seeks to develop students' ability to live and work effectively with cultural others in a dynamic global community. While international students in Australia believed that a key feature of an international education should be engagement in meaningful cross-cultural interactions with Australian as well as other international students, this was rarely their lived experience. Similarly, Australian students could see the potential value of interactions with international students but identified many barriers that collectively resulted in this potential not being realised. The Hong Kong students believed that, were they studying in Australia, they would benefit greatly from interacting with Australian students and other international students from all over the world. In summary, all students recognised the value of engagement with cultural diversity but for entirely different reasons were dissatisfied with the levels and types of interaction they had with each other.

The students involved in this study represent a small sample of the total student population. The analysis of the focus group data confirmed the findings of the literature cited earlier (as well as Harrison & Peacock, this volume) concerning the lack of interaction between international and domestic students on campus and some possible causes.

A Response at Faculty Level

The 2004 study prompted a response at faculty level. Some changes to the way in which student services were delivered to business students were implemented in 2006, 2007 and 2008. The changes aimed to internationalise the lived experience of campus life for the majority of first-year and some later-year students through direct, localised intervention. Within relatively risk-free contexts, structured and unstructured opportunities to develop both domestic and international students' intercultural confidence and competence were provided. The intention was to internationalise campus culture by moving more students towards an experience enriched by cultural diversity.

The interventions were designed to make interacting across cultures a normal part of the everyday life of a first-year student in business. Recognising that communicating and interacting with culturally different others is intense and the risks associated with failure may well outweigh the possible benefits, we sought to reduce the risks. We focused on the first year because of the critical role of peer engagement in the first year in creating a sense of belonging in the university community and trend data collected from 1999 to 2004 indicating that first-year students are less likely to engage with their peers than later-year students (Krause, 2005, p. 6).

The First-Year Experience Project in Business

In response to the data presented above, in the planning stages of the first-year experience project, strategies that would require interaction between international and domestic students in low-risk situations were included in the project plan. We also decided to measure the effectiveness of these strategies through evaluation questions asking directly about the extent to which students believed their involvement had contributed to the development of their intercultural skills and understandings.

Within the informal curriculum, a mentoring scheme 'Business Mates' was designed primarily to improve the quality of the first-year experience. Mentors were international and domestic students in their second or subsequent year of study at UniSA. The programme included the usual aims such as assisting commencing students with the transition to the social and academic culture of the university, facilitating interaction between students through social and learning networks, providing a reliable and accessible support network for commencing students and providing continuing students with the opportunity to develop leadership, communication, organisation and team work skills. However, an additional aim was included: 'Encouraging interaction between international and domestic students in particular.'

The decision to specifically incorporate an additional intercultural dimension into the project made it different from other first-year experience projects at the university. Indeed, in another faculty, a similar programme was implemented at the same time without focusing on interactions between domestic and international students, providing a useful benchmark for evaluating the effectiveness of the Business Mates programme in enhancing the student experience of internationalisation. To assist the achievement of this 'intercultural interaction aim' international and domestic student mentors were paired. Each pair of mentors was allocated a group of 40 first-year international and domestic students. The training session for mentors included an extended session on cross-cultural communication, and mentors were reminded of the importance of both modelling and encouraging interaction between international and domestic students in the context of the university's focus on the development of graduate qualities, and in particular GQ7 'international perspectives'.

At the conclusion of the first year of the programme, mentors and mentees were asked to indicate to what extent they believed the extra-curricular activities they had been involved in had assisted them to develop their international perspectives and the impact on their experiences as students. Evaluation included three statements taken from the university-wide SEQ discussed above.

1. I am happy with the level of interaction I have with other students.
2. I feel I am part of the UniSA community.
3. I feel the UniSA community values diversity.

This enabled a comparison between the satisfaction levels of the general student population with those of the mentors and mentees.

The results for mentors and mentees of 2008 were compared with those of the general student population as indicated in the SEQ 2006 (Table 1.2). This is not an exact comparative measure, but does provide an indication of the impact of the paired mentoring programme.

Table 1.2 Agreement Levels of Mentors and Mentees, 2008, and the General Student Population, 2006 (All Students in the Division of Business)

	Level of Agreement (%)						
	Mentors			Mentees			
SEQ Statement	Int.	Dom.	All	Int.	Dom.	All	General Student Population
I am happy with the level of interaction I have with other students	78	68	72	72	64	66	58
I feel I am part of the UniSA community	100	92	95	64	61	62	42
I feel the UniSA community values diversity	94	88	91	73	79	77	71

In drawing conclusions it is important to recognise that the mentors are a small cohort of students who could be perceived as already being more engaged with the university as they have chosen to become involved in the student mentoring role. However, the data suggests that:

- International student mentees are happier with the levels of interaction they have with other students, feel more a part of the community and are more likely to feel part of the university community than the general student population of 2006.
- Most mentors and mentees are more satisfied with the levels of interaction they have with other students than the general student population of 2006. The exception is the domestic student mentees.
- International student mentors and mentees are slightly more satisfied than domestic students with their levels of interaction with other students.
- Both international and domestic mentors and mentees felt more a part of the university community than the general student population did in 2006.
- Mentors felt much more a part of the university community than both mentees and the general student population in 2006.
- Mentees feel more a part of the university community than the general student population in 2006.
- Both mentors and mentees in 2008 are more likely to perceive the university as valuing cultural diversity than the general student population in 2006.
- Mentors are much more likely than mentees and the general student population in business in 2006 to perceive the university as valuing cultural diversity.
- International student mentors are more likely to agree with all three statements than domestic student mentors.

In summary, the paired mentoring programme has had a more dramatic positive impact on the experiences of the international student participants (both mentors and mentees) than on the experiences of the domestic student participants. This finding is perhaps not surprising. The programme was in part set up to overcome some of the barriers to cross-cultural interaction, including the more negative attitudes of domestic students to interaction with international students (Summers & Volet, 2008, p. 365). The data reported above does not tell us, however, whether the programme is facilitating greater interactions between domestic and international students or within the international student cohort. Thus while it appears that all students have benefited to some degree, it is not clear to what extent it will assist in 'filling the empty chairs'.

Mentors and mentees were also asked to indicate to what extent they agreed with the following statements *as a result of their involvement in the mentoring programme.* These measure their predisposition to working across cultures in the future as a result of their experiences in the Business Mates programme.

Table 1.3 Predisposition of Mentors and Mentees Towards Working in Cross-Cultural Groups

| | *Level of Agreement (%)* | | | | | |
| | *Mentors* | | | *Mentees* | | |
Statement	*Int.*	*Dom.*	*All*	*Int.*	*Dom.*	*All*
I am more likely to choose to work in class with people from a different cultural background to my own	50	68	60	76	24	40
I am more likely to socialise with people from a different cultural background to my own	50	68	60	78	27	43

1. I am more likely to choose to work in class with people from a different cultural background to my own.
2. I am more likely to socialise with people from a different cultural background to my own.

The responses from mentors and mentees are summarised in Table 1.3. It is evident that:

• The most dramatic impact on predisposition towards working in cross-cultural groups in future was on international student mentees. This may have been because the programme gave them the confidence to make connections with people from other cultures. As first-year undergraduates in a new cultural and educational environment this programme was particularly useful.

• The least dramatic impact on future behaviour was on domestic student mentees. It is important to remember that all mentees are first-year undergraduate students, for whom the early experiences at university 'are particularly important for their development of the necessary skills and willingness to engage in group work with people of other cultures' (Summers & Volet, 2008, p. 366). Clearly the impact on domestic student mentees' future behaviour was not as great as for international students; however, the fact that 24 per cent of those involved in the programme indicated that they would be more likely to choose to work with people from another culture in class is somewhat encouraging. And while we don't know what their predisposition was prior to their involvement in the programme, other research in the area suggests that it would have been low (Summers & Volet, 2008; Volet & Ang, 1998).

• The impact on the future behaviour of domestic student mentors was more positive than the impact on the first-year domestic student mentees (where 'positive' is defined in terms of being more predisposed to work and socialise with people from other cultures). This suggests it is possible and necessary to design interventions to engage domestic students with international students at all levels of study. This does not deny the importance of the first year, but rather indicates the need to reinforce the interventions with follow-up activities and opportunities in later years of study.

- The impact on the likely future behaviour of domestic student mentors was more marked than on the future behaviour of international student mentors. This could be because international students were more inclined towards this behaviour prior to participation in the programme. This finding does, however, support the conclusion above that we need to continue to focus on interventions to improve intercultural engagement at all levels of study.

Mentors in both the paired and unpaired mentor scheme were also asked to indicate to what extent their participation in the programme had assisted them to develop the seven UniSA Graduate Qualities including Graduate Quality #7, 'demonstrates international perspectives as a professional and as a citizen'. The paired mentors believed that they were much more likely to develop GQ7 'international perspectives' than the unpaired mentors (see Figure 1.1). They also believed that they were more likely to have developed GQ6, effective communication, and GQ4, working autonomously and collaboratively, than the unpaired mentors (Figure 1.1). These three Graduate Qualities are related and to some extent overlapping. Cross-cultural communication skills are associated with GQ6 and assist the development of GQ7. The paired mentors were required to work collaboratively in mixed-culture groups with mixed-culture groups of mentees, which clearly connected their experience in the programme with the development of skills required to work collaboratively across cultures and with the development of international perspectives.

This data indicates it is possible to support the work of the formal curriculum through interventions outside the classroom and that a fairly minor modification to the objectives and structure of a programme can change the outcomes significantly.

Future Research

This research has highlighted the difficulty we face in seeking to encourage domestic students to be more open to working across cultures in and out of class. They are clearly the group most resistant to having an international experience at home, yet they have potentially the most to gain. Further research into how we can more effectively engage domestic students with cultural diversity in class and on campus across the entire length of their programme of study is needed.

Conclusion

It is the extent and depth of the level of engagement with other cultural perspectives as a normal part of life at university which defines the student

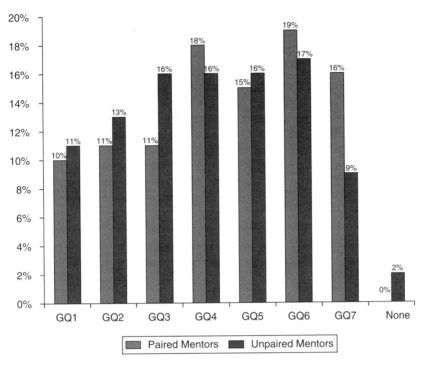

Figure 1.1 Graduate Qualities Developed by Paired and Unpaired Mentors

experience of internationalisation. However, while students may appreciate that developing their understanding of 'the world out there', openness and respect for other cultures and the ability to work effectively across cultures are important and desirable outcomes of their university education, they will not necessarily embrace every opportunity they are given to develop these understandings and skills. Strategic and carefully planned interventions over time are required if we are to 'fill the empty chairs' in our international classrooms.

Cultural diversity on campus has for many years been viewed as an important and positive aspect of internationalisation providing many valuable opportunities for students to engage positively with cultural others and develop wide-ranging international and intercultural knowledge and skills of value to individuals, nations and the world. However, even when institutional strategies are developed that support interaction, students do not necessarily engage meaningfully across cultures on campus or in class. Institutional approaches can provide valuable frameworks but they are likely to have limited impact on the student experience of internationalisation unless carefully planned strategies support their implementation.

Seemingly small local decisions can have a significant impact on the student experience of internationalisation. The everyday reality of life for university students is likely to comprise a range of formal and informal interactions with other students and staff. Many of these can be affected by small decisions about the structure and focus of activities at the local level. This study showed that the decision to require that students work in culturally diverse pairs and groups, and the provision of training and support to assist them to do this effectively, had a positive impact on the experience of internationalisation for both international and domestic students, although the impact was variable across different groups of students. The study also showed the importance of monitoring, at both institutional and programme level, the effectiveness of any interventions designed to change the student experience.

In summary, multiple responses on various levels in an institution and constant monitoring of the effectiveness of strategic interventions inside and outside the classroom are necessary if we are to ensure that the empty chairs are filled in ways that enrich all students' experiences of internationalisation.

Note

1 More information on the Graduate Qualities at UniSA is available from http://www. unisanet.unisa.edu.au/gradquals/default.asp

References

Carroll, J., & Ryan, J. (Eds.). (2005). *Teaching international students: Improving learning for all.* London: Routledge.

De Vita, G. (2005). Fostering intercultural learning through multicultural group work. In Carroll & Ryan (2005).

Fairclough, N. (1992). *Discourse and social change.* Cambridge, UK: Polity Press.

Fairclough, N. (1995). *Critical discourse analysis: A critical study of language.* New York: Longman.

Foucault, M. (1972). *The archaeology of knowledge.* London: Routledge.

Foucault, M. (1981). *The history of sexuality,* Vol. 1: *An introduction* (R. Hurley, Trans.). Harmondsworth, UK: Penguin.

Hanassab, S. (2006). Diversity, international students, and perceived discrimination: Implications for educators and counselors. *Journal of Studies in International Education, 10*(2), 157–172.

Hills, S., & Thom, V. (2005). Crossing a multicultural divide: Teaching business strategy to students from culturally mixed backgrounds. *Journal of Studies in International Education, 9*(4), 316–336.

Kalantzis, M. & Cope, B. (2000). Towards an inclusive and international higher education. In R. King, D. Hill & B. Hemmings (Eds.), *University and diversity: Changing perspectives, policies and practices in Australia* (pp. 30–53). Wagga Wagga: Keon Pubications.

Krause, K. L. (2005). *Understanding and promoting student engagement in university learning communities.* Centre for the Study of Higher Education, University of Melbourne, Australia.

Larkins, R. (2008). Higher education supplement. *The Australian,* 23 April, p. 25.

Leask, B. (2001). Bridging the gap: Internationalising university curricula. *Journal of Studies in International Education, 5*(2), 100–115.

Leask, B. (2003). Venturing into the unknown – a framework and strategies to assist international and Australian students to learn from each other. In C. Bond & P. Bright (Eds.), *Research and development in higher education,* Vol. 26: *Learning for an unknown future* (pp. 380–387). Christchurch, New Zealand: HERDSA.

Robertson, M., Lane, M., Jones, S., & Thomas, S. (2000). International students, learning environments and perceptions: A case study using the Delphi technique. *Higher Education Research and Development, 19*(1), 89–102.

Slethaug, G. (2007). *Teaching abroad: International education and the cross-cultural classroom.* Hong Kong: Hong Kong University Press.

Summers, M., & Volet, S. E. (2008). Students' attitudes towards culturally mixed groups on international campuses: Impact of participation in diverse and non-diverse groups. *Studies in Higher Education, 33*(4), 357–370.

University of South Australia (2006). *Student experience questionnaire*, University of South Australia, South Australia. Available from: http://www.unisa.edu.au/unisareport/ [Accessed August 2008].

Volet, S. E., & Ang, G. (1998). Culturally mixed groups on international campuses: An opportunity for inter-cultural learning. *Higher Education Research and Development, 17*(1), 5–23.

2
Students as Global Citizens

DOUGLAS BOURN

Introduction

Students today live in a global society – a society where they cannot ignore global interdependence and global inequalities. How are today's students going to understand and to respond to the freedoms, problems and responsibilities they are inheriting? How are today's students going to find their individual roles in a global society? And where do they start?

> Awareness of the world has heightened the curiosity of students about their role in a global society. They travel across the world, absorb news from across the world and communicate with people from across the world. Unless students find themselves roles to play, there is a risk of disenfranchisement or of disillusionment: that they are aware of global issues but do nothing about them.
>
> (Lamb, Roberts, Kentish & Bennett, 2007)

This statement is taken from a paper by representatives of three student-led organisations for discussion with voluntary organisations, policy-makers and practitioners in education. Entitled 'Students as Active Global Citizens', it aimed to demonstrate that whilst students are increasingly interested in engaging with global issues, frameworks in which this is undertaken need to recognise their right to determine the nature of their own contribution rather than merely responding to proposals from both within universities and outside (Lamb et al., 2007).

This chapter addresses the ways in which, using the rhetoric of global citizenship, universities are responding to student interest. It aims, by reviewing dialogue with students at two colleges in London, to locate how student perceptions of global citizenship compare with the agendas of policy-makers and universities. Finally it compares perceptions of the concept of students as global citizens, including issues of identity and social mobility, responses to globalisation, learning and understanding about the wider world, and forms of social activism.

Policy Support for Global Citizenship

'Being a global citizen' has become part of the rhetoric of policy-makers, non-governmental organisations (NGOs) and social commentators in recent years. UK policy-making bodies have begun to use the term in response to the government drive on citizenship and social engagement, but also because of interest in sustainable development and globalisation (DfES, 2004, 2005). Within higher education, 'being a global citizen' is referred to by the Higher Education Funding Council England (HEFCE, 2005) and the United Kingdom's Higher Education Academy (2007) in strategies on sustainable development and internationalisation. The Academy, for example, aims to encourage 'curriculum development' that would 'prepare all graduates, regardless of country of origin, to be informed, responsible citizens able to work effectively in a global, multicultural context' (Higher Education Academy, 2007).

The same term has emerged from the UK government's international development ministry (Department for International Development) in promoting and supporting development education and international development (DFID, 2007). It has also come to be seen as a way of binding communities together in terms of bigger social goals. The then UK Minister for Higher Education stated at a conference on global skills in 2008 that global citizenship is key to social cohesion:

> To deliver to its full potential, education and training has to develop citizenship, not just of Britain but in Europe and indeed of the world as a whole. It is at the heart of the benefits, not only for your learners and employers, but for the communities that you serve.
>
> (Bill Rammell, Global Skills Conference, London 2008)

In promoting a programme for international mobility for young people, the British Council stated that 'it matters for Britain that today's generation of young people grow up understanding first-hand what globalisation means for people and are confident to make the most of the opportunities of the twenty first century' (British Council, 2008). The former British Prime Minister, Tony Blair, in an address to students at Yale University in 2008, stated that globalisation is driving the modern world:

> The issues you [Yale students] must wrestle with – the threat of climate change, food scarcity, and population growth, worldwide terror based on religion, the interdependence of the world economy – my student generation would barely recognise. But the difference today is they are all essentially global in nature. You understand this. . . . You are the global generation. So be global citizens.
>
> (Blair, 2008)

Academic Discourse on Global Citizenship

The rhetoric around global citizenship has begun to be addressed in the United Kingdom within academic debates around citizenship, political and social engagement and moral responsibility. As April Carter has stated, 'the idea of world citizenship is fashionable again' (Carter, 2001). The debate within academia has tended to summarise the various approaches to global citizenship as a form of global social activism, a revival of interest in global governance, a recognition of social mobility and complex cultural identities, a response to globalisation or more instrumentally within education as addressing inclusion of citizenship within the curriculum (Carter, 2001; Cogan & Derricott, 2000; Heater, 2002; Mayo, 2005; Osler & Starkey, 2005).

The emergence of a discourse around global citizenship can be seen in both the USA (Schattle, 2008) and Canada (Abdi & Shultz, 2008) alongside debates linked to policy and practice in Australia (Stokes, Pitty & Smith, 2008) and Japan (Chan, 2008). As Schattle has stated there is evidence of interest from around the world. He notes from interviews with a range of people that key to their meaning of global citizenship is 'face-to-face interaction among cultures in everyday life' (Schattle, p. 160).

Within the United Kingdom, probably the leading academic writer on global citizenship over the past decade has been Nigel Dower. His approach is from an ethical and moral perspective with an emphasis on social responsibility. He breaks down the status of being a global citizen to three elements: normative (about how humans should act); existential (relationship to the world); and aspirational (role in the future) (Dower, 2003).

The Economic and Social Research Council (ESRC)'s booklet *From Local to Global* (Gaventa & Rootes, 2007) notes that citizens, both individually and collectively, respond to calls for support for global causes. Gaventa states, 'as citizens do engage in transnational forms of action, new identities as global citizens begin to emerge'. However, his colleague in the report, Christopher Rootes, notes that despite advances in communication and increased public engagement in initiatives such as Make Poverty History, building organisations and networks on a global scale is difficult. Rootes suggests that in the absence of a global state, it is premature to speak of global citizenship.

> Rather than risk a backlash by people who fear an influx if people from the South exercise their rights as 'global citizens', we would be better to emphasise our common humanity and embrace collective action to tackle global problems at their roots.
>
> (Gaventa & Rootes, 2007)

Such discourse has influenced a number of bodies in responding to growing public interest in the wider world. In the United Kingdom and in education, probably the most influential has been Oxfam, the NGO for development and aid, which first began using the term 'global citizen' in the late 1990s as a deliberate precursor to the inclusion of citizenship in the school curriculum. Oxfam is recognised as one of the leading NGOs in the United Kingdom providing resources and support to teachers in promoting understanding of global and development issues within schools.

Oxfam sees the global citizen as someone who:

- is aware of the wider world and has a sense of their own role as a world citizen;
- respects and values diversity;
- has an understanding of how the world works;
- is outraged by social injustice;
- participates in the community at a range of levels, from the local to the global;
- is willing to act to make the world a more equitable and sustainable place;
- takes responsibility for their actions.

(Oxfam, 2006)

Whilst this definition has had considerable impact in UK compulsory education, it has been less influential within higher education or elsewhere in the world. Bournemouth University has been one of the few in the United Kingdom to make reference to Oxfam's definition in their programme on global perspectives (Shiel, 2006).

Critics of the term 'global citizenship' suggest it is elitist, not grounded in realities of political systems and makes assumptions, usually by people in the North on behalf of the rest of the world, about best forms of global social change (Dobson & Valencia, 2005). Carter (2001) suggests the term is seen more as a way of opening up dialogue and debate and as a spectrum of theories and interpretations as the basis for constructive discourse. Andreotti (2007) makes a distinction between 'soft' or passive global citizenship versus a 'hard' or more active form linked to notions of social justice and critical thinking. This range of interpretations and approaches offers a context for analysing what 'being a global citizen' means within higher education institutions.

Globalisation, Internationalisation and Students as Global Citizens

'Global citizenship' has emerged from the discourse on internationalisation in the UK. It has been linked to pedagogical principles to develop and empower students as critical beings, to see the relevance of global issues to their own lives and demonstrate the relationship between local actions and global consequences (Caruana & Spurling, 2007; Killick, 2006; Lunn, 2006; Shiel, 2006).

Universities such as Bournemouth, Leeds Metropolitan, Leicester and University College London (UCL), are questioning the nature of the courses they offer and the extent to which they are inclusive to students from around the world in order to promote their institutions as developing global citizenship (Killick, 2006; Shiel, 2006). At Bournemouth, 'global perspective' frames their international strategy. They see this as broadening the curriculum and including pedagogic approaches that support students to develop as critical beings, able to challenge orthodoxy and bring about change (Shiel, 2006, 2007).

UCL talks about graduates who are:

• Critical and creative thinkers.
• Ambitious – but also idealistic and committed to ethical behaviour.
• Aware of the intellectual and social value of culture difference.
• Entrepreneurs with the ability to innovate.
• Willing to assume leadership roles: in the family, the community and the workplace.
• Highly employable and ready to embrace professional mobility.

(UCL, 2007)

However, debates on 'global citizenship' within universities, whether in the United Kingdom, North America, Australia or the Far East, cannot be divorced from wider issues of market forces, the cosmopolitan nature of the student body, external social and political factors and the preparation of graduates for working in a global economy. In the USA, Stearns (2009) refers to global citizenship as a way in which universities can positively and proactively respond to their role in the twenty-first century. He notes that we owe it to our students to keep pace with the changes and innovations taking place:

> More and more students, whether they anticipate this or not, will find themselves in situations where they work, their voting, their leisure interests depend on some awareness of global and comparative history and trends, and American higher education ... simply must keep abreast, which means further curricular change and further program innovation.
>
> (Stearns, p. 194)

The University of Hong Kong states in its strategic plan:

> As the world is getting smaller and more interconnected, it is important for the University to prepare its graduates as global citizens by developing an international outlook and enhancing their global competencies in terms of attitude, language abilities, knowledge and analytical skills through our curriculum, student activities and a variety of international experiences.
>
> (University of Hong Kong, 2007)

However, the tendency of most universities, particularly in North America, who use the term 'students as global citizens' is to see it as one or more of the following:

- Volunteering or International Service Learning (Annette, 2001; Brown, 2003).
- Internships and overseas work: 'international experience broadens the perspective of US students and helps them become better global citizens'.[1]
- Strategic initiatives bringing together language learning, exchange programmes and opportunities to learn with students from other countries via online groups. For example, the University of Washington (2007) states an intention to support students because they are global citizens, to enable them to understand what it means and to recognise interconnections with places elsewhere in the world.
- Specific campus initiatives that include one day or a themed week of activities that aim to create, share and apply knowledge to make the state or the university and the world a better place (Abdi, Hannemann & Shultz, 2007).
- Projects that encourage students to be aware of global issues and problems and give them the experience to translate this interest into direct learning and experience. An example of this is the Crossing Borders Global Citizenship campaign at the University of Michigan (2008) School of Public Health.

Student Perceptions of Themselves in the Context of Globalisation

How does this increased drive to promote global citizenship in universities and programmes relate to students' perceptions about their own role, learning priorities and engagement in society? Where specific studies have taken place, the relationship between students' own personal experience and their cultural backgrounds were key factors. Richardson, Blades, Kumano and Karaki (2003) studied school student perceptions in Japan and Canada of being a 'world citizen' and noted considerable support for learning and studying more about global issues. However, there were noticeable differences in student perceptions of their own role in the future, with the Japanese cohort being more negative than the Canadian. Research by Hicks and Holden (2007) with student teachers in the United Kingdom suggests that experience of the wider world via travel, or of living in a multicultural society, resulted in greater sympathy towards learning about global issues.

Little research has looked at student identities in the context of globalisation and has tended to focus on international students (Caruana & Spurling, 2007), or on reviews of the motivations behind student international travel (Urry, 2007). However, the broader discourse in globalisation, learning and identities does suggest certain themes. Ray (2007) argues that living in a globalised world does not create homogeneity or polarisation but rather a creative and eclectic mix of identities. Jarvis (2007) suggests that the global–local relationship is a key area of tension.

A small video chat-room study undertaken by University College London in 2007 on students' roles as global citizens takes on a significance beyond its original intention, which was to demonstrate the rationale for their strategy on global citizenship. Over 30 students participated in a discussion on 'your role in your community and the wider world, observations on globalisation, being a global citizen and future role in the world'. Students came from a wide range of backgrounds, a combination of undergraduate and postgraduate courses, and from different departments and faculties. Whilst it is impossible to say if the sample was representative, comments covered a wide range of views. What is less clear is the extent to which students came voluntarily, whether they felt strongly about the issues or were just asked on the spur of the moment.[2] The questions were also too open-ended and students went off at tangents. However, the responses are interesting and revealing and can be summarised as follows:

- The majority of students were ambivalent about their own identity; they were not sure how to define themselves in relation to their own community and the wider world. However, a positive feature within their wider social and cultural experience was a strong sense of enjoying living in London.
- Virtually all said they would like to learn and engage more in wider world issues and questions. Several wanted to make a positive contribution to the world and felt studying at UCL gave them additional opportunities to do this.
- Globalisation was seen predominantly as opening up communities to world trade and being interconnected with people around the world. Some saw it in terms of Western economic domination and cultural icons such as MacDonalds, Coca Cola, etc. However, for the majority it was more positive than negative. Those engaged in study that included globalisation had more to say, outlining contradictions and complexities. Few directly related their views to the role and purpose of the university.
- The majority were dubious about the term 'global citizen'. Some felt it was an elitist concept. 'Only a very few people could be considered as global citizens' was one observation. Others saw themselves as 'human beings'. For the majority, 'global citizen' was linked to globalisation. Those who were positive or at least neutral said it meant going beyond national boundaries, an ability to communicate with and learn from others. Students who had lived and travelled around the world and who came from more than one cultural background were more positive.
- Students tended to have a low opinion of their own potential contribution to the world in the future despite their interest. Those studying subjects such as medicine and engineering were more positive.

This small-scale study demonstrates that whilst University College London may be correct in recognising that more resources are needed to raise students' awareness of the wider world, this should not simply be reduced to re-creating a new identity for themselves as global citizens, without more dialogue and debate.

Being Global Citizens and Learning About Global Issues

The second area considers 'students as global citizens' within the context of specific learning discourses, particularly education. Research undertaken with trainee teachers from the geography and modern foreign languages subject areas at the Institute of Education, University of London suggests a more positive response to such debates. In the school curriculum in England, terms such as 'equipping pupils to be global citizens' are increasingly mentioned by policy-makers and practitioners. For both groupings of students in this study, 'being a global citizen' was predominantly seen as a useful term to encourage discussion amongst themselves and also within school environments. Below are some of their definitions of a global citizen:

- 'Everyone who lives in the world. All our actions affect and impact upon the world.'
- 'A person whose actions have global implications.'
- 'A global citizen is someone who is aware of their rights and responsibilities in the world around them.'
- 'Somebody who is aware of issues both locally and globally and wishes to positively improve the world.'
- 'A global citizen is someone who travels, uses the internet, mobile phones, watches TV, we are all global citizens.'
- 'Actively aware and involved in the world around them.'
- 'Acts locally and thinks globally so that they promote world prosperity and sustainability.'
- 'A global citizen is a citizen who acts for the good of the whole globe.'

Whilst these responses reflect a range of perspectives from passive to more active definitions, the majority saw the term in relation to being aware, socially conscious and wishing to see social change. These definitions equate closely with Oxfam's approach, and the student teachers' awareness of the work of this NGO may have been a factor. But it also indicates that they could be used for debate and dialogue when linked to broader learning goals and objectives; similar perspectives and approaches can be seen where students themselves wish to learn more about global issues directly relevant to their future career. Examples are in engineering, particularly through the network Engineers Without Borders, and in health, through the student group Medsin. Engineers Without Borders UK is a student-led organisation providing engineering-related placements in developing countries. Their training and educational programmes for students have the stated aim of developing 'all engineering students into global citizens by embedding human development issues into the core engineering curriculum' (Engineers Without Borders, 2009). Medsin is a network of students who have an interest in health. They aim to 'promote health as well as to act upon and educate students about health inequalities in our local and global communities' (Medsin, 2009).

U8, a student-led global university network, has attempted to bring together these interests. It 'aims to provide a non-partisan platform for students to engage, learn, voice their views, and make a positive impact in the field of global development'. U8 grew out of an initiative developed at Cambridge University by Engineers Without Borders and other student networks which created The Humanitarian Centre. A key feature of the Centre has been the organisation of one-day conferences and courses bringing together students and academics internationally across disciplines covering globalisation and international development.

Being Active Global Citizens

The third area of engagement with global citizenship relates to activism and campaigning. The growing enthusiasm for action on global social change within the UK student population can be demonstrated by significant increases in membership of bodies such as People and Planet, Development in Action (DiA) and Student Action for Refugees (STAR). People and Planet was founded in 1969 under the name of Third World First, and supports campaigning and awareness-raising within universities, colleges and schools. They campaign to end world poverty, defend human rights and protect the environment (People and Planet, 2008). Development in Action is a UK-based development NGO, founded in 1992 and run by young people for young people. They promote global citizenship by encouraging young people to engage in global issues (Development in Action, 2008), and provide volunteer placements for students, mainly in India. STAR, a student-led network founded in 1994, focuses on supporting refugees and asylum seekers through awareness-raising activities and campaigns within universities (STAR, 2008).

What led these organisations to produce the paper 'Students as Active Global Citizens', referred to earlier (Lamb et al., 2007) was their unease at the way in which leading NGOs, on the back of the success of Make Poverty History, were seeing a global citizen as someone who merely wore a wrist band or took part in specific campaigns with no reference to critical debate and dialogue: 'If you are to encourage young people to engage with development issues, beyond joining a march or paying a subscription to an NGO, then it is necessary to help them invest in their enthusiasm with local activities' (Strange 2005).

People and Planet, DiA and STAR have a distinctive emphasis on learning and development of skills for effective campaigning and social action. STAR talks about 'learning about and raising awareness of refugee issues in innovative ways' as well as supporting refugees practically and engaging in campaigns. The noticeable factor about these bodies is the extent to which they take account of the complex nature of terms such as global citizenship and the relationship between the issues and their own future careers. DiA, for example recognises the perceptions of elitism in the term which might be seen as 'buying fair-trade bananas and chocolate, choosing a bank that invests money ethically and reducing our environmental footprint'. DiA suggests that:

> If equal access to rights is placed at the heart of our definition of global citizenship, it may encourage us to make more difficult ethical consumer choices. More importantly however, it may allow us to begin to deconstruct the notion of 'deserving/ undeserving' poor and prevent the erosion of a

public and political commitment to the defence of human rights. In place of a discourse which focuses on the necessity of conforming to a particular, negatively-defined notion of good citizenship, we could build on the achievements of the Fair Trade movement and develop a perspective which emphasises equality of rights for all 'global citizens'.

(Development in Action, 2007)

Websites are emerging, set up by and run for students, about taking action on global issues. One, entitled Hands Up, was set up by a youth and student activist, Kierra Box, and aims to give students the knowledge, skills and tools to get involved in 'grassroots action' (Box, 2008). She seeks to identify ways of securing change by working with other like-minded students (Box, 2006). This area of self-directed learning and engagement through social networking is likely to be one of the most tangible forms of student involvement as global citizens in the years to come. To date it has been the subject of little research, but in the longer term may tell us much more about how students perceive themselves as 'global citizens' than the work of NGOs or universities.

Conclusion

'Being a global citizen' is a phrase used by policy-makers and universities but what it means beyond rhetoric is still open to debate. At one level it could mean equipping students to be effective graduates in the global economy, to understand the complex world in which they will be living and working. But it could also link to a process of learning, making sense of the world. It also relates to being informed social activists.

This chapter emphasises the importance of promoting and supporting critical and independent thought alongside a strong values base of social justice, regardless of the lens through which one can look at these issues. Students at UCL saw being a global citizen in sceptical terms because it was posed solely within the context of how they see themselves in the world. If, on the other hand, global citizenship is seen as facilitating learning that encourages the questioning of society, seeking further knowledge and the skills to engage in securing a more just world, then perhaps it has an important place within the policies and programmes of universities. There is clear evidence from around the world that more and more students wish to have a greater sense of global connectedness. The challenge for universities is to ensure this interest becomes the dominant voice in promoting their international outlook rather than as subsidiary to one based on market share and economic need.

Notes

1 Linked to service learning but having a distinct purpose in itself overseas work and international experience are helping students to be effective global citizens. See www.usask.ca/communications/ocn/06-apr-21/feature05.shtml
2 The evidence on which these comments are based comes from a series of filmed tapes with students in March 2007.

References

Abdi, A., Hannemann, N., & Shultz, L. (2007). Building bridges, connecting with the world: Global citizenship in post-secondary education. University of Alberta. Paper presented at Institute of Education, Higher Education Conference, July 2007.

Abdi, A., & Shultz, L. (2008). *Education for human rights and global citizenship.* Albany: State University of New York Press.

Andreotti, V. (2007). Soft versus hard global citizenship. *Policy and Practice, 4,* 40–51.

Annette, J. (2001). Global citizenship and learning in communities. *Development Education Journal, 8*(1), 10–12.

Blair, T. (2008). Students to be global citizens. Available from: http://fora.tv/2008/05/25/Tony_Blair_Incites_Students_to_Become_Global_Citizens [Accessed April 2009].

Box, K. (2006). Campus radicals. Available from: www.newstatesman.com/200606110001 [Accessed April 2009].

Box, K. (2008). Available from: www.handsupfor.org/home [Accessed April 2009].

British Council (2008). The Prime Minister's global fellowship. Available from: http://www.globalgateway.org.uk/default.aspx?page=4124 [Accessed April 2009].

Brown, N. (2003). Embedding engagement in higher education: Preparing global citizens through international service-learning. Available from: www.compact.org/20th/read/preparing_global_citizens [Accessed February 2009].

Carter, A. (2001). *Political theory of global citizenship.* London, Routledge.

Caruana, V., & Spurling, N. (2007). The internationalisation of UK higher education: A review of selected material. Available from: www.heacademy.ac.uk/assets/York/documents/ourwork/tla/lit_review_internationalisation_of_uk_he.pdf [Accessed April 2009].

Chan, J. (Ed.). (2008). Another Japan is possible: New social movements and global citizenship education. Stanford, CA: Stanford University Press.

Clarke, J. (2008). Internationalisation at home: Students as global citizens. Available from: www.heacademy.ac.uk/resources/detail/events/conference/Ann_conf_2008 [Accessed February 2009].

Cogan, J. J., & Derricott, R. (2000). *Citizenship for the twenty first century.* London: Kogan Page.

Department for International Development (DFID) (2007). Building support for development. Available from: www.dfid.gov.uk/developmentawareness [Accessed February 2009].

Development Education Association (2005). Graduates as global citizens: Quality education for life in the 21st century. Report of a conference held on 13 April 2005. London: DEA.

Development in Action (2007). Available from: www.developmentinaction.org/about_dia [Accessed April 2009].

Development in Action (2008). Making a difference. *Winter 2007–2008 Newsletter,* Issue 29. Available from: www.developmentinaction.org./downloads/newsletters/DIA_newsletter_winter_2007.pdf [Accessed April 2009].

DfES (2004). *Putting the world into world-class education.* DfES Publications. Available from: www.teachernet.gov.uk/internationalstrategy [Accessed April 2009].

DfES (2005). Sustainable Development Action Plan. London: DfES. Available from: http://publications.dscf.gov.uk/ [Accessed April 2009].

Dobson, A., & Valencia, A. (Eds.). (2005). *Citizenship, environment and economy.* London, Routledge.

Dower, N. (2003). *An introduction to global citizenship.* Edinburgh: Edinburgh University Press.

Engineers Without Borders (2009). What is EWB? Available from: www.ewb-uk.org/home [Accessed April 2009].

Gaventa, J., & Rootes, C. (2007). *From local to global.* Swindon, UK: Economic and Social Research Council.

Heater, D. (2002). *World citizenship.* London: Continuum.

HEFCE (2005). *Sustainable development in higher education.* HEFCE, UK.

Hicks, D., & Holden, C. (2007). *Teaching the global dimension.* London: Routledge.

Higher Education Academy (2007). Internationalisation. Available from: www.heacademy.ac.uk/ourwork/learning/international [Accessed April 2009].

Humanitarian Centre. Available from: http://www.humanitariancentre.org/hub/public/index.htm [Accessed April 2009].

Jarvis, P. (2007). *Globalisation, lifelong learning and the learning society.* Abingdon, UK: Routledge.

Killick, D. (2006). World-wide horizon: Cross-cultural capability & global perspectives, guidelines for curriculum review. Available from: http://www.leedsmet.ac.uk/international/Cross_Cultural_Capability_Guidelines.pdf [Accessed April 2009].

Lamb, A., Roberts, E., Kentish, J., & Bennett, C. (2007). Students as active global citizens. *Zeitschrift fur internationale Bildungsforschung und Entwicklungspadagogik,* 30 Jahrgang, 1.

Lunn, J. (2006). Global perspectives in higher education. *Project summary 2004–6.* London: Royal Geographical Society.

Make Poverty History. Available from: http://www.makepovertyhistory.org/ [Accessed April 2009].

Mayo, M. (2005). *Global citizens: Social movements and the challenge of globalisation.* London: Zed Books.

Medsin (2009). What is Medsin? Available from: www.medsin.org/ [Accessed April 2009].

Osler, A. & Starkey, H. (2005). Learning for cosmopolitan citizenship: Theoretical debates and young people's experiences. *Educational Review, 55*(3), 243–254.

Oxfam (2006). *Education for global citizens: a guide for schools.* Oxford: Oxfam.

People and Planet (2008). Annual review 2007–2008. Available from: www.peopleandplanet.org/dl/pnp_annual_review_2007_2008.pdf [Accessed April 2009].

Ray, J. (2007). *Globalisation and everyday life.* Abingdon, UK: Routledge.

Richardson, G., Blades, D., Kumano, Y., & Karaki, K. (2003). Fostering a global imaginary: The possibilities and paradoxes of Japanese and Canadian students' perceptions on the responsibilities of world citizenship. *Policy Futures in Education, IX*(2), 402–421.

Schattle, H. (2008). *The practices of global citizenship.* Lanham, MD: Rowman and Littlefield.

Shiel, C. (2006). Developing the global citizen. *Academy Exchange: Supporting the Student Learning Experience,* Issue 5, Winter, 13–15.

Shiel, C. (2007). Developing and embedding global perspectives across the university. In S. Marshal (Ed.), *Strategic leadership of change in higher education.* London: Routledge.

STAR (2008). *STAR Action Guide.* Available from: www.star-network.org.uk/images/uploads/blog/Microsoft_Word_-_1._All_About_STAR.pdf [Accessed April 2009].

Stearns, P. (2009). *Educating global citizens in colleges and universities.* New York, Routledge.

Stokes, P., Pitty, R., & Smith, G. (Eds.). (2008). *Global citizens: Australian activists for change.* Melbourne, Australia: Cambridge University Press.

Strange, M. (2005). Empowering university students as 'global citizens'. *Development Education Journal, 12*(1), 25–26.

U8. Available from: http://www.u8development.org/ [Accessed April 2009].

University College London (2007). Global citizenship. Available from: www.ucl.ac.uk/global_citizenship [Accessed April 2009].

University of Hong Kong (2007). Preparing global citizens. Available from: www.hku.hk/liaison/oise/ [Accessed April 2009].

University of Michigan (2008). Crossing borders global citizenship campaign. Available from: www.globalcitizenship.crossingbordersonline.org [Accessed February 2009].

University of Washington (2007). Available from: http://uwnews.org/uweek/uweekarticle.asp?visitsource=uwkmail&articleID=34479 [Accessed April 2009].

Urry, J. (2007). Cosmopolitanism and higher education. Paper presented at Kingston University seminar on global citizenship. Available from: www.staffnet.kingston.ac.uk/%7EKU08277/globalcitizenship/marystuart/ [Accessed April 2009].

3

The Relevance of the Internationalised Curriculum to Graduate Capability

The Role of New Lecturers' Attitudes in Shaping the 'Student Voice'

VIV CARUANA

Introduction

Recent research with UK students in higher education suggests that whilst they have a prevailing interest in other cultures and recognise the benefits of working in the 'international classroom' their experience is not tied more widely into learning or skills acquisition and benefits are often incidental, of low yield and not contextualised. Some students also feel that it is the institutions' responsibility to review policy, procedure and pedagogical practice to better facilitate communication between different student groups (Harrison & Peacock, 2007; this volume; Peacock & Harrison, 2006). Arguably this process of review is well underway and at some institutions it has prompted notions of internationalisation which embrace the concept of global citizenship (Bourn, this volume; Caruana & Spurling, 2007). At the institutional level the *rhetoric* of global citizenship is manifest in mission statements and internationalisation strategies that trumpet internationalised, intercultural and inclusive curricula (Caruana & Spurling, 2007). However, internationalisation is not a clearly defined, absolute set of 'best practices' but rather a nuanced construct which is highly context specific. In other words, internationalisation will be manifest in different ways depending upon disciplinary perspectives, whether it is viewed from an academic or administrative stance, from an institutional, faculty or department vantage point or from staff, student, employer and other stakeholder perspectives. However, the crucial factor determining the possibilities for intercultural dialogue within the student learning experience is academics' attitudes towards, and the ways in which they understand, the process of internationalisation (Hyland, Trahar, Anderson & Dickens, 2008; Schoorman, 1999).

New Academics – The Receptive Students Who Shape the 'Student Voice' on Internationalisation

This chapter draws on research undertaken at a UK university with graduates of the institution's Postgraduate Certificate in Higher Education Practice and Research (PGCHEPR), the first component of a Master's level programme, compulsory for all new academic members of staff. The programme is informed by a philosophy of transformative learning and critical pedagogy that provides a counterweight to the conservative (rather than expansive), instrumental (rather than evidence-informed), common-sensical (rather than scholarly) approach to teaching and learning often encountered in the immediate practice setting (Knight, Tait & Yorke, 2006).

There is an element of 'how to' but the programme is based on Habermas' (1972) notion that knowledge is communicative and emancipatory, therefore participants are encouraged to question critically and reflect on what they do, how it works, to consider alternatives, why they believe it is important, etc. Participants are introduced to internationalisation in higher education in the second of two core modules 'Learning Design and Enquiry'. Participants may well be more receptive to the 'internationalisation agenda' than more experienced colleagues since they are learners who acknowledge that curriculum innovation and development is a complex, messy and problematic process requiring dialogue between educational theory, research and policy initiatives.

Whilst most academics appreciate how curriculum processes are influenced by disciplinary and collegial norms and allegiances, the programme heightens awareness of *institutional* allegiances and norms. A steep learning curve may be experienced in understanding institutional values and ethos and the interface between institutional policy and strategy and the operational context of practice. However, this is a learning curve that more experienced colleagues may not have encountered so directly and so intensely, if at all (Caruana & Murrell, 2006; Cranton & King, 2003). New members of staff on this programme tend to value the opportunity afforded for cross-fertilisation with other course members: 'perhaps the most satisfying aspect was the freedom to engage and listen to colleagues and share stories and solutions to the everyday issues we face'; 'The group discourse, the broader understanding of the workings of the institution outside my particular school and the encouragement to take risks has made me stronger in my conviction that I have what it takes to teach.'

Reflections on PGCHEPR experience also suggest that the opportunity to diversify thinking about higher education by taking on the persona of a student is valued and in this sense also, participants are key members of the academic community who will not only shape the internationalised curriculum but will also be influential in shaping how their students perceive the international and global dimension of their learning (Prosser et al., 2006): 'Part of my action research project has involved considering how the students "see me" …. I feel I am now better equipped to actively seek feedback, reflect upon the student/teacher relationship and understand its bearing upon teaching and learning.'

Shaping Academics' Perspectives on Internationalisation – Institutional Strategy and Academic Discourse

This research assumes that institutional policy is a significant factor shaping participants' attitudes to the international/intercultural dimension in curriculum development. The organisation in question has assumed a very traditional and conservative *target-driven* approach in the past despite an emerging debate surrounding alternative approaches (Caruana, 2004; Caruana & Hanstock, 2003, 2005, 2008). However, this approach is challenged in a recently published internationalisation strategy which acknowledges that rather than being enabling, it might have distorted reality by exaggerating local successes in curriculum innovation and development (University of Salford, 2008a; 2008b).

Internationalisation strategy now anticipates a long-term process of evolution and development embracing eight key elements. Global citizenship and partnerships are prioritised for development since they are regarded as impacting upon and feeding into the other six strands: international students; international research; student exchange, mobility and work experience; staff internationalisation; internationalisation of the curriculum; and brand recognition (University of Salford, 2008b). Regarding the concept of global citizenship and in particular, how it relates to the internationalised curriculum, current strategy documents are brief and quite vague, assuming that curriculum development is a core activity of faculty in the disciplines: 'It is essentially about ensuring that all our students benefit from the internationalisation of the University' (University of Salford, 2008b).

Whilst this kind of approach is not uncommon in UK higher education (Caruana & Spurling, 2007), experience in Australian universities suggests that dependence on departments and faculties to internationalise the curriculum means less coverage in institutional actions and sometimes confusion over what exactly is meant by 'internationalising the curriculum' (Stella & Liston, 2008).

Locating a Data Collection Tool to Engage Faculty in What Might Be Unfamiliar Territory

A major challenge in data collection was to design a tool which would facilitate synergy between related concepts irrespective of individuals' knowledge of the field. The work of colleagues at the University of South Australia (UniSA) and Leeds Metropolitan University was invaluable here. UniSA has done much over the years to challenge the prevailing tendency to view internationalisation and the process of intercultural learning as separate entities. Betty Leask has worked extensively with UK institutions like Leeds Metropolitan University (known for its *values-driven* approach to internationalisation) to promote awareness of the UniSA perspective on internationalisation which embraces the notion of 'levels' and 'layers'. In effect, discussion of levels, layers and values provides a useful counterweight to the 'marketisation discourse' which emphasises the economic rationale and encourages a *target-driven* approach focused on 'activities' (Leask, 2003; UniSA 2004).

UniSA's Internationalisation Information Kit and Simon Mercado and John Leopold's (2007) AOPI (Assessment of Programme Internationalisation) Framework were adapted to form the basis of an online questionnaire made available to past and current cohorts of the PGCHEPR. Six sections prompted engagement with principles and aims of the internationalised curriculum;

potential 'enablers' of international/intercultural dimensions in curricula and the learning outcomes, content, teaching, learning and assessment strategies which might be appropriate in the international/intercultural context of study. The questionnaire also asked respondents to consider how they thought their students might regard the relevance of an international/intercultural dimension to their learning experience and the relevance of cross-cultural capability to their future lives and careers. The questionnaire was supplemented by a 'wiki' where respondents could post and comment on each others' reflections.

Responses were generated from a relatively wide range of disciplines/subject areas including information systems, business, management and economics, construction law, art and design, aviation and gas engineering, psychology/social sciences, audio visual computing and enterprise, social work, media (performance and journalism), health, exercise and physical activity and IT training and facilitation. Analysis of the major themes emerging from the questionnaire and 'wiki' follows.

Principles and Aims of the Internationalised Curriculum

Respondents were asked to select which of three statements relating to the principles of 'internationalising the curriculum' most nearly reflected their understanding. The majority selected Statement 3 which emphasised a curriculum designed to enable students to understand the global context of their studies, to develop awareness of how knowledge is globally linked and to prepare them for viewing change as positive and managing it effectively in a global context. Remaining respondents selected Statement 2 which referred to education for global citizenship and leadership; teaching and learning informed by the global context and a curriculum which enables students to explore their subject from an international perspective. No participants selected Statement 1 which simply referred to embedding international perspectives in curriculum content.

Respondents were then asked what they feel the principal aim of the internationalised curriculum *should* be. Responses were fairly evenly split between equipping graduates with the requisite cross-cultural skills, knowledge and attitudes to enhance their employability and developing graduates as global citizens, who are aware of world issues and are empowered to bring about change towards a more just, sustainable society. Postings to the wiki included:

- '[T]he role of education is paramount to prepare students to live and work in an environment where people have different values.'
- 'Internationalising the curriculum should include cultural awareness, analysis of social and political implications for different human clusters (in the subject area), analysis of different perspectives.'
- 'I think students interacting with the local community is important although I understand that that's not all there is to internationalisation.'

Since no respondents selected the statement that the aim of the internationalised curriculum is to 'provide support to enable students to assimilate' it is clear there is a perception that internationalisation is about more than acculturating international students to UK higher education. Seemingly, the internationalised curriculum is also about more than introducing 'international content' into learning. The preference for a definition which emphasises the development of appropriate skills to challenge knowledge in a global context (Statement 3) suggests a tendency towards strong or 'transformative' internationalisation rather than the weak or 'symbolic' internationalisation suggested by Statement 2 which simply engages the rhetoric of 'global citizenship' prevalent in institutional mission statements (Appadurai, 2001). At the same time though, data on the principal aim of the internationalised curriculum points towards a conflation of pragmatic and liberal ideological educational rationales. Pragmatism is apparent in seeking to offer a curriculum which develops competencies that enhance graduates' employability, and the ideological is manifest in the emphasis on lifelong learning skills for a largely unknown but increasingly inter-related, future world.

Enabling the Internationalised Curriculum?

Internationalisation of the curriculum cannot take place in a monocultural classroom in isolation of the wider world and where the student body, staff, curriculum content and supporting materials all reflect a single dominant culture. In effect, 'enablers' need to be present providing the raw material and potential richness of cultural experience which can be strategically blended into teaching, learning and assessment practices to provide an international/intercultural dimension. Participants in this research were asked to rate the significance of each of the following factors in their practice:

- the presence of international students and/or home students with diverse ethnic and cultural backgrounds in their classrooms;
- international collaborations and partnerships;
- links with organisations in the community (business, industry, voluntary sector, public sector, third sector, etc.) which are either representative of cross-cultural interests or are involved in work which has a cross-cultural dimension;
- international accreditation of programmes;
- international staff who are contractually available to teach;
- learning materials and resources which originate outside the United Kingdom;
- opportunity to learn languages.

In some subject areas/disciplines cultural and ethnic diversity is apparent in cohorts with large representation of international students *or* home students with diverse backgrounds. Indeed, *both* groups may be well represented (business, management, information systems). However, in law, media, psychology and the audio/visual branch of computing at this UK university cultural and ethnic diversity is conspicuous by its absence. It is interesting to consider that whilst many universities are pre-occupied with issues of equality and diversity, integration and inclusivity across campus the 'multicultural classroom' is a phenomenon quite alien in some disciplines. Furthermore, the absence of diversity in cohort profiles is compounded by the unavailability of learning materials and resources originating outside the United Kingdom and the absence of international staff (these factors were rated low in significance (0–2) by the majority of participants). Similarly, international accreditation, the opportunity to learn languages and international collaborations and partnerships were under-rated (0–2) in most cases.

The evidence regarding international collaborations and partnerships is interesting since the university has identified this as an area for priority strategic development. What is perhaps of concern is that in the interim, there seem to be equally limited possibilities in terms of developing 'internationalisation at home'. Fifty per cent of respondents felt that cross-cultural opportunities based on existing links with organisations in the local community were relatively insignificant and, perhaps more importantly, these were the same individuals who had rated international collaborations and partnerships low too. Only in tourism management were clear aspirations towards international collaborations and partnerships, links with community organisations with global interests or affiliations, international accreditation of programmes and the opportunity to learn languages apparent.

It seems that developing the internationalised curriculum across disciplines at this university poses a real challenge in all areas outside business and management/information systems, due to the absence of enablers. Furthermore, the driving force for the internationalised curriculum remains the perceived needs of the discipline or subject area (significant drive in tourism management), rather than any broader notion of cross-cultural capability or global citizenship for *all* students irrespective of disciplinary or professional orientation.

Defining Learning Outcomes for Cross-Cultural Capability

UniSA developed their G7 graduate attributes in the 1990s (Leask, 2001) and in the United Kingdom, David Killick and colleagues have been active in developing the notion of cross-cultural capability since the first UK conference on the subject was held at Leeds Met in 1996 (Killick & Parry, 1997). Designing learning outcomes for cross-cultural capability is central to the internationalised curriculum and respondents in this research were asked to consider what they felt were appropriate outcomes in the cognitive, behavioural and affective domains of engagement with the international/intercultural dimension of the student learning experience. Four levels of engagement were put forward from 'scoping' through 'enabling' and 'training' to 'relating' including:

- defining the scope of the cross-cultural dimension by identifying the range and significance of cultural and national perspectives on past and/or current issues, understanding how culture and nationality influences attitudes, values and actions and the way in which one's own cultural and national perspectives influence attitudes, values and actions;

* enabling cross-cultural engagement through developing skills to communicate effectively across national and cultural boundaries;
* the training or professional practice-based domain – embracing aspects of cross-cultural engagement, including understanding the relationship between cultural and national contexts and different approaches within the discipline area and/or understanding international standards within the discipline area;
* relating learning to new and unfamiliar contexts and adapting behaviour to different contexts by, for example, using cross-cultural communication skills to negotiate outcomes and generate 'new' knowledge within the discipline and/or reflecting on the relationship between international standards, benchmarks, etc. in the discipline in both their local and global contexts.

The majority of respondents tended to rate each level of engagement in a similar range, some rating all four levels low (0 or 1) whilst others rated them all high (4 or 5). These responses could reflect individuals' general perception of the importance of the international/intercultural dimension within the broader student learning experience. Alternatively, they might conceal a fundamental difficulty in differentiating between each level of capability. Certainly, Leask (2003) argues that judging achievement of student learning outcomes related to internationalisation is a significant challenge for academic staff, particularly since students may not progress from one level to another in a linear fashion but rather move backwards and forwards between levels as their knowledge and skills develop. These alternative possibilities aside, what is clear is that for those who did differentiate between the levels the emphasis tended to be on lower-order scoping ability and skills acquisition rather than aspiring to the relational, a position which is consistent with the emphasis on skills acquisition when considering the principal aim of the internationalised curriculum.

Teaching, Learning and Assessment Strategies Appropriate for the Internationalised Curriculum

In this section of the questionnaire respondents were asked to consider a number of possible options within their teaching, learning and assessment practice which they felt would facilitate intercultural learning. Respondents favoured a broad mix of material encompassing international and UK-based curriculum content, including case studies from a range of cultures, detailed international case studies from more than one country, analysis of recently published international articles, texts, etc. It was agreed that content should afford students the opportunity to recognise how knowledge is constructed differently from culture to culture. Content considered less relevant to the internationalised curriculum included material exploring critical global environmental issues, topics on ethical issues in globalisation and accounts of the historical background to current international practices.

Participants were asked to consider and prioritise a range of teaching and learning activities which might be included in the internationalised curriculum. A favourable response was registered in the following initiatives:

- utilising international contacts and networks, such as simulations of international or intercultural interactions and input from guest lecturers with international experience;
- requiring students to consider issues and problems from an international perspective and to analyse issues, methodologies and possible solutions associated with current areas of debate within the discipline from a range of cultural perspectives;
- requiring students to explore cultural and regional difference in values and assumptions affecting the discipline and how these might impact on the actions of individuals;
- establishing working relationships with fellow students from diverse backgrounds and cultures with a view to locating, discussing, analysing and evaluating information from a range of international sources.

Finally, participants were presented with a range of possible strategies which could be deployed in assessment of the international/intercultural dimension of their students' learning. The most favoured strategies were problem-solving exercises and/or research assignments with an international component, a range of group and individual projects where students would be assessed on their ability to work with others and to consider others' perspectives in comparison with their own, and tasks comparing local and international standards. There was also significant support for engaging students in assessment tasks involving simulated international professional environments, collecting data or gaining feedback from a cross-cultural audience, applying reflective writing skills to intercultural or international matters, and tasks involving assessment criteria explicit to cross-cultural communication skills.

Wiki postings included:

- '[T]he students who come to study with us are predominantly international, so if the learning material was predominantly UK based it would be difficult for them to engage in the discussions.'
- '[I]n some cases where international issues are concerned my knowledge is not necessarily of much help to the students but it is not possible to get all nationalities to be represented in one module.'
- 'On our programme, a number of international students apply for the postgraduate course [but] I am not sure we actively integrate consideration of different cultural perspectives into our teaching and learning activities … . Although the diverse intake of students means that there are potentially a rich spread of experiences students can share with each other … I am not sure as lecturers … we consciously facilitate this.'

These postings, all from business and management/information systems, tend to suggest a pre-occupation with content coverage alone rather than any desire to develop the multicultural classroom as a learning space which invites the sharing of multiple perspectives in order to challenge and understand one's own perspective. Applying McLaren's (1994) model of ideological positions (as cited in Warren & Fangharel, 2005) to the data as a whole, suggests some aspiration towards a curriculum which rises above conservative multiculturalism (paying lip-service to cultural pluralism). However, the almost wholesale rejection of material exploring critical global environmental issues, topics on ethical issues in globalisation and accounts of the historical background to current international practice is consistent with liberal and left-liberal notions of multiculturalism, whereby society is viewed as a 'forum of consensus' and culture as a 'soothing balm' to gloss over issues of power and privilege, conflict and domination.

Overall these responses mirror the perspectives evident when considering the principal aims of the internationalised curriculum. That is, qualities of criticality and empathy in the context of multiple perspectives were espoused, but there was relatively little evidence to support the conceptualisation of the global citizen as the agent of global democracy. The willingness on the part of some respondents to engage cultural interpretations of social, scientific, or technological applications of knowledge, which may be divisive and inequitable and to encourage students to analyse the construction of knowledge and cultural practices within their discipline demonstrates some aspiration towards critical multiculturalism. However, there seems to be only limited support for the internationalised curriculum as the curriculum for global citizenship which exposes how power, inequality and oppression operate via the dominant culture and seeks to develop notions of 'unity in difference' (Warren & Fangharel, 2005).

Academics' Perception of the Student Perspective on the Internationalised Curriculum

The internationalisation literature has traditionally been dominated by research into the international student experience (Caruana & Spurling, 2007). More recently, concerns regarding integration on campus have prompted research involving home students too as evidenced by Hyland et al. (2008), as well as Harrison and Peacock and others in this volume. It is paradoxical that much of this research is conducted with groups of home and international students in isolation of each other. Whilst the lack of integration needs to be understood through research involving students, attempts to engage students in authentic discussion and debate are hampered by a perceived lack of skills to enable effective cross-cultural discourse, the very skills that would be developed within the internationalised curriculum based on integration of multiple perspectives.

In contrast with the current thrust of research in the field, participants in this research were asked to consider the reactions they would anticipate from their students if they were to open up a conversation regarding the significance of cross-cultural capability in their learning and future lives. The data from the questionnaire survey suggests a widely held perception that students (home and international alike) value study and placement abroad as enhancing their future employability and broadening their horizons more generally. This is also reflected in contributions to the wiki:

- 'I am aware that some students do value the importance of an international experience for their future career, whilst others might not find it interesting. It probably depends on their view of life and their aspirations. However, interpersonal skills and cross-cultural skills could be fundamental to any graduate.'
- '[t]hey do ask me if the material taught in the module was of relevance to other countries – this is certainly an indication for me that they are interested in using that information to increase their chances in future employment.'
- 'I consider the student to have a range of views. There are real opportunities working globally for my students and many of the students are open to these.'

Very few respondents felt that their students might express the views that 'cross-cultural expertise is an essential graduate attribute, most workplaces are multicultural after all' and 'I value the experience of working with international students'. At the same time some felt that students might regard global citizenship as 'OK but it has nothing to do with my degree'; 'There is nothing intercultural about my discipline or what I hope to do when I graduate so it's irrelevant' and 'I don't want to be assessed with international students in groups because they will bring my average marks down.'

Academics at this university feel that students have a very traditional outlook on internationalisation focused on international mobility and a diversity of content designed essentially to enhance their employability in an increasingly global labour marketplace. The relatively negative perception of cross-cultural capability and global citizenship which accompanies this traditional view may be the product of students' intellectual stage of personal growth and development where their own fairly single-minded view of the world is accepted as a true representation, rather than as a particularised view conditioned by their historical period, culture and place in nature (Gerdes, 2002).

Higher-order learning is undoubtedly associated with intellectual openness and the ability to adopt a critical perspective on one's own, as well as others' beliefs, values and positions and perceived student attitudes may, in this sense, also be characteristic of the ethnocentric stage of Bennett's Developmental Model of Intercultural Sensitivity (DMIS) where denial of cultural difference may manifest in a disinterest in international affairs which don't impinge on oneself (Bennett, 1986; Engberg, 2004). Seemingly, the paradox is once again apparent – students may undervalue cross-cultural capability and notions of global citizenship because they have not experienced the internationalised curriculum which broadens their horizons encouraging intellectual openness.

Academics' Perception of the Intellectual Challenge of Constructing the Internationalised Curriculum

Whilst the questionnaire survey did not directly address academics' perceptions of the challenge of the internationalised curriculum all of the reflective postings to the wiki were unanimous in their expression of uncertainty and lack of confidence when encountering the phenomenon:

- 'Internationalisation takes extra effort … [and] has to be a concept that staff really understand so it flows as part of the learning without standing out … I think staff would need to really buy into the idea and incorporate it right through their work but need to be at the point where it comes naturally. Otherwise, learners might resent work that they see as not being part of their course.'
- 'If anything … I perhaps underestimate the openness of students to consider issues internationally and this can be addressed by my developing my own awareness of the transferable aspects of my own discipline.'
- 'I wouldn't really know where to start internationalising a curriculum without having much more time to digest the concept and reflect on it … I need to understand more about the concept to buy into it and I need time that I don't have to learn about the concept.'
- '[N]ot feeling confident that I have strong 'cross-cultural capability' myself, making it difficult to think about how to facilitate experiences for others. I suppose using the strengths of the students' different experiences is one way of developing this and therefore devising learning opportunities that encourage this interchange of perspectives as an integral part of the course.'
- 'Personal attitudes, values and beliefs are discussed in part of the programme but this can be scary/difficult for lecturers and students at times, especially when attitudes and values conflict.'

Perceiving Internationalisation and Global Citizenship – A Way Out of the Fog of Consensus and Confusion?

The attitudes of new lecturers engaged in this research are characteristic of Warren and Fangharel's (2005) 'modernisers' who see the main function of education as producing the workforce to enable employers to compete globally, with some – albeit limited – evidence of 'progressive' tendencies in viewing education as a means for creating and supporting change. It seems (in contrast with Rowland, 2003) that the combined forces of globalisation, marketisation and internationalisation do not represent a point of fundamental discontinuity between lecturers, students and management at the institution studied here. Rather, a consensus emerges around the focus on graduate employability and the potentially contradictory predisposition to conservatism in conceptualising the internationalised curriculum.

Whilst the study fails to engage the 'silent majority' of academics who in the face of internationalisation in its current globalised manifestation, have assumed a position of 'resistance and cynicism' (Robson & Turner, 2006) the 'willing converts' in this study share a clarity of aim and purpose which blends the pragmatic and ideological rationales for internationalisation. However, what is striking is the uncertainty encountered when considering learning outcomes and differentiating between different levels of cognitive, behavioural and affective engagement. In essence these new academics steeped in the philosophy of the scholarship of teaching and learning schooled in reflexive practice and eager to provide the best possible student learning experience are clear about the internationalised curriculum as a distant, objective phenomenon pursued by the institution but struggle with the concept in the more proximate, subjective territory of their own learning and teaching practice. Another clear message from this research is that preparing graduates as global citizens across the range of disciplines is likely to be a challenging task, given the apparent lack of enablers in disciplines outside business, management and information systems. Compounding this practical limitation is a philosophical issue whereby (rather than cross-cultural capability being viewed as a generic quality for all students) the discipline assumes exclusive significance in shaping the curriculum.

This study shows that discussing internationalisation strategy as part of a formal programme of study or encountering it within the informal operational context of disciplinary practice are equally lacking when it comes to understanding the complexity of the internationalised curriculum and global citizenship. This probably reflects the assertion made at the start of this chapter, that internationalisation is a construct rather than a set of 'best practices'. Internationalisation strategy is correct in anticipating a long process of evolution and development but more important is the form which the process will take. It is likely (particularly in light of Australian experience) that assigning curriculum development exclusively to individual schools and departments will not deliver the internationalised curriculum which will benefit *all* students. Rather institutions need to encourage the broad based cross-faculty dialogue characteristic of the PGCHEPR in shaping institutional strategy and broadening staff and students' horizons beyond a traditional outlook based on periods of study or placement abroad. Development is likely to be iterative, if not incremental, and a 'diffusionist' or 'middle-out', centrally co-ordinated and facilitated approach encompassing 'the bringing together of faculty and students for discussion of processes' in the spirit of collaboration and insider perspectives characteristic of action research seems to offer more potential for authentic engagement than either of the tried and tested top-down (from senior management) or bottom-up (from students) approaches to internationalising the curriculum (Campbell, 2007; Caruana & Hanstock, 2008; Chang et al., 2004).

References

Appadurai, A. (Ed.). (2001). *Globalization.* Durham, NC: Duke University Press.
Bennett, M. J. (1986). A developmental approach to training for intercultural sensitivity. *International Journal of Intercultural Relations, 10*(2), 179–195.

Campbell, F. (2007). Hearing the student voice: Enhancing academic professional development through the involvement of students. *Educational Developments, 8*(1), 4–8.

Caruana, V. (2004). International mission impossible? ICT and alternative approaches to internationalising the curriculum. *Proceedings of the 4th International Networked Learning Conference,* July 2004, Lancaster University.

Caruana, V., & Hanstock, J. (2003). Internationalising the curriculum: From policy to practice. In *Proceedings of the Inaugural Education in a Changing Environment Conference,* September 2003, University of Salford, UK.

Caruana, V., & Hanstock, J. (2005). Internationalising the curriculum at home or far away? A holistic approach based on inclusivity. Paper delivered to the *Education for Sustainable Development: Graduates as Global Citizens Conference,* September 2005, Bournemouth University, UK.

Caruana, V., & Hanstock, J. (2008). Internationalising the curriculum: From rhetoric to reality at the University of Salford. In A. McKenzie & C. Shiel (Eds.), *The global university: The role of senior managers* (pp. 31–35). London: DEA.

Caruana, V., & Murrell, K. (2006). Masters in higher education practice and research: The education development unit, University of Salford. In H. Urponen, V. Mitchell, D. Rutkauskiene, R. Mark, F. Moe & M. Brennan (Eds.), *The managers' handbook for European university lifelong learning* (Case Study no. 7.1). Available from: http://www.eullearn.net/ [Accessed April 2009].

Caruana, V., & Spurling, N. (2007). The internationalisation of UK higher education: A review of selected material. Available from: www.heacademy.ac.uk/assets/York/documents/ourwork/tla/lit_review_internationalisation_of_uk_he.pdf [Accessed April 2009].

Chang, R., Wahr, F., De Pew, D., Gray, K., Jansz-Senn, A., & Radloff, A. (2004). Knowledge, wisdom and a holistic approach: A case study of change management in academic development. Available from: www.herdsa.org.au/conference2004/Contributions/RPapers/P019-jt.pdf [Accessed September 2008].

Cranton, P. & King, K. P. (2003). Transformative learning as a professional development goal. *New Directions in Adult and Continuing Education,* 98, Summer.

Engberg, M. (2004). *Using the intercultural development inventory to assess liberal arts outcomes.* Wabash, IN: Center of Inquiry in the Liberal Arts. Available from: http://liberalarts.wabash.edu/cila/home.cfm?news_id=1809

Gerdes, E. P. (2002). Disciplinary dangers. *Liberal Education, 88*(3), 48–53.

Habermas, J. (1972). *Knowledge and human interests.* Boston: Beacon Press.

Harrison, N. & Peacock, N. (2007). Understanding the UK response to internationalisation. *World Views,* Summer, Issue 23. London: UKCISA.

Hyland, F., Trahar, S., Anderson, J., & Dickens, A. (2008). A changing world: The internationalization experiences of staff and students (home and international) in UK higher education. Available from: http://escalate.ac.uk/4967

Killick, D. & Parry, M. (1997). Developing cross-cultural capability: *Proceedings of the conference at Leeds Metropolitan University,* 16 December 1996, Leeds Metropolitan University, UK.

Knight, P., Tait, J. & Yorke, M. (2006). The professional learning of teachers in higher education. *Studies in Higher Education, 31*(4), 319–339.

Leask, B. (2001). Bridging the gap: Internationalising university curricula. *Journal of Studies in International Education, 5*(2), 100–115.

Leask, B. (2003). Beyond the numbers: Levels and layers of internationalisation to utilise and support growth and diversity. Paper presented to the *17th IDP Australia International Education Conference,* 21–24 October, Melbourne.

McLaren, P. (1994). *Life in schools.* White Plains, New York: Longman.

Mercado, S. & Leopold, J. (2007). Assessing curriculum internationalisation: Reflections on the experience of two UK business schools. Presentation to University of Salford Awayday, 31 May.

Peacock, N. & Harrison, N. (2006). Understanding the UK student response to internationalisation. Paper presented to *Going Global 2* conference, British Council, 6–8 December. Available from: http://www.britishcouncil.org/goingglobal-2_-_4e_-_neil_harrison_and_nicola_peacock.pdf [Accessed September 2008].

Prosser, M., Rickinson, M., Bence, V., Hanbury, A., & Kulej, M. (2006). Formative evaluation of accredited programmes. Available from: http://www.heacademy.ac.uk/research/Formative Evaluationreport.rtf [Accessed April 2009].

Robson, S., & Turner, Y (2006). Conceptions of internationalization and their implications for academic engagement and institutional action: A preliminary case study. *Second International Chinese and Asian Learners* conference, University of Portsmouth.

Rowland, S. (2003). Teaching for democracy in higher education. *Teaching in Higher Education, 8*(1), 89–101.

Schoorman, D. (1999). The pedagogical implications of diverse conceptualisations of internationalization: A U.S.-based case study. *Journal of Studies in International Education, 3*, 19–46.

Stella, A., & Liston, C. (2008). *Internationalisation of Australian universities: Learning from cycle 1 audits.* Melbourne, Australia: AUQA.

University of Salford (2008a). Internationalisation away day, group sessions and discussions. 2 April 2008. Unpublished.

University of Salford (2008b). *Evolving our internationalisation strategy.* Unpublished.

University of South Australia (UniSA). (2004). Intercultural teaching and learning resource project. Available from: http://www.unisa.edu.au/tu/learningconnection/staff/practice/internationalisation/documents/intro.pdf [Accessed September 2008].

Warren, D., & Fangharel, J. (Eds.). (2005). Approaches to the challenge of student cultural diversity: Learning from scholarship and practice. In *International conference on the scholarship of teaching and learning: Proceedings 2003 and 2004* (pp. 237–253). London: City University, Education Development Centre.

4

Student Voices, Internationalisation and Critical Conversations in Initial Teacher Education

JON TAN AND CHRISTINE ALLAN

Introduction

The role of the professional educator is undergoing fundamental change. Across Europe, national commitments to the development of internationalisation require a corresponding investment in the professional learning of students of initial teacher education (ITE). As Persson (2004) identifies, at a European level, the impact of internationalisation is a significant influence, manifest in a strong obligation to identify vital competences for the future teachers of Europe. The scaling up of associated policy expectations for teachers and teacher education across Europe has been evident, certainly in the years following the Bologna declaration of 1999. Yet, whilst there has been much encouragement of reciprocal international partnerships between European countries and their schools, colleges and universities, in the field of teacher education there has been limited systematic examination of students' experiences. It is in the interests of extending research knowledge and informing future development that this chapter makes its contribution.

Drawing on original research conducted by the authors, this chapter puts the students' voice at the centre of an understanding of international reciprocal placements in France and the United Kingdom. One of the project's aims was to provide an evaluation of student experiences of a bilateral exchange programme and their perceptions of its value to their own professional development in pedagogical and intercultural terms. In doing so, it aimed to contribute to a currently limited field of knowledge and inform further strategic and practice development working from this student perspective.

In this chapter we focus particularly on students' development of a professional awareness and how they talked about the international placement changing them personally and professionally. We start with a review of current literature and policy, in order to situate these student experiences. Against this backdrop, we then explore some of the experiences and development of a group of ab initio educators, training to become teachers of young children aged 3–11 in schools in France and the United Kingdom.

Looking to International Partnerships in Initial Teacher Education

Meeting the needs of children, young people and their communities, is a complex undertaking. It requires professionals that have a highly developed awareness of social, educational and welfare needs, and that have close inter-professional relations that facilitate knowledge-sharing and professional working.

Furthermore, if schools are to become central to education and welfare provision for children and young people, arguably, they will need to develop further as social and culturally inclusive communities, and be institutions that facilitate globally educative experiences. These challenges are ones that extend to higher education and particularly for those engaged in ITE. As Bash, Shallcross and Stewart (2007) highlight, the Universities Council for the Education of Teachers (UCET) in the United Kingdom make this association clear: 'if education is to make an authentic, critical and productive response to these issues in the future, the international and global dimension must figure much more prominently in teacher education programmes' (Bash et al., 2007, p. 1).

Similarly, the draft Common European Principles for Teacher and Trainer Competencies and Qualifications (European Commission, 2003) further emphasises the need for new knowledge, developed through research and evidence-based practice; the facilitating of mobility projects for teachers and trainers that is integral to professional learning; and fostering of initial and continuing professional development programmes that ensure that teachers and trainers have the knowledge and expertise of European co-operation to enable them to value and respect cultural diversity and to educate learners to become EU citizens.

The expectations at social, cultural and educational levels are obvious. For teacher educators and student teachers, a key document in the development of partnerships between France and the United Kingdom has been the 'Common Reference Framework' (DfES, 2005a), written and published through collaboration between the Teacher Development Agency (TDA), Higher Education Institutions in England, and the French Ministry of Education and CDIUFM (Conférence des Directeurs des Instituts Universitaires de Formation des Maîtres). As it states: ·

> The trainees are at the forefront of a Europe-wide vision, via teaching and learning modern languages, for the entrenchment of intercultural respect among sovereign nations. The children in European primary classrooms are the vehicles for the realisation of this vision and these teacher trainees are the inspirational catalysts in the development of the children's cultural understanding.
>
> (p. 9)

In the United Kingdom, the importance of having an international component in the education that children and young people receive has gained impetus in recent years (DfES 2004, 2005b). As such, there are clear expectations communicated through a range of policy directives. The challenge to bring an international component to the school curriculum, and indeed to higher education, has been firmly set for teachers, their schools and those engaged in ITE.

Policy Expectations and Internationalising the Curriculum

Through the UK presidency of the European Union and in the G8 Conference in 2005, there was a significant emphasis on the building of international partnerships between schools, colleges and universities at many levels. A key policy driver in this encouragement of pan-European partnerships related to education has been the Bologna declaration, signed by Ministers of Education from across the European community, and containing a number of objectives associated with the greater comparability and mutual recognition of qualifications; more effective arrangements for credit transfer and quality assurance; and promoting increased mobility in a flexible and responsive system of higher education. In the United Kingdom, such a vision of international connectedness and mobility has filtered into national policy responses that have placed intercultural awareness and exposure to foreign languages high on the agenda.

A good example of the policy directives in the United Kingdom is the Department for Education and Skills' publication, *Putting the World into World-Class Education* (DfES, 2004). This set out the vision of a strong international dimension across the education system in the United Kingdom, forged by developing international partnerships to enable people of the United Kingdom to have 'the knowledge, skills and understanding they would need to fulfil themselves, to live in and contribute effectively to a global society' (DfES, 2004, p. 1). As it stated: 'One cannot truly educate young people in this country without the international dimension being a very significant and real part of their learning experience' (p. 1).

Furthermore, *Developing the Global Dimension in the School Curriculum* (DfES, 2005b) considered how a global dimension could be incorporated into the National Curriculum for compulsory education. The Government envisaged that by 2010 every school in England would be partnered with a school overseas via an Internet Global Gateway.

How the development of cultural and international awareness should be central to education provisions for children and young people was further emphasised by the United Kingdom's languages strategy, *Languages for All: Languages for Life* (DfES, 2002). As it states: 'In the knowledge of the 21st century, language competence and intercultural understanding are not optional extras, they are an essential part of being a citizen' (p. 5).

This key document within the United Kingdom is indicative of the commitment to making progress towards fulfilling the recommendations of the Barcelona European Council (European Commission, 2003) with regard to language teaching and learning in schools. With a strong emphasis within policy, the active encouragement of exchange programmes within ITE has fostered reciprocal European partnerships that enable students of ITE to gain experience of teaching in another country, combining the development of linguistic and inter-cultural skills. Such initiatives have gathered pace across Europe but we have lit-tle understanding of how these international placements contribute to students' pedagogical and intercultural development.

The Study: Focus and Methodology

It was with such questions in mind that we set out to examine the student expe-rience of international placements and how trainee teachers perceived its value in terms of their own professional development. Whilst the professional devel-opment of in-service practitioners has been the focus of significant rhetoric, little research has specifically set out to capture the professional learning of those who could be considered nascent professionals. Even more limited has been research that has focused on the association between international teaching placements and professional learning for trainees. The research presented in the chapter adopted a case study approach that utilised a range of qualitative meth-ods of data collection. There was clear rationale for such an approach: Focusing as we were on the experiences of student teachers undertaking placements in France and the United Kingdom, we wanted to capture what were their own frames of reference through which they made their assessments of value and challenge. Not satisfied with obtaining a largely descriptive account through more quantitative means, such as the use of survey-based attitudinal scales, from the outset the study was designed to yield a richness of data. In accordance with Bryman (1993) and Walker (1988), we thus considered a qualitative approach essential to being able to examine students' experiences with this rich contextual data intact.

Methods for obtaining data included the use of semi-structured group inter-views, classroom observations and set pieces of reflective writing. Adopting this range of data collection methods was important in a number of ways. First, the combination of focus group interviews and observations enabled the researchers to probe student answers to questions concerning classroom expe-riences with reference to specific examples. This was useful in establishing a level of shared contextual knowledge about their schools, their classrooms and significant others (such as host teachers). Second, this combination further sup-ported our interpretation of students' responses and the subsequent under-standing of their experiences in context. Finally, using a combination of methods enabled us to establish trustworthiness in our data analysis through a process of triangulation (Bryman, 1993, p. 131; Flick et al., 2004, pp. 180–181).

The following analysis provides an account of one aspect of their experiences, namely their professional learning. Drawing from the data obtained from two cohorts of trainee teachers – a group from France, teaching pupils aged 3–11 in UK primary schools, and a corresponding group of trainees from England teaching in France – it provides a rich account of their experiences, their assess-ment of the value of international exchanges and comments on how such place-ments enrich professional learning in teacher education.

Findings: Culture 'Shocks', Pedagogical Reflection and Professional Learning

Perhaps most apparent in the responses of participants were their comments about the classroom contexts in which they taught. Alongside descriptive commentary on these experiences, more significant was the degree to which their accounts contained reflective and self-analytical statements about their professional identity. Here we share Boud, Keogh and Walker's (1985) view of reflection as being 'a generic term for those intellectual and affective activities in which individuals engage to explore their experiences in order to lead to a new understanding and appreciation' (p. 19).

All participants in the study explored their experiences with a range of analytical, reflective lenses. It was clear from pre- and post-placement focus group work, classroom observations and students' later reflective writings, that the teaching placement in France represented a major challenge. Unsurprisingly, concerns about their own linguistic competence figured significantly in their considerations of what this challenge involved:

'I think the problem is though that I think we're all, well I am, I'm quite worried that I'm going to get over there and I know how to teach and I have you know strategies in place to do everything but the language, I'm just going to be so busy concentrating on thinking of the right words to say.'
(Pre-placement interview, UK student)

'And also our teacher, the first kind of two weeks she was speaking so fast and she kept going "I speak really fast", but she didn't really make the effort to slow down!'
(Post-placement interview, UK student)

Stepping up to such challenges, however, brought significant professional and personal reward. As one French student working in an English primary school reflected:

'The big challenge of these weeks was to try to do a lesson in English. I was very very afraid and I thought it was … impossible. I did it, with my poor abilities and it was a fantastic experience … I would like to do other lessons in English because it was very exciting and very constructive. In my vocational training, it was a very important moment.'
(Reflective writing, French student)

At the same time, the 'culture shock' effect to which Byram, Gribkova and Starkey (2002) refer also seemed to give participants a different lens with which to make sense of their experiences and their professional development. Being located within a different educational context provided opportunities for the comparison of professional and pedagogical approaches. In doing so, they were often reflecting on and analysing their own practices:

'Another interesting thing to say, is the way of introducing a new topic to the pupils. In France nowadays, we are trying to let the children discover how things are working on their own, whereas here [in England] the teacher is giving the pupils the rule, he's explaining it to the class, and then the pupils are doing exercises in their books to practice. It reminds me of when I was in school … I tend to think that, sometimes, it's maybe better than to leave the children in the middle of something they just can't understand alone because they've never seen it before! Teaching in England seems to be more directive so, compared to France, but it looks like it's working, this is the most important, isn't it?'

(Reflective writing, French student)

And again:

UK student: When I came back I felt so positive about being a teacher and the possibility of me being a teacher abroad even more … the whole experience encouraged me … being a teacher and about being able to communicate with children who … didn't speak my language.

Researcher: Mmm.

UK student: … and that really encouraged me I think. The [concern] I think is … the implications for back here, just thinking about how I can be more child-focused … in terms of the lessons. But that's hard because you've constantly got people above you telling you what you should be doing ….

Researcher: OK.

UK student: Mmm, yeah. So I think those, those things in particular but I did, I did learn, I was challenged a lot while I was there but I wouldn't have been necessarily over here [on a UK teaching practice].

(Post-placement interview, UK student)

Extended in-depth dialogue such as this was very typical across the group and it is interesting to see how the opportunity to tell of their experiences contained references to many aspects of professional practice and pedagogy. In a number of examples we were able to identify messages about notions of assessment and ability; about different learning styles and appropriate activities; about the role of the teacher and working with other staff; about maintaining motivation and challenge; and about the challenges in balancing whole class teaching and one-to-one support for pupils.

To completely step outside of one educational context and to be immersed in an unfamiliar one also prompted participants to reflect on different approaches to learning and the use of resources. The following example is typical of the types of cultural and context-related 'shock' that students encountered, and later thought deeply about, relating it to differing professional approaches:

'[W]ithin the first week the biggest culture shock was the amount of school trips and educational visits that the children took part in. It was amazing to see that the children used public transport to get to local attractions and were well behaved because they were used to learning outside of the classroom and interacting with the public …. It was surprising to see that the class teacher was relaxed and not stressed about the whole process of taking the children out …. In the UK it takes too long to get forms signed by parents, which deters teachers from taking children on school trips. I think the French system of one signature at the beginning of the year, giving a brief outline of where the children may be visiting is a time-saving and stress-free way … educational trips in France [are] an essential part of learning, school visits are compulsory because they offer children different ways of learning and they help address all learning styles.'

(Reflective writing, UK student)

And commenting on the use of other adults in the classroom and the pedagogical possibilities, one student from France commented in their reflective writing:

'The first thing which surprised me is that in each class there are at least two adults. The teacher can teach quietly because the teaching assistant is here to take care of the pupils who are in difficulties … because [there are] many adults in a class, pupils can work in work-groups. This is really interesting: In France we used to work like this with young pupils (3–5 years old), because the teacher is helped by an assistant.'

(Reflective writing, French student)

Other students, on returning from their placements in France made direct connections between their own development of a cultural awareness and how education policy initiatives within the United Kingdom might be seen to have broader, European focus:

'The 4-week placement in Montpellier was an opportunity to experience living and working in another country, within the French education system. What was experienced on a week-to-week basis was a gradual coming to terms with the culture of the classroom, the school, the community and the country. Some weeks after the placement, following a period of reflection, it is easier to understand how the benefits of the experience can be used to teach the [Intercultural Understanding] strand at KS2 [Key Stage 2] …. Living in different cultures and sub-cultures encourages an examination of one's own culture and promotes empathy and tolerance of others. If the European ideal for the education of children is to encourage tolerance, remove stereotypes and work towards common goals, then the learning environment in the classroom must reflect that.'

(Reflective writing, UK student)

Clearly then, the responses of these trainee teachers indicate that the teaching placement in one of the international host primary schools represented a major challenge, and one that carried with it a sense of being resituated as an educator. Immersed within a different cultural, educational and professional context gave them an opportunity to analyse their prior experience with significant depth. Out of the 'shock' of being resituated came both a gaining of new professional knowledge and also the development of a critical lens with which to reassess their existing pedagogy.

What is also apparent from their reflections was the ways in which such international experiences represented major, critical moments in their personal and professional development. A number of participants referred to how the experience promoted their empathy for children from other cultures entering a new school environment in another country, for example:

'I've broadened my own knowledge to teach about difference in cultures. As well as an outsider … we've been that different person …. You can't understand what it's like to be completely different until you've done it. It helps you in that way because at least you understand in a very small way how they [children coming from other cultures] must be feeling.'
(Post-placement interview, UK student)

Such responses have resonance with Newman, Taylor, Whithead and Planel (2004) who suggest that benefits to trainees are twofold, both in helping them to reflect on their own education, culture and language, as well as understanding and appreciating the differences of another.

Conclusion

This chapter has provided a brief insight into the ways in which a group of student teachers experienced and evaluated an international teaching placement. The challenge for them, particularly teaching across the curriculum for 75 per cent of the time in the target language, was immense. Yet linguistic factors represent only one aspect of how they assessed their development. Clearly, their personal and professional development figured greatly in their reflections and the ways in which they considered the international experiences as meaningful. Other researchers have suggested that international exchange programmes change perceptions and that student-teaching-abroad programmes can make a long-term difference (Swiniarski & Breitborde, 2001).

For us as professional educators engaged in teacher education, perhaps most significant was how this international placement provided an opportunity that enabled students, as nascent professionals, to develop a range of critical, reflective lenses with which to interrogate their pedagogies. Drawing conceptually from Loughran (2006), such international experiences may be considered a catalyst for professional, critical conversations between schools, host teachers, university academic partners and students where the voices of learners and pedagogues all act equally to illuminate the complexities of the pedagogical relationship. This, we would argue, lies at the heart of real, productive partnership, professional learning and the co-construction of knowledge.

References

Bash, L., Shallcross, T., & Stewart, Y. (2007). *Internationalisation of teacher education*. London: UCET.

Boud, D., Keogh, R., & Walker, D. (1985). *Reflection: Turning experience into learning*. London: Kogan Page.

Bryman, A. (1993). *Quantity & quality in social research*. London, Routledge.

Byram, M., Gribkova, B., & Starkey, H. (2002). *Developing the intercultural dimension in language teaching – A practical introduction for teachers*. Council of Europe.

DfES (2002). *Languages for all: Languages for life. A strategy for England*. Nottingham, UK: DfES Publications.

DfES (2004). *Putting the world into world-class education*. DfES Publications. Available from: www.teachernet.gov.uk/internationalstrategy [Accessed April 2009].

DfES (2005a). The common reference framework. Available from http://publications.dcsf.gov.uk/ [Accessed April 2009].

DfES (2005b). Developing the global dimension in the school curriculum. Available from http://publications.dcsf.gov.uk/ [Accessed April 2009].

European Commission (2003). *Summary of the first report on the activities of the working group on languages (July 2002–June 2003)*. Brussels: European Commission.

Flick, U., von Kardorff, E., & Steinke, I. (Eds.). (2004). *A companion to qualitative research*. London: Sage.

Loughran, J. (2006). *Developing a pedagogy of teacher education: Understanding teaching and learning about teaching*. London: Routledge.

Newman, E., Taylor, A., Whithead, J., & Planel, C. (2004). 'You just can't do it like that – it's just wrong!' Impressions of French and English trainee primary teachers on exchange placement in primary schools abroad: The value of experiencing the difference. *European Journal of Teacher Education, 27*(3), 285–298.

Persson, M. (2004). *Towards the teacher as a learner*. The Learning Teacher Network Publications.

Swiniarski, L., & Breitborde, M. (2001). Teacher formation: Beginning with oneself, changing the world. Presentation for the *2001 Annual ACEI Conference on Education*, Toronto, Canada.

Walker, R. (Ed.). (1988). *Applied qualitative research*. Aldershot, UK: Gower.

II

The Impact of Study Abroad and International Volunteering

5

Beyond Immersion

Global Engagement and Transformation
Through Intervention via Student Reflection in
Long-Term Study Abroad

GABRIELE WEBER-BOSLEY

Literally as well as metaphorically, the man accustomed to inverting lenses
has undergone a revolutionary transformation of vision.

Thomas Kuhn (1970)

The student voice as a reflection of internationalization efforts on our campuses
around the globe is the focal point of this chapter. While internationalization begins
with the institutional vision and mission, it combines curricular reform, faculty
development, international student recruitment, study abroad and of course student and faculty exchanges in support of learning abroad, with systematic assessment
as an integral part of all of these efforts. The product of this considerable institutional
investment must be a *globally engaged student* on the road to develop into a *global
citizen*, empowered by high-impact learning. It is encouraging that the long overdue
support from the academy, as well as the testimony of leading executives is finally
assisting the efforts on our campuses to involve our students and faculty in global
and intercultural learning. In addition, data from sources like NSSE (National Survey
on Student Engagement, 2007) support what international educators have of course
known anecdotally, namely that it is the *experiential* aspects of the college years
which impact students more than any other tertiary pedagogical experience, with
one of these critical high-impact learning experiences being study abroad.

With accreditation agencies looking for 'measurable' outcomes, employers
looking for a more easily adaptable and integratable hire domestically as well as
abroad, and parents and students expecting accountability for their 'investment',
this chapter will present one of the options available to educators to maximize
a study-abroad experience by examining the effectiveness of a formative on-line
course designed to aid students in the development of target culture behaviour
and transformation while on long-term study abroad around the globe, predominantly via direct enrolment at foreign universities. It will focus on student
narratives as student voices providing testimony of reflection, intercultural
adjustment and transformation brought about by the general, everyday experience of cultural immersion, as well as critical, salient events, forcing students
into a confrontation with cultural difference.

While the course which produced the student narratives in this chapter integrates the 'laboratory' of study abroad with the US home-campus curriculum, it also examines the limitations of an on-campus intercultural course versus this cultural immersion variant and offers effective intervention techniques, enabling students to maximize their experience abroad. This instructor-guided intervention is informed by development theory and guided by the combination of quantitative assessment tools like the Intercultural Development Inventory (IDI) and Global Perspectives Inventory (GPI), and long-term qualitative assessment of student writing assignments. Learning outcomes are evaluated employing these quantitative tools via pre- and post-assessment and through the qualitative assessment of the semester-long documentation process of meta-level analysis, as well as pre- and post-study-abroad workshops where students have an opportunity to share their voices face to face.

Surveys have revealed that the primary reason for going abroad is to 'learn about oneself' and to 'challenge oneself' with 'living in another culture' and 'stepping outside one's comfort zone' following closely behind (Bosley, 2008, Bellarmine Globe Trotter Survey: Learn about/Challenge myself (80 per cent), Live in another culture (76.8 per cent); Step outside my comfort zone (75 per cent); Experience different political/social perspective (67.9 per cent); Meet new people (66.7 per cent); Become more self-reliant (63 per cent); Enhance future career (54.7 per cent); Take a course in my major/minor (40.7 per cent); Get away from BU for a while (34 per cent); Experience different academic systems (23.6 per cent)).

Informed by these student *voices*, the content of this on-line course, which has its roots in a 1994/1995 prototype course first delivered at Bellarmine University (in German and via e-mail at the time), is being adjusted continually, reflecting national research and surveys in the course assignments, as well as the incorporation of the latest techniques in curriculum delivery modes across the globe.

Most international educators would probably expect empirical evidence to support the premise that intensified cultural immersion leads to improved intercultural learning. But, Janet Bennett (2008) reminds us that

> cultural knowledge does not equal cultural competence, language learning may not be sufficient for culture learning, cultural contact does not necessarily lead to competence, cultural contact does not always lead to significant reduction of stereotypes, and disequilibrium need not lead to dissatisfaction.
>
> (pp. 16–17)

Mounting evidence, anecdotal and empirical, is revealing that intervention invigorates the experiential learning that underlies the purpose and richness of study abroad.

There are many possible approaches for intervention depending on a variety of factors including programme types, durations and learning outcomes. This chapter provides a look at one specific approach that has met with considerable success, by connecting students, via computer-networked Blackboard software, to home culture peers who are themselves situated in cultural immersion programmes in other countries around the world, as well as to home university instructors *and* international students attending the home university. The initial focus will be a reflection on the purpose of the course in the context of 'value added' study-abroad and intercultural learning outcomes. Next will be a brief look at the course structure, followed by a collection of student voices through excerpts from a sample of assignments, including original student narratives, demonstrating student reflection, engagement and growth resulting from intentional intervention. The chapter will conclude with some closing observations regarding the use of the IDI (Hammer & Bennett, 2001) as well as the GPI (Braskamp, Braskamp & Merrill, 2008) as two of the many instruments and inventories designed to measure specific knowledge, skills, attitudes, traits, qualities and developmental outcomes.

Intervention Rationale, Goals and Learning Outcomes

Contrary to conventional, depersonalized forms of cognitive learning and knowledge acquisition, this course's approach is highly personalized, affective learning via self-reflection and direct experience with cultural difference including epistemological explorations regarding alternative ways of knowing and validating what we know. Progression through the different stages of development challenges students' sense of self, cultural identity and world view. Thus, the overall intent of this writing-centred course is for students to develop intercultural skills while immersed in another culture and thereby capitalize on the transformative experiential learning potential of study abroad. Accordingly, the course is organized to facilitate and intensify the experiential learning process in a cultural immersion context with two major goals: (1) to introduce students to the value of understanding, accepting, and adapting to cultural difference and (2) to improve the overall cultural immersion experience by providing essential predeparture, during-semester, and re-entry learning designed to help students develop intercultural skills during all stages of the intercultural experience.

Learning outcomes derived from these course goals are (1) to understand the advantages and disadvantages of culture study, including the contrast of internal versus external perspectives, and the concept of critical self-consciousness; (2) to encourage critical thinking about culture and to develop perspective-taking abilities; (3) to examine similarities and dissimilarities between and within cultures; and (4) to explore forces that contribute to the development and changes of cultures, including social, economic, political, geographic, environmental, agricultural and religious factors.

The need for a course reflecting these learning outcomes arose from the experience and recognition that, without explicit and intentional intervention into the study-abroad experience, students, in general, will limit themselves to surface-level observations and experiences abroad. In much the same way that service-learning distinguishes itself from volunteering, the intercultural learning process requires a framework within which students reflect on their experiences, analyse behaviours and values, suggest tentative conclusions or generalizations, and apply such to the next set of experiences. Repetition of this experiential learning cycle (Kolb, 1984) throughout the immersion experience is critical for the development of intercultural skills, not the least of which is an emergent understanding of how the student's own cultural identity is socially constructed. With both theoretical work and related research underscoring the importance of facilitating the development of intercultural competence in order to optimize the transformative nature of study abroad, this course is a response that combines both research and application. Institutional empirical data, derived from the IDI being administered to all students on long-term study abroad, pre and post their experience, substantiates the national research findings that, students left to their own devices will tend to gain very little in the way of intercultural development as the Georgetown University Consortium Project with 1,300 student participants (Vande Berg, Balkum, Scheid & Whalen, 2004) confirms. This study found that study abroad without intervention results in consistent, but rather *modest*, intercultural development of an average of a 2.22 gain on the IDI's developmental scale, an assessment tool that is employed to measure intercultural development and inform both general course goals and individualized learning objectives.

Application and Intervention in Cross-Cultural Learning as Reflected in Student Voices

With this book's primary focus on *student voices*, I will offer in this chapter excerpts from student writings which reflect the four learning outcomes mentioned earlier, guided by pre-departure seminars and reflection assignments capitalizing on the *laboratory of the other culture* to develop intercultural competence.

While culture as civility and culture as solidarity are at times at odds with one another, T. S. Eliot, though a connoisseur of high cultures, perhaps sums it up, when he says culture is 'first of all what the anthropologists claim: the way of a particular people living together in one place', but also 'the *whole way of life* of a people, from birth to the grave, from morning to night and even in sleep' (1948, p. 31). The latter is significant in that so much of when and how we engage in culture is unconscious rather than conscious. It is the gap between the two that we as international educators must seek to bridge and/or close by raising the level of consciousness and reflection which a student left to his own devices might not engage in. As Heidegger puts it, it is the set of 'pre-understandings' which allow specific acts of understanding to happen. In fact, Heidegger replaces the word 'subject' with the word '*Dasein*' which translates into 'being-there'. *Dasein* is determined by the world and the horizon in which we are placed. Thus, *Dasein* is by definition a 'being-in-the-world'. As a result, the way we project ourselves is to a large extent dictated by our context. At the anthropological level, Heidegger's philosophy consequently undermines any claim to universalism and the concept of man as an autonomous being with definite properties and an identity. Instead, he prefers to describe *Dasein* as an 'ability-to-be' (*Seinkönnen*) and as an always unfinished project. One of his favourite statements was, 'possibility is greater than reality'. It is here where our students abroad will find themselves, in this '*Dasein*', in this '*Seinkönnen*' by not merely immersing themselves into another culture, but by immersing themselves with intent and reflection, taking the focus on the *self* during the first month, to the *other* during the second month, then to the *synthesis* or integration of the two during the third and generally last phase abroad, with guidance in the form of ethnographic and interculturalist–constructivist methods, focusing on a progression of critical analysis of the three focus areas and culminating in a research paper.

Specifically, students are provided with a series of ethnographic assignments designed to stimulate engagement with the host culture in a basic participant–observer mode designed around specific learning outcomes capitalizing on the laboratory of the other culture to develop intercultural competence. The following truncated excerpts reflect learning outcomes 1, 2 and 3 (above).

Samantha – Spain

Assignment Week 1: Splash!

I am exhausted physically, mentally and somewhat emotionally, which is rather odd for me.

Mary – Spain

Assignment Week 2: Culture-Shock

It may sound odd, but the cultural practice that has 'astonished' me the most so far is the daily 'night-life'. Every night, starting at about 18:00, the people of Salamanca – seemingly all of them – take to the streets. Every night, there are gatherings in parks, at cafes, at the bars, and at the stores. People come out by themselves, with their dogs, with their friends, and with their families – even the members that are not old enough to walk, and those too old to walk far. And the center of this night-life is another cultural attribute – the Plaza Mayor.

No matter where you go in Spain, every city and town has a Plaza Mayor (though it may go by a different name), and it is always – almost literally – the center of the city, and the center of these nightly socials. …

The reason behind the popularity of these nightly shopping trips is easy for any observer or participant to understand – it's a social activity. Even if you go out alone, you're surrounded by crowds of people. If you don't run into someone you know, it's easy to engage people in the stores or in a café or bar over a drink. In short, these nightly outings are an amazing social practice in a culture that values society, socializing, and even just the practice (and exercise) of walking.

Conclusions and Observations (Myself and Patricia): Compared to both of our home cultures, the nightlife here is very different …. It fulfills both personal and social needs, and as such is as practical as it is diverting. And while it may be odd, and even overwhelming for foreigners at first, it is easy to adapt to, and enchanting – if not almost addicting – once one becomes accustomed to the nightly outings ….

Assignment Week 3: Experiential Learning Cycle

Positive Experiences: Good roommates, meeting Paloma and others, ISEP program, tour of Murcia, Erasmus soccer games

Negative Experiences: Sitting at the airport alone for several hours, my housing and the bill, showering, language barrier with French roommate, inconvenience of stores

Assignment 3: Experiential Learning Cycle

Although I have had some pretty funny negative experiences, one of my positive experiences has probably shaped my entire experience here. I have reflected on this one event many times and I have come to the conclusion that I am very lucky for this to have happened.

 … I heard someone say, 'Hello' – not hola but actually hello. Again, this is not very uncommon late at night; however, it is usually a man that is trying to talk to us. This voice was a woman.

 A long dialogue played out in my head. Should I turn around? I thought this person could not possibly know me. I was scared …

 As it is pointed out in the article, 'Towards Ethnorelativism: A Developmental Model Of Intercultural Sensitivity', the history of cross-cultural interactions tended to end badly for at least one party, if not both … or at least hurt feelings. Then I recalled a generalization I had heard from another exchange student that had been studying here for the past five months. She said that Murcians are very nice and they are excited to meet Americans because there are so few Americans that actually visit Murcia. I had nothing to lose so I tested this generalization; I turned around and said, 'Hola.' This is how I met Paloma, Miguel and Maria …. I was so excited about actually meeting the locals and for now the generalization about Murcians being nice stands. However, this event launched my Experiential Learning Cycle.

Experience: I was approached by locals on the street. … Although the experience could be considered somewhat anti-climatic, my reflection of this night has put many things into perspective for me. Before this experience I had not spoken to anyone I did not know or did not speak English. I was terrified that the locals did not like me because they really tend to stare …. I was scared that people would judge me based on the actions and the sentiments of the former president of the United States, George W. Bush. Maybe it is the American cultural trait of individualism in me that just wants to, 'resist being thought of as [a] representative of any homogenous group,' (Being An American Abroad, 24), or perhaps I am just scared of the stereotype. However, this experience has given me confidence. The three Murcians proved to be nice and generally interested in Americans. They were so welcoming…. Maria and I talked politics for a long time. … They made me feel very comfortable and gave me the boost of confidence I needed in order to actually speak Spanish in public. … The other interesting point to note is that this event began in the street and ended in a bar – two places I am weary of. … Contrary to the United States, the college students in Spain go to the bars for socialization and to have a couple of beers. I like the idea of conversation being more important than the actual drinking …

Reflection: It was a perfect night that gave my troubled mind some comfort…. Before I left the States I had already been reviewing stereotypes and generalizations. Therefore, I was not surprised that before I even acted I had analyzed the situation based on both positive and negative generalizations. This event has helped me to relax and put much less emphasis on the stereotypes…. Also, the experience solidified what the other exchange student had said about the sincerity of the Murcians' interest in and caring about Americans …

Generalization: Although Murcians know a lot about other cultures, the city is small and tired of the same people. They want to experience something new.

Applying the things I have learned from this experience should be rather easy. I now know that people are not staring to be mean. They are simply curious…. I plan on using this experience as a guideline for how to behave in a social setting and know that I can be at ease. I have more confidence with my Spanish and I now know that I can speak in public. I can apply the genuine willingness of the three Murcians to help me through my journey of learning Spanish. No one is going to make fun of me …

Application: I can relax in my interactions with locals …

Students are asked to reflect weekly on and write about their experiences by posting these on the home university's Blackboard site. The work is accessible to the instructor at the home campus *and* to the other students in the course. The students are then required to review their peers' postings on the same assignment and provide feedback. The key here is that the students' peers are located in many different cultures around the globe, not at the same programme/university site or even in the same host culture. Advancing discussion of intercultural concepts with peers in other cultures as opposed to discussion with peers in the same host culture avoids the common pitfall of soothing one another's discomforts with judgemental references. Instead, it forces each student to focus on the essence of each situation taking the learning to a meta-level, that is, above the specific host culture and its idiosyncrasies. This feature enables the students and instructor to examine how similar cultural processes are at work in different settings with dissimilar outcomes.

Megan – Ghana

Assignment – Week 3: Experiential Learning Cycle

Positive Experiences:

- Learning that my dorm room was much bigger than most in the States, even though I feared it would actually be a mud hut.
- Successful navigation through international airports for the first time.
- Realizing that the new currency system makes conversion from the American dollar much easier.
- Going on 'shopping sprees' that cost less than 10 dollars.
- Having not yet seen one snake. Anywhere.
- Learning to adapt to the laid back, stress free approach to academics.
- Travelling to Elmina Castle, one of the first ports ever erected, and a vital spot on the slave trade triangle.
- African fabric! It's gorgeous, colorful, and LOUD. There are also seamstresses everywhere, you could have a wardrobe made within a week.
- Learning the Twi language. The acquisition has been much easier than I anticipated since most locals speak a mixture of Twi and English infused together.

Negative Experiences:

- Not being able to accurately explain my experience to those at home. I feel as if they simply have no idea what I'm going through.
- Being shunned by most Ghanaian girls in class. A friendlier female explained to me that they are taught to do so, because American girls have no principles.
- Realizing that you are the 'white spot' in any social situation. Others' interest in you feels less genuine, and as if it's purely for their amusement.
- Being harassed by military officials at check points. This doesn't occur with all of them, but when it does it's terrifying. Large men with military uniforms and semi-automatic weapons strewn about their person is scary enough, when you add sexual harassment to the mix, you feel helpless.
- Being pick-pocketed!!!!
- Realizing that everyone/everything seems to have a price. The western cultural influence is devastating in this respect. It makes me wonder if money really does make the world go 'round.

- Feeling a distinct separation between races/ethnic backgrounds within the ISEP group. It's like the huge pink elephant in the room that no one wants to discuss.
- Having 'oboruni' shouted at you EVERYWHERE you go. Oboruni this, oboruni that. Literal translation = white man. However, it has come to mean 'foreigner' in most cases.

My Experience: At first, I hated being called 'oboruni'… it made me nervous simply because I didn't know what it meant. After the meaning was explained I felt relieved that they were simply pointing out that I was American, and not something horribly offensive. However, it begins to feel like you're constantly being called out in a crowd. It's difficult to assimilate when there are always strangers pointing at you and yelling 'foreigner', and inevitably everyone within ear shot turns to look. Some days I try to realize that I look just as strange to locals as they might to me. Other days, it would be nice to be able to fade into the crowd …

Reflection: Overall, I don't see this as entirely negative because the intention is not to embarrass or harass. Whenever this is shouted it is generally accompanied by a wide eyed look of sheer amazement. It's as if they are so surprised to see you that they just can't control shouting out about what they've discovered. Though I may receive/interpret it a number of different ways depending on my mood, I know that it generally comes from a good place …

Conclusion: In Twi, we addressed the issue with Dr. Kofi (our instructor). He explained the connotation and origin, as well as the intention. It put us all at ease. He also taught us the term for 'local' … so that now we have a running joke with some of the merchants: whenever they yell 'foreigner' we just point right back and yell 'local'. They always laugh, and then commend us for learning the language. It's been a good ice-breaker, and even gotten me a few deals on purchases as well as an impromptu language lesson.

Applying the Knowledge: I feel as if this is simply another example of how critical it is to examine the background and nature of what you are experiencing while abroad …. At home, shouting anything at anyone is considered rude, offensive, and inappropriate. In Ghana, you shout if you're happy or mad, excited or bored. It's just another way to express oneself.

As Heidegger maintains in his main work, *Sein und Zeit* (1927), where he develops a holistic epistemology according to which all meaning is context-dependent and permanently anticipated from a particular horizon, perspective or background of intelligibility. This particular horizon is important for students to identify in order to then expand this horizon, taking in the perspectives of the host culture. Again, it is important to remember that all students enrolled in this course are reading each others' writings, thus enabling cultural comparisons beyond the cultural contexts of one's own host culture's horizon, a horizon that is marked by human *effort*.

This effort then produces acts and practice, most often predictable practices, because culture, according to cultural theorist Stuart Hall, is 'a process, a set of practices' (1982, p. 2). It is these social interactions which are most often cited as constituting 'culture shock' or 'cultural bumps', ranging from language-barrier issues, to personal-space issues, to getting-acquainted rituals, to seemingly simplistic matters such as navigating public transportation, shopping, eating in and eating out, negotiating living space and cooperative encounters, managing new concepts of time, etc.; as T. S. Eliot puts it, 'the *whole way of life* of a people, from morning to night and even in sleep' (1948, p. 31). The everyday is linked to modes of being, modes of encountering understanding, modes of responsibility and modes of being human.

El Medhi, on Exchange in United States from Morocco

Assignment – Week 3: Experiential Learning Cycle

My Experience: One of the most important differences between American and Moroccan youth culture is partying. In Morocco, we do not have house parties because all university students can go to clubs. In my second weekend at Bellarmine, I went with some international students to a house party for the first time in my life …

Reflecting on My Experience: At the time we got to the party, I found that the house was full of people. The thing that I liked the most about this party is that most people study at Bellarmine. I also noticed that all people knew each other, which was the good side of this party, so I was introduced to a lot of people, and I made many new friends …

My Conclusion: American house parties are one of the ways that students use to socialize. All international students told me that they made a lot of friends through house parties. In my point of view, these kinds of parties that are organized every weekend give students the chance to see each other and have fun after busy study days. Socializing is one of the most important aspects of the Moroccan culture …. The difference that exists is that in Morocco, we do not have loud music and a lot of people; we mostly have house parties between close friends …. I think the house parties in US are the equivalent of clubs in Morocco.

Application: I had a good experience attending my first house party; therefore, I will attend more parties in the future …. I also learned that I do not have to be shy and feel free to talk and introduce myself to learn about new people.

Evelin, on Exchange from Bulgaria in United States

Assignment Week 4 – Cultural Bump

One of the observed things which bother me is the division between fresh-man and students with other standings. At first I did not notice that, but now, when I get to know more people my observation is becoming more justified.

First time I noticed the division when I was hanging out with my American friends and some freshmen stopped by to meet me. I felt very excited that these guys not only were willing to meet me but they also knew my name and were very friendly. But at the same time it was awkward to see my friends being cold to these young kids.

I thought about that for a while but then I decided that it just was my wrong perception. However, the similar situation happened again. I … to my big surprise, my American friends, majority of who are juniors and seniors, had a face expression of disapproval, it seemed as I was guilty, as I have done something very bad. I was trying to get that through my mind, why they do not like my new friends, what the reasons are. … I talked to my friends to find the reason what causes such a behavior, why there is such a division of people according to their statuses … my friends simply answered: 'They are freshmen. You do not mess with freshmen, they are miserable and unpop-ular' …. It was shocking for me since I have never encountered such a trend. America in my mind has always been associated the high awareness of human rights and very strong anti-discriminatory policies …. I have been asking myself all sort of questions, what can be the cause of such behavior and determined that it is cultural values and perceptions which differenti-ate people, depending on the environment and customs they have been growing up in …

While initial assignments focusing on the *self* (culture shock reflections, cul-tural bump explorations. experiential learning cycle activities, etc.) point in the direction of learning outcome 1, the remainder of these learning outcomes are achieved through a combination of experiential and research based assignments on topics involving the *other* which include the host culture's concept of time, play, institutions, organizations, systems, and values, followed by the synthesis of the self and the other, including the final research paper which most often addresses learning outcome 4 *to explore forces that contribute to the development and changes of cultures, including social, economic, political, geographic, environ-mental, agricultural, and religious factors.*

The titles of some of the students' research papers might serve to offer insight into the student voices reflecting this course segment as well: 'The Struggle of German Social Democracy in the Era of Globalization'; 'How the Educational System in Ireland Has Helped Maintain Class Inequality'; 'Significance of the

Didgeridoo in Australian Aboriginal Music'; 'Evolution of a Crime Free Land: The Formation of Contemporary Japanese Justice'; 'The Basque People and Their Place in Spanish Society Today'; 'Death Toll – 26 and Rising: The Problem of Gender Violence in Spain'; 'The Reality of Globalization; A Comparison of Australian Aboriginals and Native Americans'; 'Patriarchy in Ecuador'; 'A Quiet Voice: Hong Kong'; 'Scarification in West Africa: Tradition versus Modernity'; 'Education and Democracy in Sweden and the USA'.

Conclusions

The above course excerpts serve as examples of the potential of reflective, empathetic engagement in transformative learning in study abroad through critical inquiry, the intellectual practice of being the subject and object by going beyond being the silent observer returning home with little to share, particularly in terms of *self* reflection on someone or something *different*, i.e. the *other*. Daloz (2000) examined individuals' experiences with someone they viewed as different and pointed out the important role that empathy plays in engaging with this otherness:

> For the experience to be more than simply an encounter, for it to be a constructive engagement, there had to be some sense of empathic connection with people different from themselves. In some significant way the inner experience of the other was engaged, a bond was formed, and some deep lesson about connection across differences was learned.
>
> (p. 110)

While various research assignments on broad cultural topics have their place in this course, and constitute about 50 per cent of the grade, it is important to note that the other half of the course focuses on the experiential aspects of the cultural immersion experience, emphasizing that the everyday is distinctive in not being distinctive, but in need of reflection. Thus, assignments capturing critical incidents which trigger events that engage students in the social and historical matrix of language, relationships, the exchange of necessities, and the basic ordering of society are the focus of these student excerpts, linking the everyday to ontology, epistemology, ethics, and anthropology.

The transformative learning that takes place by crossing these boundaries between 'us' and 'them' are skills that are transferable into everyday life not only while abroad, but upon return to the home culture. What is more, we have instruments that can measure these 'personal gains', this 'value added' aspect of a study-abroad experience. The IDI (intercultural Development Inventory) and GPI (Global Perspectives Inventory) are incorporated into pre- and post-experience workshops, allowing us to measure student gains which have proven to be substantial for participants in this course vis-à-vis the research reflected in the Georgetown Consortium Project and its marginal gains without intervention. Ideal would be for an institution to be able to compare the gains on both instruments with data taken from their administration to all freshmen and seniors, in addition to pre- and post-study-abroad groups (an effort currently underway at Bellarmine University). Furthermore, it is fair to say this course also addresses quite successfully the five primary reasons for assessing education-abroad outcomes: tracking student learning, personal growth, participant satisfaction/attitudes, programme development, and the need for institutional data (Sutton & Rubin, 2004).

References

Bennett, J. M. (2008). On becoming a global soul. In Savicki (2008).

Bosley, G. W. (2008). *Globe trotter survey.* Louisville, KY: Bellarmine University.

Braskamp, L. A., Braskamp D. C., & Merrill K. C. (2008). *Global perspective inventory (GPI), its purpose, construction, potential uses, and psychometric characteristics.* Chicago: Global Perspective Institute. Available from: www.gpinv.org [Accessed April 2009].

Daloz, L. A. P. (2000). Transformative learning for the common good. In J. Mezirow & associates (Eds.), *Learning as transformation: Critical perspectives on a theory in progress* (pp. 103-123). San Francisco: Jossey-Bass.

Elliot, T. S. (1948). *Notes towards the definition of culture.* London: Faber & Faber.

Hall, S. (1982). Culture and state. In *Popular culture.* Milton Keynes, UK: Open University Press.

Hammer, M. R., & Bennett, M. J. (2001). *Intercultural development inventory.* Portland, OR: Intercultural Communication Institute.

Heidegger, M. (1927). *Sein und Zeit.* Tübingen: Max Niemeyer Verlag.

Kolb, D. A. (1984). *Experiential learning: Experience as the source of learning and development.* Englewood Cliffs, NJ: Prentice Hall.

Kuhn, T. S. (1970). *The structure of scientific revolutions* (p. 112). Chicago: University of Chicago Press.

National Survey of Student Engagement (2007). *Experiences that matter: Enhancing student learning and success: Annual report 2007.* Bloomington, IN.

Savicki, V. (Ed.). (2008). *Developing intercultural competence and transformation: Theory, research and application in international education.* Sterling, VA: Stylus.

Sutton, R. & Rubin, D. (2004). The GLOSSARI project: Initial findings from a system-wide research initiative on study abroad learning outcomes. *Frontiers: The Interdisciplinary Journal of Study Abroad, 10,* 65-82.

Vande Berg, M., Balkum, J. A., Scheid, M., & Whalen B. J. (2004). The Georgetown University consortium project: A report from the halfway mark. *Frontiers: The Interdisciplinary Journal of Study Abroad, 10,* 101-116.

6
Discovering the World –
Discovering Myself

DANUTA DE GROSBOIS, JOHN KAETHLER AND
ALEXANDRA YOUNG

Introduction

Brock University, a mid-size Canadian university, has during most of its 44-year history had an unofficial internationalization mandate. From its inception, Brock hoped to achieve this by teaching courses with international content and by accepting fee-paying international students. With the advent of globalization, this passive approach was replaced by a mission statement designed, amongst other things, to develop students to become global citizens. Hence, student exchanges and experiential learning programmes became the engines for driving this change.

The number of exchange programmes has grown rapidly, providing Brock students with opportunities to study on six continents. While participation in exchange programmes has increased, some students have been deterred from spending a semester or two abroad by the expense, while others have been deterred by the time commitment. To engage this group, Brock developed short-term experiential learning programmes, called Solidarity Experiences Abroad (SEA). The originator of these programmes is Raoul Masseur, Catholic chaplain at Brock University. He approached John Kaethler, Brock's Director of International Services, with the idea, and together these offices have developed and run two- to three-week summer experiential learning programmes in Peru, Brazil, Ecuador and Namibia.

Brock University is a public and secular institution, so while Campus Ministries is the main organizer of SEA programmes, they are open to all university students. To develop a successful programme, organizers must ensure that participants understand the programme's objectives. Participants are expected to partake in volunteer placements as guests, not as experts, and to learn from the people of that country rather than to teach them our ways. In brief, SEA programmes are designed to open the minds of Canadian participants to other people and their cultures in the belief that it is more important what you do for the rest of your life in Canada than what you do for several weeks in a foreign country. Alexandra Young, a Brock Tourism and Environment student participated in the SEA-Namibia programme in May 2007 and subsequently conducted research for her honours thesis on how similar or dissimilar the motivations, experiences, and personal growth of participants on Brock's exchanges and SEA programmes were.

The Role of International Travel in Student Education: Literature Review

The impact of international travel has received substantial attention in academia for a long time. Research examines numerous potential benefits for international travel; however, these are believed to depend on the traveller's personality, travel motivations and expectations, or the activities and interactions abroad. The motivation to travel is especially important in determining the impact of the experience in the traveller's life.

Travel Motivations of Study-Abroad Participants and Volunteers

Research in travel motivation has been important in understanding and predicting travel decisions and choices. Motivation is conceptually viewed as 'a state of need, a condition that serves as a driving force to display different kinds of behaviour toward certain types of activities, developing preferences, arriving at some expected satisfactory outcome' (Cha, McCleary & Uysal, 1995). Travel and tourism researchers have been exploring two forces associated with motivation, push and pull factors. Push factors are the intrinsic motivations and desires that are perceived by the individual which 'push' them into making a travel decision, such as personal escape, thrill and adventure, and social interactions, while 'pull' factors are the more tangible aspects of the destination which attract the individual to a particular site, such as a destination's natural or artificial attractions (Kim, Jogaratnam & Noh, 2006; Mannell & Kleiber, 1997). Seminal work on these factors was conducted by Crompton (1979) who identified nine motivational factors influencing the selection of vacations and destinations. Socio-psychological motives included escape from a perceived mundane environment, exploration and evaluation of self, relaxation, prestige, regression, enhancement of kinship relationships, and facilitation of social interaction, while cultural motives included novelty and education.

Extensive prior research on travel motivations of study-abroad participants and SEA participants indicates substantially different motivational factors for these groups. For study abroad participants, the desire to obtain better education, learn a foreign language, or learn about another country are very important, while SEA participants can be considered volunteer tourists. The latter are usually defined as

> tourists who, for various reasons, volunteer in an organized way to undertake holidays that might involve aiding or alleviating the material poverty of some groups in society, the restoration of certain environments or research into aspects of society or environment.
>
> (Wearing, 2001)

Volunteer tourism is an important and growing type of tourism that has considerable impact both on the host community and its participants (Gray & Campbell, 2007; McIntosh & Zahra, 2007; Singh & Singh, 2004; Wearing, 2001, 2002). There is disagreement regarding the nature of volunteer travellers' motivations. Several authors argue that volunteer tourism is a tourist's altruistic behaviour that potentially benefits both host community and tourist through personal development and growth, increasing understanding of the world, acceptance of other cultures, and influencing lifestyle (Gray & Campbell, 2007; Singh & Singh, 2004; Tikkanen, 2007; Wearing, 2002). Some authors, however, argue that volunteer tourists' 'selfless' contributions to local communities and environments are actually self-serving attempts to build their own cultural capital in order to have better chances of finding jobs, etc. (Gray & Campbell, 2007). This argument is strongly discussed with respect to student volunteers who travel either before entering post-secondary education or after, prior to starting a job in the 'real' world when this kind of experience can 'enhance one's access to both social spaces and employment' (Duffy, 2002).

Experiences Abroad

To understand the impact of an international experience a traveller must understand his/her motivations to travel, the kind of activities engaged in, the challenges faced, and the feelings and emotions experienced abroad. There is agreement in the literature that the experience of travelling is subjective and stems from how one interprets and adjusts to new environmental surroundings (MacCannell, 1976). The benefits are greater when the traveller engages in the community and interacts with locals. These cross-cultural encounters are becoming highly valued as 'a rich source of narrative, learning, appreciation, inspiration, cultural respect, solidarity, and equality in the search for sustainable models of tourism' (Butler & Hinch, 1996; McIntosh & Zahra, 2007).

Prior research indicates that 'being there' may develop travellers' feelings of attachment to the new place. 'Place attachment' has been widely studied (Lengkeek, 2002; Trigger & Mulcock, 2005) and is described as 'a fusion of human and natural order ... defined less by unique location, landscape and communities than by focusing of experiences and intentions onto particular settings' (Relph, 1976). According to Trigger and Mulcock (2005), place attachment can become a motivational force for individuals to act on their feelings towards a particular place, if for any reason it is threatened or damaged. Travelling abroad might also bring feelings of anxiety and uncertainty (Stier, 2003) and cause culture shock (Westwood, Lawrence & Paul, 1986). Oberg (1960) defined culture shock as 'a disease precipitated by the anxiety that results from losing all familiar signs and symbols of social intercourse'.

The existing literature on international experiences strongly suggests that they are highly individualistic and personalized, result from a combination of many factors and can be influenced by decisions that can drastically change ones' perspective upon reflection, particularly after the experience.

Re-Entry

Often when travellers return home, there may be a period of reflection accompanied by reverse culture shock. Martin hypothesized (1984) that it is during the re-entry culture shock when travellers become aware of personal changes as they readjust to their familiar culture. A vast literature discusses perceived benefits of an international experience (Emanoil, 1999; Guoqing, 2003; Lindsey, 2005; Stier, 2003). Some of these include: an increased commitment to peace; more interest in international affairs; increased empathy; the development of a new worldview; increased willingness and participation in studying other languages; spending more time in college while also becoming higher-achieving students; developing more analytic ways of thinking; increased cultural awareness; increased desire to travel or live abroad; increased cultural sensitivity; enhanced self-awareness; values and beliefs; better understanding of their own country; opening the mind to new ways of thinking; awareness and insight into personal values and beliefs; social awareness and challenges to societal values and beliefs; appreciation of differences; cultural sensitivity and anti-discriminatory practices; social justice and professional identity development. When students are the tourists, many even claim their international experiences to be 'life-changing' (Cushner, 2004), yet there is limited research available to either support or challenge such statements.

Methodology

To investigate the similarities and differences between the personal experiences of international volunteers and study abroad participants, quantitative and qualitative data were collected through a combination of interviews and a self-administered questionnaire. Participants were Brock University students and some recent alumni who had taken part in study-abroad or international volunteer programmes within the past 5 years for a minimum of 2 weeks and a maximum of 1 year in duration.

Questionnaires were administered to a sample of Brock study-abroad and volunteer participants, recruited through a variety of means. Interested students were then asked to reflect upon their most recent international educational activity and to fill out the survey based on memories of that activity as well as indicating availability for a follow-up interview. In total, 52 usable questionnaires were collected. Interviews were held with selected participants (3 involved in study abroad and 3 involved in volunteering programmes). Interview participants were randomly selected from those who indicated willingness to participate in a follow-up interview.

Descriptive Statistics

Half of survey respondents participated in study abroad and half as international volunteers. Their average age was 22.7 years, and the majority were female, with a higher proportion among volunteers than study abroad. Participants studied in different faculties at Brock. It is noteworthy that volunteers came mostly from faculties of Social Science, Applied Health Sciences and Humanities, while the study-abroad participants came from faculties of Business, Humanities, Applied Health Sciences and Social Science.

The international programmes differed markedly in duration, from 2 weeks to 12 months. The majority of volunteer programmes were 2–4 weeks long, while study abroad programmes were usually at least 3–4 months long, with most between 5 and 12 months. Students travelled to diverse destinations, including South America, Europe, Africa, Asia, Oceania, North America, Caribbean and Central America. For the volunteer participants, the two most popular destinations were South America and Africa, while the study-abroad participants preferred Europe followed by Oceania.

The majority of respondents indicated they had previously travelled internationally, mostly for tourism. Among the study-abroad participants, only two had previously studied abroad (both during high school), so for the overwhelming majority the programme was their first study-abroad experience. Among the volunteers, six participants had previously volunteered internationally.

Travel Motivations

The most important motivational factors for taking part were to: have new experiences; see the world; experience a new culture; and give one a new perspective (Figure 6.1). The interviews confirmed further that 'experiencing something new' is among the most important motivating factors (mentioned by 5 out of 6 interview participants). The importance of motivating factors did not differ markedly between the two groups.

Although the two groups did not rank differently the four most important motivating factors, there were significant differences in the importance they assigned to several other motivating factors. An important factor for study abroad participants and ranked fourth was to have fun; however, it was less important for volunteers. Study-abroad participants also considered the following factors more important compared to volunteers: career advancement; travel without parents; try new foods; and relaxation. Volunteers, however, considered 'to help others' to be among the most important motivating factors (ranking fourth after 'to have new experience', to experience a new culture' and 'to see the world'), while for study abroad participants this factor was less important and ranked as fifteenth. Volunteers also considered the fact that the programme took place during the summer break as a more important motivating factor than study abroad participants (Figure 6.1).

Participants reported financial considerations as their greatest concern prior to taking part. According to one SEA participant, '[It] seemed kind of an absurd concept to spend $3000 to go help someone abroad when you could just send the money.'

Although both groups were concerned about finances, study-abroad participants were more concerned about running out of money while abroad; however, volunteers were more concerned than study-abroad participants that

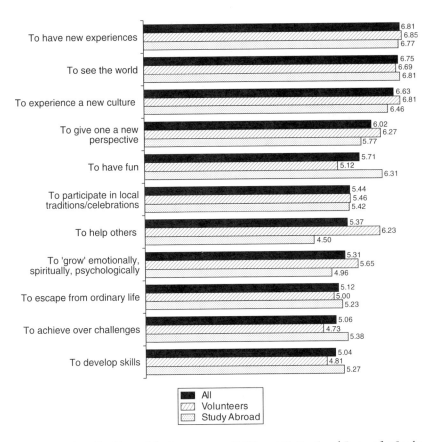

Figure 6.1 Mean Rankings of the Importance of Different Motivational Factors for Study Participants

family and friends were worried about their safety. Issues such as self-doubt, being away from family and friends, cultural differences, getting time off work or school were hypothesized to play an important role, but turned out not to be major concerns for either group.

It is noteworthy that despite expressed higher levels of worry about concerned family and friends, volunteers indicated that they received a lot of support from families and friends for their participation, as did study-abroad participants. Additionally, the interview participants stressed the important role family and friends played in encouraging them to travel either by strongly recommending it or by sharing their own travel experiences.

Prior to departure, participants considered themselves adventurous and extroverted, friendly, and outgoing. However, they did not feel very knowledgeable about what they would be doing while abroad. One volunteer indicated this lack of understanding of the programme's purpose in the following words: 'I didn't really know what to expect, the whole "solidarity" part of it, because really

I hadn't known [that] the purpose was to make bonds with the community instead of just go and provide services for them.' Also, on average, participants did not feel very knowledgeable about the country they were travelling to; however, study abroad participants indicated higher knowledge than volunteers.

In-Country Experience

The second stage of an international experience is when the participant becomes a sojourner. During this stage, it is important to examine the student's feelings, activities engaged in, and any difficulties encountered (Figure 6.2).

Upon arrival at their destination, study-abroad participants felt great excitement and happiness yet also somewhat nervous and overwhelmed. However, they felt neither sadness nor regret. There were no significant differences between volunteers and study-abroad participants with respect to feelings upon arrival at their destination. As a volunteer participant reflected on arriving in the host country:

'I was really excited, I had no idea about what to expect, I was exhausted, my luggage was lost. [...] I didn't know what we were going to be doing because we didn't really have a firm itinerary for the first couple of days when we were getting into the community, and we got in pretty late'.

However, for a study-abroad student it was about being independent and on his own:

'I went to Peru, I had to establish myself. It's like you have a brand new, fresh start. And you get to pick your own friends, you get to pick your own extra-curriculars, and stuff like that down there. So I got to set up my life'.

While abroad, the students participated in numerous activities and events. The most popular activities were: spending time and interacting with locals; eating local, culturally traditional foods; visiting sites of historic, political or religious importance; visiting sites of environmental significance or to see wildlife; and travelling for personal fulfilment or to accomplish a personal goal. There were no substantial differences between study-abroad participants and volunteers in these most popular activities; however, a number of differences were found regarding less popular activities.

Study-abroad participants involved themselves in the following activities more often than volunteers: completing homework or students' schoolwork; travelling to country/countries beyond the borders of where you were living; travelling for the purpose of participating in a local/national event, ceremony or holiday; and participating in national holiday celebrations. However, volunteers participated more often in: fundraising events; religious ceremony events; health awareness campaigns; and travelling to cities/towns/areas that were less developed (Figure 6.2).

During their programmes, volunteers had to deal with situations which many found very challenging, as one volunteer confirmed, '[it] will test your boundaries.

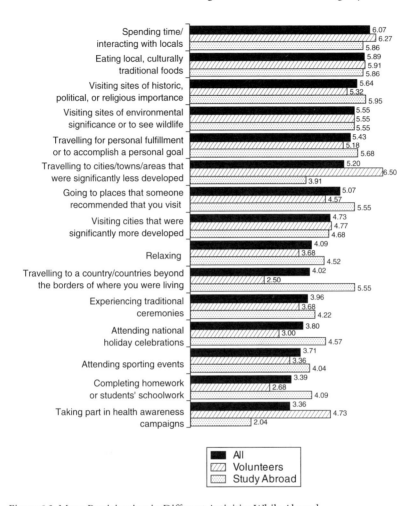

Figure 6.2 Mean Participation in Different Activities While Abroad

You will have to conform to different circumstances. [...] You will be put into a different social structure, with different norms'. When asked whether anything was difficult to deal with or comprehend, 44 per cent of all respondents indicated they did. The proportion of students facing difficult situations was much higher in the group of volunteers (82.3 per cent of questionnaire respondents) than the study-abroad participants (47.6 per cent).

While abroad, study-abroad participants remembered most often experiencing feelings of happiness and excitement; however, volunteers reported higher levels of happiness than study-abroad participants. The feeling of excitement was the most often remembered emotion by those interviewed: 'I remember waking up every day and being so excited to be over there' and 'Every day was memorable!' The third most frequent feeling was nervousness, experienced equally by both groups.

Participants rarely reported feelings of relief, confusion, sadness, home-sickness, heartbrokenness, or regret. However, while these were infrequent, volunteers indicated higher levels of sadness and being heartbroken than study-abroad participants. This may be because volunteers came across more situations of extreme poverty and more people living with disease or illness treatable with modern medicine. Despite these different experiences, study-abroad participants indicated they felt very connected to the people/city/country with no marked differences between volunteers and study-abroad participants.

Re-Entry

Upon returning home, the predominant feeling shared by volunteers and study-abroad participants was to see more of the world while also longing to return to their place of sojourn to visit friends they made while abroad. However, this did not diminish their excitement at seeing family and friends again.

It is widely stated in the literature that international travel can be 'life-changing' in many ways. Participants in this study (both at questionnaire and interview stages) strongly confirmed this. The survey responses indicated overwhelming support for the statement: 'I believe that the trip and my experiences abroad have changed my life.' Interviewees further reinforced this statement, saying: 'I just think in a completely different way now that I'm back'; 'I never thought that it would change me as much as it did […] Certainly my outlook on life changed'; 'It would be impossible for someone to go on a trip like this and not be changed or affected in some way.'

Life changes due to international travel can have very different manifestations: they may be related to personal development, changes in beliefs, career changes or particular actions that would not be otherwise undertaken. To investigate these in more depth, respondents were asked to rank their agreement with 22 statements describing perceived changes in their goals, actions, knowledge and beliefs that could result from international travel (Figure 6.3). The highest-ranked changes indicated were: 'I have travelled more, or have plans to, as a result of my experiences with this trip'; 'my experiences abroad have become a part of my identity'; and 'I have a broadened multicultural perspective'. There were no significant differences between volunteers and study-abroad participants; however, they differed in perceptions of other changes in their lives. Volunteers reported higher levels of agreement with statements: 'I plan on volunteering or working while travelling abroad in the future'; 'I spend more time volunteering or working with similar organizations to those I gained experience with while abroad'; 'I am more aware of social issues' and 'my perception about standards of living have changed'.

Self-Discovery

Personal development and self-reflection are widely recognized as desired outcomes of international travel in general, relevant to volunteers and study abroad

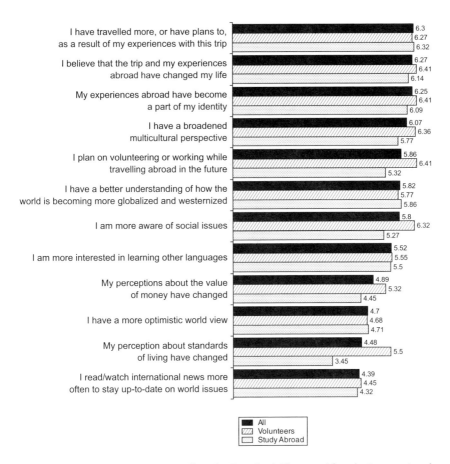

I have travelled more, or have plans to, as a result of my experiences with this trip
6.3
6.27
6.32

I believe that the trip and my experiences abroad have changed my life
6.27
6.41
6.14

My experiences abroad have become a part of my identity
6.25
6.41
6.09

I have a broadened multicultural perspective
6.07
6.36
5.77

I plan on volunteering or working while travelling abroad in the future
5.86
6.41
5.32

I have a better understanding of how the world is becoming more globalized and westernized
5.82
5.77
5.86

I am more aware of social issues
5.8
6.32
5.27

I am more interested in learning other languages
5.52
5.55
5.5

My perceptions about the value of money have changed
4.89
5.32
4.45

I have a more optimistic world view
4.7
4.68
4.71

My perception about standards of living have changed
4.48
5.5
3.45

I read/watch international news more often to stay up-to-date on world issues
4.39
4.45
4.32

All
Volunteers
Study Abroad

Figure 6.3 Mean Responses Regarding the Perceived Changes After the International Experience

participants. Survey respondents strongly agreed that their experiences abroad have become part of their identity and that they reflected on them often. One of the volunteers further explained how reflection played an important role in his personal development:

'It helped me figure out where I was in my present time in life [...] after that [experience] there was a period of reflection, not only for what I had done on the trip, but also how it had affected me, and how these new emotions that I was feeling and the new experiences I was feeling, how I was going to integrate that into my life.'

Another volunteer stressed the importance of international experience in understanding oneself:

'It opens your eyes to the world, to new experiences. It's never wrong to experience something new. [...] It allows you to reflect on different things. And it forces you to understand. [...] How are you expected to pick a career if you don't know who you are?'

This was echoed by two study-abroad participants: 'through travelling you can begin to understand more of the world, of who you are, and what you want from your life, and who you are to other people'; 'By travelling abroad you learn so much about yourself and the world!'

In some cases, international travel not only helps the traveller to better understand him/herself, but can also help them overcome personal crisis and self-doubt and make a new start. This can be illustrated in the following quotes:

'Before I left for Brazil I'd told people that I was on the verge of [being] broken, before I left I wanted to escape, clean my life up. So it [the trip] taught me how to lighten up, joke around with people.'

'In the past, I had wondered and was a little confused about what I wanted to do with my life. [...] It gave me perspective.'

The need for personal changes and the role of self-reflection is strongly illustrated in the following quote:

'[W]hen you see what you are really like, out of context, in another society, and you come back after being away for so long, you start to get a sense of who you really are as a person, you get to really know yourself and you don't want to be the person you were before you left.'

Discovering One's Career

Another potential change is the discovery of a new career path. Respondents in this study indicated moderate overall level of agreement with the statement 'My career path/goals have changed as a result of my experiences abroad'. It is noteworthy that the answers to this question ranged from 1 (not at all) to 7 (very much) with 20 respondents (out of 52) indicating substantial change of career path. The interviews provided some examples of career changes made due to the international programme. One volunteer indicated new interest in making documentaries on Third World countries, while another explained how he withdrew from the university in order to join a seminary and become a priest, as a direct result of two trips to South America, during which he was a student assistant in a service learning programme.

Discovering What We Have

A major theme emerging from the qualitative data analysis related to discovering what we have. Many respondents indicated that travelling abroad and seeing poverty and challenges that people face in other countries made them appreciate their own country and their life:

'I was walking down with the little girls who kept pointing at houses at varying degrees of being built. Some were just a tarp, held up by an umbrella, and they were saying 'look, look: peoples' homes, peoples' homes' and I realized that some people would kill to have the life I have. Why am I squandering it? Why am I, why don't I actually get my butt in gear and finish my degree, be happy, and move on from some of the things I haven't dealt with, and it just made me want to live life more fully.'

'We should be more grateful for what we have. They have nothing down there. You know, we saw the little kids sitting there reading their little books, trying to read, and they are exactly like us, except they just don't have the nice clothes. I just learned to really appreciate what I have more and just seeing how other countries work.'

Scope of the Discovery

The current study indicates that the self-discovery and personal development that take place while on programmes abroad are very subjective and differ by participant. While the overwhelming majority believed this had had a significant impact on their lives and enabled them to discover more about themselves and the world, other respondents did not feel the same. As one of the participants indicated: 'The impact [the experience] had on my life in general was rather minimal. In my practices I was the same both before and after the trip.'

However, the majority of the respondents mentioned important changes in their lives and beliefs related to the international experiences:

'When I came back, my mentality changed, my career direction changed, my focus changed. It's still with me, it follows everything I do.'

'I just think in a completely different way now that I'm back.'

'I matured a lot, and now I see things in a whole different light.'

'I became a lot more independent, and more self-confident.'

'My time abroad definitely changed my life in terms of my own personal development – educationally, psychologically, emotionally.'

'I have grown so much since travelling. I am so much more confident, out of my shell, spiritual, thankful, and more.'

'[This experience] truly allowed me to have some time to get to know myself in ways that I never would have been able to by living in Canada.'

It is interesting to note that, while for the majority of participants the experiences were life changing, they did not lead to great changes in their religious beliefs, degree of pessimism, or changes in academic goals.

Factors Affecting the Discovery

The scope of self-discovery varied significantly. A number of factors can be identified as causes of this diversity: participant's personality; motivation to travel; expectations and attitudes; the nature of the experience itself; and participant's degree of maturity.

In terms of attitude, the interviewed students stressed the importance of being open, flexible and adaptable. Namely, they indicated that people who expected their life abroad to be the same as their life at home and expected the locals to adapt to them did not have as beneficial and enriching experiences as those who were open and adaptable:

> 'I was very open. I was going into a different country, where I didn't speak the language, didn't know anybody, and so the expectations that I had were sort of: what ever happens, happens, and I'll have to deal with it.'

> 'It depends on how you go: if you don't want to go and to learn, then you're not going to have that type of experience.'

Overall, the programmes were perceived by the interviewees, both volunteers and study abroad, as an important and indispensable part of their education, very different from their university studies:

> 'Even though it was short, I learned more from it, about the world and myself, than I have in three years of university.'

> 'What you learn and experience cannot be taught in a classroom!'

> 'Travelling abroad has provided me with an education no undergraduate degree could ever compare with.'

In general participants were supportive and enthusiastic about recommending others to participate in similar international programmes:

> 'To people who come up to me now, saying "oh, I might be going to Honduras", or "I'm thinking of going to Namibia" I say "go in a heartbeat". Go in a heartbeat, it will change your life. You will not regret it. It was just incredible, absolutely incredible.'

Interview respondents mentioned difficulty readjusting to cultural norms, missing friendships they had developed while abroad, and feeling like their life had changed: 'You leave your job for a while and your friends for a while, and when you come back [...] things are different, they don't go back to what they were.'

Conclusions

This study examined study abroad and volunteer programme participants to understand their motivations and experiences and how those impact on their lives afterwards. The study results confirm that international experience can enable students to discover more about themselves and be life changing; however, the degree is very subjective, depending on many factors.

The study indicates that students take part primarily because they want to have new experiences and to see the world. Whereas volunteering participants are also motivated by a strong desire to help others, study-abroad participants are more interested in fun and recreation. These motivations are reflected in the activities in which the two groups are most often engaged. The study further indicates that there can be profound impact on study-abroad participants and volunteers. The changes encompass discovery of oneself, one's career and one's environment. Finally, participants gave enthusiastic testimony to the importance of international experience to their personal development.

The results of this study will be used by international programme organizers to better promote the programmes and to develop pre-departure orientation programmes that place more emphasis on student motivation, attitudes and expectations. As well, they will be able to design better re-entry programming to assist returning participants to enhance their global citizenship. The study suggests that study-abroad and international volunteer programmes complement students' academic programmes, rather than provide academic tourism opportunities. Hence, the study will be helpful in promoting the value of such programmes to Brock faculty. The *raison d'être* of universities is to educate students, and these international programmes have become an integral part of fulfilling that mandate at Brock University. Its student participants are proving St. Augustine perceptive when he said: 'The world is a book, and he who does not travel reads only one page.'

References

Butler, R., & Hinch, T. (Eds.). (1996). *Tourism and indigenous peoples.* London: International Thomson Business Press.

Cha, S., McCleary, K. W., & Uysal, M. (1995). Travel motivations of Japanese overseas travelers: A factor-cluster segmentation approach. *Journal of Travel Research, 34*(1), 33–39.

Crompton, J. L. (1979). Motivations for pleasure vacation. *Annals of Tourism Research, 6*(4), 408–424.

Cushner, K. (2004). *Beyond tourism: A practical guide to meaningful education travel.* Toronto: Scarecrow Education.

Duffy, R. (2002). *A trip too far: Ecotourism, politics and exploitation.* London: Earthscan.

Emanoil, P. (1999). Study abroad expands cultural view, life skills, and academic experience. *Human Ecology Forum, 27,* 10–14.

Gray, N. J., & Campbell, L. M. (2007). A decommodified experience? Exploring aesthetic, economic and ethical values for volunteer ecotourism in Costa Rica. *Journal of Sustainable Tourism, 15*(5), 463–482.

Guoqing, Z. (2003). Study abroad, study abroad! *Chinese education and society, 36*(4), 85–90.

Kim, K., Jogaratnam, G., & Noh, J. (2006). Travel decisions of students at a US university: Segmenting the international market. *Journal of Vacation Marketing, 12*(4), 345–357.

Lengkeek, J. (2002). A love affair with elsewhere: Love as a metaphor and paradigm for tourism longing. In G. M. S. Dunn (Ed.), *The tourist as a metaphor of the social world.* USA: CABI publishing.

Lindsey, E. W. (2005). Study abroad and values development in social work students. *Journal of Social Work Education, 41*(2), 229–250.

MacCannell, D. (1976). *The tourist: A new theory of the leisure class.* New York: Schocken Books.

Mannell, R. C., & Kleiber, D. A. (1997). *A social psychology of leisure.* State College, PA: Venture Publishing.

Martin, J. N. (1984). The intercultural re-entry: Conceptualization and directions for future research. *International Journal of Intercultural Relations, 8,* 115–134.

McIntosh, A. J., & Zahra, A. (2007). A cultural encounter through volunteer tourism: Towards the ideals of sustainable tourism. *Journal of Sustainable Tourism, 15*(5), 541–556.

Oberg, K. (1960). Cultural shock: Adjustment to new cultural environments. *Practical Anthropology, 7,* 177–182.

Relph, E. (1976) *Place and placelessness.* London: Pion.

Singh, S., & Singh, T. V. (2004). Volunteer tourism: New pilgrimages to the Himalayas. In T. V. Singh (Ed.), *New horizons of tourism: Strange experiences and stranger practices* (pp. 181–194). Wallingford, UK: CAB International.

Stier, J. (2003). Internationalization, ethnic diversity and the acquisition of intercultural competencies. *Intercultural Education, 14*(1), 77–91.

Tikkanen, I. (2007). Maslow's hierarchy and food tourism in Finland: Five cases. *British Food Journal, 109*(9), 721–734.

Trigger, D., & Mulcock, J. (2005). Forests as spiritually significant places: Nature, culture and 'belonging' in Australia. *The Australian Journal of Anthropology, 16*(3), 306–320.

Wearing, S. (2001). *Volunteer tourism: Experiences that make a difference.* Wallingford, UK: CABI.

Wearing, S. (2002). Re-centering the self in volunteer tourism. In G. M. S. Dann (Ed.), *The tourist as a metaphor of the social world* (pp. 237–262). Wallingford, UK: CABI.

Westwood, M. J., Lawrence, W. S., & Paul, D. (1986). Preparing for re-entry: A program for the sojourning student. *International Journal for the Advancement of Counseling, 9,* 221–230.

7

'Don't Worry About the Worries'
Transforming Lives Through International Volunteering

ELSPETH JONES

Introduction

In countries around the world, universities promote study abroad and other initiatives to enable students to benefit from meaningful international experiences. In the USA in particular tens, if not hundreds, of instruments such as the Intercultural Development Inventory (IDI) (Hammer & Bennett, 2001) are available to measure quantitatively the impact of such activity on inter-cultural skills. Academics have developed innovative ethnographic and other approaches to support student learning during experience abroad (see Savicki, 2008; also Bosley and Russell & Vallade, this volume). In support of such work, large-scale studies such as the Georgetown University consortium project (Vande Berg, Balkum, Scheid & Whalen, 2004) seem to suggest that, 'students left to their own devices will tend to gain very little in the way of intercultural development' as measured by instruments such as the IDI (Bosley, this volume). As a linguist who studied abroad, I tended to support those who consider a full year to be the gold standard, with three months the 'minimal time in which significant culture learning may take place' (Martin, 1987, quoted in Hoff, 2008). A recent initiative in my university, and my research into its impact, have caused me to question some of those assumptions.

Study abroad, in the sense of one- or two-semester study at a university overseas, has long been available at Leeds Metropolitan University. Study tours led by academic staff and work placements, or internships, are other international experiences on offer. However, financial and personal factors often prevent students from taking part in longer programmes, so in 2007 we initiated an additional short-term opportunity in the form of a university-wide international volunteering programme. This aimed to develop the global perspectives of students and staff through community and conservation projects across six continents. Leeds Met contributed 50 per cent of the costs and in the first year 148 volunteers took part in 15 projects in 10 countries. This financial support was sufficient to enable many to take part who otherwise would have found the expense too great, and gave an incentive for students to raise the other 50 per cent with our support. We introduced bronze, silver, gold and platinum Global Citizen Awards to recognise participation where the volunteering was not credited within the student's main programme of study.

The projects chosen were, in most cases, developed with existing partners around the world, either partner universities or charitable foundations we already supported through fundraising. We intended to sustain these relationships and committed to continue sending volunteers in future years, where the experience worked well. A careful selection process for those taking part resulted in excellent feedback from project hosts, who commented on the outstanding way our students represented the university. Projects in that first year included building sustainable tourism trails in Indonesia, providing education, training and support for former leprosy sufferers in India, working with Roma children in Transylvania, supporting a community centre in New York State, helping to develop tourism in South Africa in advance of the 2010 World Cup, supporting conservation projects in Australia and raising aspirations of Brazilian children from the 'favelas' through sport.

Volunteering provided students with a more flexible overseas option than study abroad which, given the typical three-year bachelor degree in the United Kingdom, needs to be undertaken in the second year. Volunteering projects generally take place during vacation periods and so are not limited to a particular year of study. In some cases, students were to be housed with local families which offered close cultural contact and the need to develop communication strategies where students' language skills were limited. This represented another dimension which was generally not part of the study-abroad experience.

Returning students and accompanying staff talked of their lives being transformed by these experiences. Most volunteering projects were of only two or three weeks' duration and it seemed surprising that such relatively short periods could produce the intense, life-changing impact described, so it seemed appropriate to investigate the stories in more detail. I selected eight students with a range of experiences for a small qualitative research project. All had been international volunteers and some had also studied abroad for one semester or one year. There was an equal number of men and women, three students originally came from overseas, and the countries where their experiences had taken place were Australia, Brazil, Ethiopia, India, Indonesia, Japan, Jordan and Thailand, all within the previous two years. Two students had already graduated and were now in employment. A range of open-ended questions without prompts were provided in advance, to form the basis of structured 60- to 90-minute interviews, which were recorded and transcribed. Students were asked about their preparation and expectations, their actual experiences, cultural 'surprises' and coping mechanisms including with language, skills developed and the degree to which these were transferable to other contexts including other cultures, academic study and the world of work. Those who had also studied abroad were asked to compare the differences between this experience and volunteering and whether they would recommend either to other students.

Student Voices

Preparation and Expectations

Although the students were selected largely as a sample of convenience, it was surprising to learn that every one of them had travelled overseas prior to undertaking this trip, even if only for holidays with family. Some had sought out the study abroad or volunteering opportunities, while others had been recommended to take part by teaching or support staff. It was notable that all those undertaking study abroad had done detailed research into the country they were going to and the university where they would study. Prior research was less frequently reported by volunteers. Many took pains not to pre-judge the experience:

'I didn't have a fear about Ethiopia because I never think you should have expectations or judge things until you actually go and see it for yourself … I was just really willing to see whatever there was there.'

'I feel that Islamophobia is being created in Britain and I wanted to go and kind of see this world that I hear so much about.'

'I just thought it was going to be a learning experience.'

'I tried to go with a pretty open mind because I didn't know a lot about the place … I'd not really met the people I was going with, I'd obviously not met the people I was staying with, I thought it was important to go with as open a mind as possible so that I could get the most from the experience. If I went expecting something and it didn't happen I'd be disappointed.'

All those volunteering took part in preparation sessions including on language, culture and safety. Several reported anxiety and concern to do the right thing, especially those who were to stay with families, 'when you got introduced to somebody, you just wanted to be sure you were going to do the right thing'.

Others reported feeling anxious as the departure date got closer and some degree of questioning whether they would cope. Concerns included, weather, food, cultural issues, language, personal safety and appropriate clothing.

'[A]lthough I was excited and desperate to go and I predicted that it would be a kind of life changing experience, you know a really good opportunity, I was quite nervous before I was going out, really kind of apprehensive.'

Several reported a general tendency in themselves to seek out 'otherness':

'I look for those moments constantly in my life and in this country I am always trying to … understand what it is like for other people and find links with different people.'

'[I want to meet] people who are different from me really, rather than just sitting in my comfort zone of people who I grew up and went to school with, and share exactly the same background.'

A surprising factor was that every student interviewed reported enjoying risk or being out of their comfort zone and that the experience had enhanced this.

'I was sort of prepared for the worst but all of that just served to excite me really because I wanted to be just flung somewhere completely different.'

'I have always tried to challenge myself and you know the kind of key things people say ... you need to really come out of your comfort zone and I've always tried to do that in other things I've done.'

'We were the first people to have done this and the fact that it was pioneering was very exciting.'

Given the students' expressed plan to remain open-minded, it is crucial that pre-departure interventions and briefings recognise this, as well as the 'mindset, skillset, and heartset' (Bennett, 2008) which students bring to the international experience. Taylor outlines 'a contiguous series of components that reflect the long-term process of learning to become interculturally competent', the first of which is 'setting the stage'. This recognises 'that each person comes to the inter-cultural experience with former critical events in his or her life, personal goals, varying amounts of intercultural training, and previous intercultural experi-ence' (Taylor, 1994, p. 160). The following sections should be read bearing in mind the risk-taking, boundary-crossing predispositions of this group of students and the fact that they had all had prior international experiences.

Lived Experiences

All students reported being keenly aware of potential cultural differences, some of which turned out to be less of an issue than they had thought, including dress-ing more conservatively for fear of causing offence or being especially cautious with their host family:

'I was thinking right I'm just going to eat whatever they're going to put in front of me because I want to try my best to be ... culturally aware.'

'I sometimes think we mistake their shyness, or ... how they react to situ-ations when actually they're just being polite and, when you understand that, it's much better.'

But often they wanted to learn more: 'almost every day I did something wrong and didn't know about it and then they're too polite to tell me, so that was really difficult'.

Coping strategies included staying calm, being adaptable and open-minded, planning to try everything and see it as a learning experience: 'I quite happily changed who I was ... to suit what they wanted or what they expected because I think if we'd got off on the wrong foot they would have had a bit of apprehension.'

The communication strategies reported by those staying with host families included smiling, speaking slowly, gesturing, drawing, copying others, listening and observing:

> 'I couldn't understand what they were saying about me to each other, ... so I was trying to smile all the time ... but just trying to create that impression that, look I'm quite a nice person I want to enjoy the experience, I want to do the best I can with you. I'll abide by your rules. To get that across but not speak the language is quite difficult ... and I thought well in England if ... they didn't speak my language how would I be able to tell that they were a nice person or decent? So I was trying to think about what I would expect from them and try and put that back in myself ... it seemed to work anyway.'

Several of these comments indicate that students are in the 'ethnorelative' stages of Bennett's intercultural sensitivity model (Bennett, 1993). There seems to be an understanding that one's own culture is only one way of experiencing the world, while using knowledge of similar situations as a bridge to shift into other cultural frames of reference.

Transferability of Skills Developed

Students report having developed patience, sensitivity, mediation skills, team work and organisational skills. Several described how their skills would be transferred to new countries or cultural contact:

> 'It's now easier for me to ... meet people from places like Japan or other places in Asia, because I've ... been there and I sort of understand why they are the way they are.'

> '[Adapting skills to another country] you sort of just accept it and get over it and you go, "well actually it's a little bit different", but you carry-on and see what the ... change is.'

And how the cultural differences had affected their attitude:

> 'I think as soon as you are in Africa the culture brushes off on you and you're a lot more carefree and relaxed.'

> 'You could be sitting there in a chair in a restaurant and a rat runs under your feet ... [you think] I've got to get out of here, but then you ... just take it in your stride and you say well, I'm in Thailand ....'

'[B]eing prepared, being open to the way that a journey leads you rather than worrying about planning it all, just being open to new things. Listening and learning and just trying to focus on that and listening to other people when they speak.'

All students reported that, one way or another, the skills learned had been useful when they returned to university life or tried to get a job:

'[I've had] quite a few different interviews ... and it helps ... 300% to have the opportunities of going abroad ... there are a lot of graduates everywhere ... [so of] these five hundred people ... you go into your differences and how life's affected you and when you come out with, "oh I went to India and taught kids how to speak English, how to play football, how to have a better quality of life, helped design playgrounds," they ... [say] ... that's really great.'

Others described how the experience had already impacted on their future, including career decisions:

'[W]hen I leave uni I want to go into this sector in humanitarian aid work with sport in developing countries.'

'I learnt that I need to respect and be more open to difference in other people.'

'I hate myself because I can't speak their language.' (This student went on to study the language after the visit.)

Four students are keeping in touch with the charities they worked for:

'[I'm] helping them out fundraising as well and I'm doing the Amsterdam half marathon in October because I'm over there on business ... and I'm doing another military ten kilometre run for charity as well which goes to the India charity.'

These responses suggest that, rather than a uni-dimensional notion of learning about another culture, the students are demonstrating cross-cultural capability skills independent of any individual culture. One student referred to having developed cross-cultural mediation and negotiation skills in working with people from different countries on the same project in Thailand. David Killick defines cross-cultural capability as the ability 'to communicate effectively across cultures, to see one's discipline and subsequent professional practice in cultural perspective, and to recognise the legitimacy of other cultural practices in both personal and professional life' (personal communication, 2009).

Personal Transformation

All those interviewed reported some degree of personal transformation and rethinking of previously held views or stereotypes, including those which might have been perceived as idealised: 'I thought [it] would be much more child orientated out there and it's not.' These can be categorised into three groups; learning about self, learning about cultural 'others' and learning about group empathy.

Learning About Self

'I remember when I came back from Australia thinking, there are so many people in the world that I've never met and I will never meet and it was *so* frustrating … I just want to meet people that are completely different to me and maybe challenge me a lot more.'

'My … interest in Islam is concerning the issue of women and women's rights … it just opened up new … ways of thinking for me.'

'So that was a big learning thing for me … if there is anything I want to find an interest in, I'm going to go and experience it.'

'You meet people from different countries that have totally different views of everything and then you start to question your own … [how you have] … been brought up.'

'I feel like I'm a better communicator. I feel I have made more effort, I think it has opened my eyes a little bit to our naivety as a country.'

'[C]onstant comparisons between my life, their life, the pressures on them, the boundaries on them and the pressures and boundaries on me.'

'I think the volunteering had a deeper effect on me because it changed my perspective on things. [I] had an idea that I would go to the parts of the developing world just hating everything that we've done to them … ruined … their land and ripped them off … with trading … and once you go out there you realise that it's not actually all our fault. They do make a lot of bad decisions themselves and I think that's the main thing. I have learned not to hate us so much … maybe we're not as bad and they're not as innocent as you think.'

'[Y]ou know we often see it as, these Muslim women, they don't have a choice, they have to cover up. But … when in my Western life do I have a choice *not* to be judged physically? … I don't have the choice to cover up when I want to and just be taken for who I [am].'

One student talked of the realisation that she needed close friendships:

'I think it's a different thing when you go away for that length of time. You sort of learn that it's not as easy to meet people. It's hard to put into words but basically … it's hard to go through emotions and things with people that you haven't known for a long time. And you realise it when you've been away, you don't realise it here because you just take it for granted … It wasn't enough to actually send me home and … you learn to become more independent and more open to just meeting people and letting people close to you, so that you can just confide in them.'

Learning About Cultural 'Others'

'There is just something about taking yourself away, putting yourself in a situation . . . .. Theoretically I should have respect for other people and ethically. For example, respect for ethnic minorities in this country. But it's not until you actually feel what it is like to be in the minority that you can ever truly sort of understand.'

'I am not saying that all developing countries are the same as that but at least I know they're not the same as I thought they were.'

'Everything you see on the TV and stuff is manipulated to look in a certain way. And you go out on a volunteering trip and, however well organised the place is, you see how this country works and how people live and how people see our world as well as their own, and how people just basically want our lifestyle. All they want is to live like us and to have our clothes and look like us.'

'We saw people out there and they didn't have all the things we have and they were what we would consider poor ... they don't have any money and they are not self-sufficient. [But] ... they're content with everything and they've got everything they need and they're so happy and it really makes you question what you've got over here. Which I was shocked by because I didn't think I'd think like that.'

'If you look at classical pottery in England, it's very ... stiff and very precise and that's how it has to be. Whereas in Japan they ... think that ... an accident has to make it and that's how you create a beautiful piece and if you can replicate it it's no good . . . .. That was a different perspective in general of what beauty can be.'

Learning About Group Empathy

These volunteering programmes differ from the study-abroad experience in one key respect. Groups are formed in advance of the trip, sometimes several months earlier, meaning that there is an opportunity for bonding through the cultural and linguistic preparation process for this diverse group of individuals. Once overseas, in a strange environment with limited reference points, the group assumes a significance of its own and participants develop a deep and strong sense of identity, collaboration and mutual support beyond the individual. For Daloz, such 'constructive engagement with otherness' relates to empathy:

For the experience to be more than simply an encounter, for it to be a constructive engagement, there had to be some sense of empathic connection with people different from themselves. In some significant way the inner experience of the other was engaged, a bond was formed, and some deep lesson about connection across differences was learned.

(Daloz, 2000, reported in Bennett, 2008, p. 19)

'The next day we all got on the bus and told each other our stories and I think everyone had been touched in the same way.'

'[A]s well as getting to know all the Brazilians there I was also getting to know the English people I was with.'

Several described helping others in the group who were not coping as well:

'[A] lot of the girls were quite shocked and quite tearful about [the poverty] and I said, you know, this is their way of life and it broadens your mind you ... see things for what they are. I was able to say... that we're making a difference and we are helping people out and trying to get people out of these situations. So let's not look at ... how terrible it is but think of the positives.'

Six students reported being in volunteer groups which grew very close and have stayed in touch through Facebook and regular reunions:

'We went over there a group of people who hadn't really met each other and when you come back you're like a small family.'

'The English girl that I was sharing a room with ... we didn't fall out but we got a bit tense at times ... and it was strange though because we had such a bond from the beginning it was almost like falling out with a sister.'

'I really do feel that we're probably all very aware that we have shared something very special.'

Mezirow notes that, 'transformative learning may be epochal or incremental and may involve objective (often task-oriented) or subjective (often self-reflective) reframing. Subjective reframing often requires the support of others, a positive self-concept and freedom from intense anxiety' (Dirkx, Mezirow & Cranton, 2006, p. 125). This is facilitated through the possibility of immediate reflection with other members of the group. Two students commented on such epochal moments of realisation, which in Mezirow's terms would be described as 'subjective reframing':

'I put on the Hijab ... to show respect but also just really wanted to feel what it was like to be them. And ... the sun was setting and the call to prayer was just echoing around the city ... I was one person in their world compared to in this country ... [where I'm] in the majority and ... I thought ... this is a milestone in my life.'

'The mother just appeared smiling all the time but didn't say a word, brought me a dictionary out to the table as a present ... . Then she waved her own at me and then went out ... it must have been twenty minutes, half an hour and then she came back in [and said], "Joey I happy to have you stay", and that was it. It wasn't the greatest English ... but it was at that point that just settled everything. I thought if she's willing to go out and make that effort, I don't know if my mum would do it ... and because

I don't know how educated she was ... so that, to take half an hour to learn that line was a big task for her. But because she did, that really kind of settled me in and I thought, well if they are willing to make that effort then I can't sit here nervous about anything, and you know I'll do my best now to try and go from there.'

These experiences not only caused students to think differently but, in one case at least, there was evidence that existing beliefs were validated. Bennett's ethnocentric 'defence' stage on the scale of intercultural sensitivity involves validating currently held beliefs (Bennett, 1993), but the evidence, from this student at least, challenges the notion that it is negative attitudes and cultural traits which are reinforced:

'Before I went on the trip I was beginning to think about multi-culturalism ... but ... it's actually meeting people who are different and ... sharing experiences with them in the rawest human form. It's just completely cemented my faith ... in the fact that we are all equal and different and that this should be celebrated. And now that's cemented all I can do is build on that with what I do with my life.'

Some of the factors which have brought about the personal transformations students have described include putting oneself in the shoes of others, being in the minority, sharing humanity, finding connections, reviewing one's own cultural assumptions and considering other perspectives, including concepts of beauty. The student voices here demonstrate both 'international' and 'intercultural' education as defined by Selby, with a number of students clearly showing evidence of 'doubt[ing] the superiority of their own cultural values' (2008, p. 4).

Volunteering Compared With Study Abroad

All those who had studied abroad as well as volunteered felt the experiences were entirely different and found the volunteering experience to have had more personal impact.

'It's a very ... different level of satisfaction that you get out of it, because you're not just studying somewhere new.'

'[Studying in Japan is interesting but] you kind of live in a place that long that it becomes routine'. However, this student did learn, 'respect and how a different culture still has much deeper layers of hierarchy and how people sort of talk to each other ... Japanese culture is obviously very different to our culture but in a sense you're still ... in a similar environment ... still surrounded by people who have more or less the same financial background because they can afford to be there and ... you're all academics, you're all in university. But if you do volunteering, you meet people from very different walks of life who maybe don't have the opportunity that you have. I think in a way it sort of shows you what is important in life and what isn't.'

'I think the difference is, I learnt in Australia I personally learnt how to meet people, how to deal with people, how to get close to people who are completely different to me from different parts of the world with a completely different view on anything … it was more of a personal aspect in Australia … whereas in Indonesia I learnt about how countries like that actually work.'

Several reported that studying abroad made them want to travel more and to volunteer in future, whether overseas or back at home:

'It did make me just want to travel more and that was why I went to Indonesia.'

'It's probably one of the top sort of experiences I've ever had you know, and that's gone into a lot of other things now. Think of that as a starting block.'

'Although I loved being at the university I thought I was a bit wasted while I was there. Any chance I got I took to travel. But the rest of the time I was going to university like I would have being doing at home. I was living in accommodation and I was in like a safe place and I met people who had gone out there and [volunteered] and I sort of missed that a bit. I think I promised myself when I was out there that next time I went away I would do some sort of volunteering.'

'[With volunteering] you're really put to the test.'

Study abroad had helped them learn about themselves but the focus of volunteering was on others, with the resulting pressure to 'get it right'. For those interviewed, the key factor was not being out of their comfort zones but, feeling that they were making a difference:

'You just sort of feel humbled that you've actually helped out.'

'In Australia I learnt a lot about myself, like about who I am, but in India I've actually impacted on other people.'

'You're not thinking as much about you as you are other people. Like everyday I'd wake up and think, what am I doing with the kids today? I'd go through my lesson plan, do a few notes, make a few changes, you know, what words can I teach them? … If you mess up [your own] learning you can always re-learn it but if you make mistakes when you are teaching kids stuff it's going to affect their outcome, so you want to make everything perfect.'

'It was three weeks full on, where we worked everyday and you got something very different out of it. It was kind of like you were part of some exchange, you know when you build something and you see someone play on what you have built, it's a very different level of … achievement.'

'Sewing is not my forte ... [so] they then suddenly became teachers ... "you do this", "you do that" you know and trying to listen to them trying to demonstrate and it was great for us to see them have to adapt ... so here they are in their poor area and they are able to actually teach these Europeans something and so I think that gave them a sense of pride as well.'

'You actually see yourself making a difference and like directly impact people's lives .... I took over twenty rugby balls, twenty footballs, twenty Frisbees and all sorts of games equipment and the kids, before I was there ... were throwing them to each other and just dropping them everywhere and then [I] taught them to catch and just to see them do that was ... you know like I've helped them do that ... so that's what you get a lot out of.'

It is clear from the interviews that students perceive the experiences to have had an impact on them and, in most cases, on their future direction. One student decided to devote her design studies not to artistic work but to supporting the developing world. On returning from Indonesia she designed a solar-powered water heater made from readily available drinks cans and standard copper tubing. She returned to Indonesia with the second group of volunteers a year after her initial experience in order to help the villagers make their own water heaters based on her model. She has since visited The Gambia and done the same.

Conclusion

It is recognised that this was a small-scale study from which limited inferences can be drawn. This is also a largely unplanned evaluation – we focused on setting up the opportunities without specific learning outcomes in mind, as the volunteering initiative is not tied to any individual programme of study. Essentially it was the anecdotal feedback which initiated the research. As noted in the introduction, volunteers received preparation sessions for their visits but there was no conscious academic intervention. It might have been interesting to assess them using, for example, the IDI to see whether their scores might have improved. However, it is argued that such measures are useful as performance indicators or management tools but they are more limited when seeking to capture the nuances of personal development and transformation. It seems undeniable that most of these students have experienced the kind of 'golden growth' envisaged by Lou and Bosley (2008). A future direction for research is now clearer following this study, as we aim to avoid programme evaluations which are, 'little more than measures of customer satisfaction' (Selby, 2008, p. 3).

It is likely to be significant that all these students happen to have had prior international experiences leading to ethnorelative sensitivity (Bennett, 1993). Taking into account the importance Taylor (1994) ascribes to 'setting the stage', noted above, such risk-taking and boundary-crossing students might respond differently on encountering the 'disorienting dilemma' which Mezirow says can lead to perspective transformation (Mezirow, 1991). This may be one contributing factor in the extent of results described from just a short three-week

programme. Although the students were chosen largely as a sample of convenience for this study, it may be that programmes like this attract a certain type of
student and rather than widening the range of students taking part in international opportunities, as was the planned outcome, we are merely providing more
opportunities for those who are already engaged.

For a number of these students, reflection on their experiences took place
some time after the event, yet for others the experience was relatively recent. In
one case the student asked for his interview to be postponed as he hadn't had
sufficient time to reflect on his trip. Another wrote to me some time after the
interview listing skills he felt had been developed which continued to be of value
to him. One benefit of the *International Reflections* web page (Jones, 2007) is
that it enables reflection to take place when the writer is ready to do so. Many
students who have taken part in international volunteering programmes have
taken this opportunity and, while none of their reflections feature in this chapter, it is clear that similar stories have emerged from their experiences.

Hoff calls for increased research through longitudinal studies so that, 'the international education field may actually come to know the true "life-changing effect"
of study abroad' (2008, p. 70). The research undertaken here represents a middle
way between a longitudinal study and immediate re-entry reflection and merits
further follow-up one year after the initial interview with those who haven't yet
graduated.

Re-entry interviews have a purpose to serve, however, and might be particularly useful if those who haven't taken part are involved in meaningful discussion with their peers who have. Sharing can aid reflective processes (see Thom,
this volume) and, in addition to enhancing the experience for the volunteer,
might encourage others to take part. It could also form the basis of useful group
work. Studies in this volume and elsewhere report the difficulties of engaging
international and home students in cross-cultural group work, which rarely
seems to happen naturally. Cornwell and Stoddard talk of the two separate
movements of internationalisation and 'diversification' coming together 'in a
new paradigm of higher education in which diversity would be taught as the
historical result of multiple overlapping diasporas created by the evolving
process of globalisation' (1999). Sharing in groups the authentic international
experiences discussed in this chapter could introduce an additional dimension
to cross-cultural activity and enhance internationalisation at home. This might
offer a 'safe' environment in which to encourage other students to crosscultural
boundaries and rise above notions of political correctness in their dealings with
cultural 'others' in their daily lives.

So where does this current study go next? In addition to ideas for enhancing
the subtlety of pre-departure preparation and post-visit reflection, a series of
subsequent questions are raised for further work and consideration:

1. Establish whether programmes as they stand, or the selection process,
   are merely attracting 'risk junkies'. If so, how can we widen the range
   of students participating?

2. Seek to understand predisposition for taking part in international volunteering. Establish simple measures of prior international experience, including 'gap' years before university to consider patterns of participation.
3. Investigate whether the transformation is enduring. Follow up research with some of the same individuals to consider longitudinal effects.
4. Consider how the impacts described as a result of international volunteering can be replicated domestically and offered to those who are unable to travel overseas.

It seems that even without focused intervention, for this group of students real transformation has resulted from their international experience. Volunteering programmes can be seen as a viable alternative to full academic exchange programmes or work placements for students who cannot take such a long time out of their studies or away from the United Kingdom. More work needs to be done to ensure that a wider group of students can reap the benefits evident from these experiences and that in attracting those who may be towards the 'ethnocentric' end of Bennett's (1993) scale, we ensure sufficient support to enable the experience to be transformational.

My final question to the students interviewed was, 'what advice would you offer those who might be thinking of taking part in a volunteering experience?' This reply encapsulated the tone of their responses:

'Choose a project and a country that you want to go to. Choose a project that actually inspires you and that you believe in. And if those two things together excite you then go for it and *don't worry about the worries* because they are all part of it.'

Acknowledgements

With thanks to Lucie Charlton, Chris Dawes, Andrew Henderson, Joe Milner, Amani Omejer, Joe Rossiter, Anne Schiffer, Kathryn Wilson and to Sally Clayton for her excellent transcripts.

References

Bennett, J. M. (2008). On becoming a global soul. In Savicki (2008), pp. 13–31.

Bennett, M. J. (1993). Towards ethnorelativism: A developmental model of intercultural sensitivity. In R. M. Paige (Ed.), *Education for the intercultural experience*. Yarmouth, ME: Intercultural Press.

Cornwell, G. H., & Stoddard, E. W. (1999). *Globalizing knowledge: Connecting international and intercultural studies*. Washington, DC: Association of American Colleges and Universities.

Daloz, L. A. P. (2000). Transformative learning for the common good. In J. Mezirow & Associates (Eds.), *Learning as transformation: Critical perspectives on a theory in progress* (pp. 103–123). San Francisco: Jossey Bass.

Dirkx, J. M., Mezirow, J., & Cranton, P. (2006). Musings and reflections on the meaning, context, and process of transformative learning: A dialogue between John M. Dirkx and Jack Mezirow. *Journal of Transformative Education, 4*, 123–139.

Hammer, M. R., & Bennett, M. J. (2001). *Intercultural development inventory.* Portland, OR: Intercultural Communication Institute.

Hoff, J. G. (2008). Growth and transformation outcomes in international education. In Savicki (2008), pp. 53–73.

Jones, E. (2007). International reflections and culture change. In Jones & Brown (2007), pp. 25–41.

Jones, E., & Brown, S. (Eds.). (2007). *Internationalising higher education.* London: Routledge.

Killick, D. (2009). Personal communication.

Lou, K. H., & Bosley, G. W. (2008). Dynamics of cultural contexts: Meta-level intervention in the study abroad experience. In Savicki (2008), pp. 276–296.

Martin, J. N. (1987). The relationship between student sojourner perceptions of intercultural competencies and previous sojourn experience. *International Journal of Intercultural Relations, 11,* 337–355.

Mezirow, J. (1991). *Transformative dimensions of adult learning.* San Francisco: Jossey-Bass.

Savicki, V. (Ed.). (2008). *Developing intercultural competence and transformation: Theory, research and application in international education.* Sterling, VA: Stylus.

Selby, R. (2008). Designing transformation in international education. In Savicki (2008), pp. 1–12.

Taylor, E. W. (1994). Intercultural competency: A transformative learning process. *Adult Education Quarterly, 44*(3), 154–175.

Vande Berg, M., Balkum, J. A. Scheid, M., & Whalen B. J. (2004). The Georgetown University consortium project: A report from the halfway mark. *Frontiers: The Interdisciplinary Journal of Study Abroad, 10,* 101–116.

8

Guided Reflective Journalling

Assessing the International Study and Volunteering Experience

MARK RUSSELL AND LINDA VALLADE

Introduction

This chapter provides a case study assessing the outcomes and impacts of short-term international study and service learning at a large American Land Grant university. Most universities attempting to internationalize their curriculum have traditionally provided encouragement for home students to gain international experiences and have claimed many global and worldview perspective benefits from this experience.

The College of Agriculture, Purdue University has a long tradition of overseas collaborative research and institution building in developing countries ranging from Brazil, Honduras, and now Afghanistan, Niger and Burkina Faso. Lacking was participation of its students in any type of overseas study. In 1990, the college made a decision to make an overseas academic experience a priority for all graduating students. The goal was 10 per cent student participation by 1995; this was increased to 20 per cent by 2005. In 2006–07, 25.4 per cent of undergraduates participated. The College of Agriculture's international programme leads Purdue University in these experiences.

While the number of students studying abroad has increased, one concern of any such programme is that it should be academically sound and culturally informative. Are the students learning cultural sensitivities as well as how to absorb and incorporate this information within themselves and their daily lives? A challenge faced by all institutions is effectively measuring the outcomes of study abroad whether long- or short-term, group or independent study. As more students are participating in shorter programmes/courses it becomes critical to determine whether the desired outcomes are being met. The college received a grant from the United States Department of Agriculture to analyse this.

> On many US campuses, international education consists of a series of disconnected activities that are weakly integrated into the core academic mission … the result is a fragmented hodgepodge of programs and activities that are rarely significantly integrated to create maximum institutional impact or to advantage learning.
>
> (Green, 2003)

Our model is designed to address strategies for internationalization highlighted in the American Council on Education project 'Spotlighting Excellence in Comprehensive Internationalization' and the 'Internationalization Collaborative' (Green & Olson, 2003).

The focus of this chapter is less the quantitative analytical methods, but rather the qualitative heuristic inquiry (Moustakas, 1994) of phenomenological analysis using guided reflective journalling to elicit the impact of experiences in the students' own words. We will share the results of such reflection in two undergraduate international experiences in the College of Agriculture at Purdue University. These reflective journals illustrate the growing intercultural competence of individuals within a group of American students undertaking a service learning experience in Ecuador and on a study tour of agriculture in Central Europe. An additional finding is that the process of responding to specific guided questions and keeping a journal also helped to develop students' actual observation, learning and that which they seek to describe.

University Context

The University's main campus is in West Lafayette, Indiana, with around 39,000 students from all 50 US states and 124 other countries. In 2007–08 there were 4,994 international students, 2,042 of whom were undergraduates. The total enrolment across five campuses is roughly 70,000. For the past five years, Purdue has ranked first or second in the United States in total international student enrolment among public research institutions (Purdue University facts, 2008).

Purdue is striving to be a world-class comprehensive university, with a mission stated in the 2008–14 New Synergies Strategic Plan as

> Commitment to People: Purdue University serves diverse populations of Indiana, the nation, and the world through discovery that expands the frontiers of knowledge, learning that nurtures the sharing of knowledge, and engagement that promotes the application of knowledge.

The three articulated Goals of the University are:

- Launching Tomorrow's Leaders

Promote excellence in learning experiences and outcomes, fostering intellectual, professional, and personal development to prepare learners for life and careers in a dynamic, global society.

- Discovery With Delivery

Advance the frontiers of knowledge, innovate technologies that address the grand challenges of society to serve humanity, and improve the quality of life around the world.

• Meeting Global Challenges

Address the critical needs of society, and catalyze economic development and entrepreneurship consistent with a public research university of the 21st century with global impact.

Purdue was one of five institutions in the country to receive the 2006 Senator Paul Simon Award for Campus Internationalization. The award, given annually by NAFSA, honours colleges and universities for overall excellence in internationalization efforts.

College of Agriculture (COA)

Targeted graduate outcomes for the 2,535 full-time students in the College of Agriculture include:

• Demonstrate knowledge of a range of cultures and an understanding of human values and points of view other than their own.
• Demonstrate ability to apply social, economic, political, and environmental principles to living in a global community.
• Demonstrate awareness of civic responsibility to community and society at large.

Undergraduate students, regardless of major, take nine-credit courses in International Understanding. They are also required to take three credit hours of a Multicultural elective on cultures and people different than themselves. An International Studies Minor is also offered.

The mission of agricultural study abroad at Purdue is to 'help prepare agriculture students for the global nature of our modern world by increasing opportunities for participation in study abroad, overseas internships, and international studies'; 25.4 per cent of Purdue COA undergraduates study abroad, the highest percentage of any college or school at Purdue University. Programmes include semester- and year-long exchanges, summer courses or work, three-week Maymester, and one-week spring break or winter session group study courses. Purdue COA students can choose from 33 study-abroad and internship programmes, partnering with 31 institutions in 19 countries specifically developed for COA students. They also participate in over 200 campus-wide programmes.

Such success has been rewarding for students, but, as Deardorff says, 'Demonstrating the success of our internationalization by relying on the numbers of students studying abroad, international students on campus, etc. fails to address the student learner's behavior, attitude, and knowledge gained' (Deardorff, 2004). Even at an internationally engaged scientific research and educational institution like Purdue University, until recently little had been done to assess the outcome of our internationalization efforts and claims of their benefits.

Objectives of International Experiences

The COA lists learning objectives for international programmes under Personal Development, Education and Employability. Both courses in this case study are three-week travel courses led by Purdue professors and hosted by our international partners in the respective countries. Learning objectives for these courses include:

'Exploring International Animal Agriculture':

Gain appreciation and understanding of the culture and the people of developing countries and their dependence on agriculture and animals.

Increase the students' comfort traveling internationally such that they are empowered to participate in longer international study opportunities and explore career opportunities in global agriculture.

'Serving International Communities':

help students develop intercultural skills through working as part of diverse teams in both a domestic and an international setting

encourage students to develop a servant leader attitude by using service-learning as pedagogy to help communities build on their assets to address critical issues.

connect students to the ideas and people who can instill habits of thought and practice that embrace larger vistas, worldwide challenges, and opportunities to serve the global community.

The real challenge for higher education is defining and measuring such lofty ambitions. Developing values, behaviours, attitudes and competencies is a much larger task than assessing technical knowledge gained and skills. The good news is that

in the 21st century international labour market the development of employability skills and attributes through adopting international perspectives is essential to the enhancement of the employment prospects of the students of any nationality. Employers in many countries world-wide share the same sorts of required graduate employability skills and attributes. Spending a period of time studying or working in another country permits students to develop these skills.

(Leggott & Stapleford, 2007)

Purdue students said:

'I learned to focus more on people and events rather than the time.'

'I now feel that I can work effectively with anyone and am much more patient with people.'

'I know now that the regulations and procedures of work are different everywhere and you need to take time to understand the setting.'

Assessing Impact/Outcomes of International Experiences

Most international educational programmes are designed to either discover new science and research technologies or to expand awareness, knowledge or skills in understanding a different culture. Agricultural universities are conducting diverse international programmes for study abroad, extension and discovery, but with little evaluation of how international initiatives help students, faculty and staff acquire an understanding of the international, cross-cultural and trade implications of their studies. Comprehensive internationalization affects the hearts and minds of students, faculty and staff, requiring voluntary change. We believe the most valuable benefit of internationalizing learning, discovery and engagement is the return on our investment measured by the strengthening of student capabilities. Ashwill suggests that many education-abroad experiences are more akin to an introduction to country X rather than a meaningful opportunity to become interculturally competent. He highlights growth in awareness of cultural differences, in knowledge of cultures, and in skills based on interacting across cultures. These can be set as expected learning outcomes of the international programme and then measured. Ashwill shares best practices in developing intercultural competencies for students, faculty and staff (Ashwill, 2004).

As a result of the funded project, 'Strategies to Enhance the Integration and Assessment of International Education in Colleges of Agriculture' from the US Department of Agriculture, we became more focused on assessment. We are evaluating the usefulness of widely available assessment instruments to measure change. It is beyond the scope of this chapter to discuss the use of quantitative measures such as the Cultural Orientation Indicator, the Intercultural Development Inventory (IDI[Reg]), Culture Active Scale[Reg], or the internally developed Openness to Diversity Questionnaire and the Global-Mindedness Scale. The IDI has proven very helpful in establishing baseline worldviews of our students for the purpose of curriculum development, training, and course design but limited in other respects. Incremental changes in individuals cannot be attributed to the experience alone and group averages do not change significantly. Maybe Emotional Intelligence assessment and the Multicultural Personality Questionnaire[Reg] will prove useful to assess individual student development and growth. Traditional quantitative methods have limitations. Additionally, Boyd, Felton and Dooley (2004) conclude that 'courses that include an international dimension should consider the use of reflective writing, both as an instructional tool to improve learners' cognitive models, as well as an assessment tool to measure changes in attitudes, beliefs, values, and motivations'.

Internally developed surveys and questionnaires are proving useful for assessing international study abroad programmes. Incoming first-year and graduate exit surveys can provide baseline data of the whole population relative to the proportion of students with previous international experience, self-perceived benefits of these international experiences, worldview in general, international plans while at the university, and the primary obstacles/barriers that prevent participation in an international study experience. Approximately 60 per cent of freshmen entering the COA indicate intention to study abroad. A similar exit questionnaire for outgoing graduates can evaluate the whole programme for students who studied abroad and those who did not.

Qualitative Phenomenological Analysis

Anyone who has travelled with or known the students beforehand or witnessed their growth upon return can testify to anecdotal change, but how should this be measured? We have found the best measures to be qualitative, not quantitative. We examined the changes in students' skills, attitudes, and behaviours as a result of participating in three-week international experiences utilizing a qualitative methodology, 'naturalistic inquiry, the use of non-interfering data collection strategies to discover the natural flow of events and processes and how participants interpret them' (McMillan & Schumacher, 1997, p. 391). This helped uncover evidence difficult to obtain using quantitative methods. 'Qualitative researchers study things in their natural settings, attempting to make sense of, or interpret, phenomena in terms of the meaning people bring them' (Denzin & Lincoln, 1994, p. 2). Phenomenology allows researchers to understand and elucidate 'the meaning, structure and essence of the lived experience of a phenomenon for a person or group of people' (Patton 2002), while heuristic inquiry (Moustakas, 1994) is a highly personal process allowing 'voice' to be exhibited throughout a study, personalizing the experience.

Nicodemus (2006) suggests a written objective or subjective journal as a qualitative method to determine the attitudes of students participating in an overseas course:

> The objective journal is generally a chronology of events, or data collection. The subjective journal goes beyond what one has observed or experienced or read. The subjective journal will give a better insight into the students' personal growth, reactions, and thoughts.

We have called ours a reflective journal and we expect more critical thinking and personal thought than the objective journal referred to here.

Student Voices

Central Europe

In Exploring International Animal Agriculture, student assignments were originally open journals without guiding questions. This allowed instructors to evaluate content but most students used the journals either to detail a chronology of their experiences, or to communicate with instructors about ongoing trip issues. We subsequently designed preflection and post-experience assignments linking directly to the learning objectives (Jones, 2005). Preflection included:

- What do you hope to gain by completing this course?
- How do you expect the culture in central Europe to be most different than home and how do you plan to deal with these differences?

- In what way, if any, do you expect that the experiences of this course will cause you to view other people, cultures, practices, and beliefs differently?
- What do you think is the role of the United States and of the American people relative to the rest of the world?
- How do you anticipate that this course will help you in your career objectives upon graduation?

Asking questions beforehand increases the intentionality of the consciousness or the 'orientation of the mind to its object' thus deepening the experience (Jones, 2005). With basic guiding questions it is possible to follow those themes throughout the experience. To assist in understanding the method, actual questions from the Central European travel study course are given here:

Journal 1 – When Leaving Warsaw

- How have you found the culture here to be most different than home and how are you dealing with these differences?
- Give examples of 'uncertainty' that required you to be flexible. How have you handled this need for flexibility?
- In what way have the experiences of this course caused you to view other people, cultures, and beliefs differently?

Journal 2 – When Leaving Krakow

- What cultural attitudes are different here than Warsaw or home and how are you dealing with these differences?
- How have you communicated with our hosts, students, local residents here? How do you feel about your success with communications?
- How have the experiences of this course caused you to view other people, cultures, and beliefs differently?

Journal 3 – When Leaving Nitra

- How is the culture in this country different/similar to that of Poland and how does that make you feel?
- How are the relationships within our group changing? What have you learned about group dynamics and yourself?
- How have the experiences of this course caused you to view other people, cultures, practices, and beliefs differently?

Journal 4 – When Leaving Brno/Prague

- How is the culture in the Czech Republic most different than home and how are you adjusting to these differences?
- Give examples of 'uncertainty' that required you to be flexible. How have you handled this need for flexibility?

- How have the experiences of this course caused you to view other people, cultures, practices, and beliefs differently?
- What do you now think is the role of the United States and of the American people relative to the rest of the world?

An example of sequenced responses from a single student on this course follows.

Preflection – Four Months Before Trip

How do you expect the culture in Central Europe to be most different than home and how do you plan to deal with these difference?

'I expect the culture to be less dependent on technology and computers and less modern. I feel that I will need to be patient as life will not be as fast paced.'

Journal 1 – One Week into Trip When Leaving Warsaw

How have you found the culture here to be most different than home and how are you dealing with these differences?

'I have been hearing faculty say "It isn't right or wrong, just different" for a long time, however it never really sinks in until you get to experience that culture, talk to the people, and try to practice these beliefs. I'm seeing now that people here do indeed live differently than me and that is ok. I've never been in a place where I'm a minority. I've always been in a place where the "different" people look different than me. I don't think I've been rude to them just curious, but now I see people look at me and wonder what I'm doing in their country. I think I will be more open-minded and interested in different people now.'

Journal 2 – When Leaving Krakow, Poland

What cultural attitudes are different here than Warsaw or home and how are you dealing with these differences?

'I view the culture as something that needs to be appreciated. I now have a greater appreciation for the practices studied and realize that Americans aren't the only ones with an amazing story to tell. My experiences have made the words I've read in a text book and heard on TV real and I now have something to associate them with and will always try to appreciate them more'.

Journal 3 – Three Weeks into Trip When Leaving Nitra, Slovakia

How is the culture in this country different/similar to that of Poland and how does that make you feel?

'Getting to know the culture and history of places we go truly make me appreciate their culture more and in some ways my own. To understand this culture you really have to better evaluate and understand yourself. Going to the ballet/opera and taking city tours shows the deep roots of history but at the same time realize there is a lot of history in our home country that we take for granted and don't appreciate. Much of it came from Europe.'

Journal 4 – End of Trip When Leaving Prague, Czech Republic

How have the experiences of this course caused you to view other people, cultures, practices, and beliefs differently?

'I didn't think that they were as advanced as we are but especially after Prague it is obvious that they are. I really see life in general in a new way after this trip. There is usually not one right way to do anything. I think that my view of Europe has definitely changed. I especially think my view of people changed a lot because of the interactions with students and leaders of the universities. I was very impressed by how welcoming and genuine all of our hosts are, and I will always remember their hospitality.'

Final Exam – One Week Post-Trip

How did this experience help you better understand different cultures and people at home? Use specific examples.

'In each country I learned that people are somewhat different and in many ways similar. For instance they listen to much of the same music and movies, but on the other hand they show more respect to elders than we do, especially teachers, but they seem more distant from their instructors. Paying to use the restrooms is different and was a pain but then you realize that this supports employment for people. Cultures are based on traditions, like toasting before meals and drinking more beer, but it is in these traditions and understanding why people do what they do that you really begin to understand and appreciate them. I also learned that the technology and customs of others are often equally alternative ways of doing things. I have learned to think in a different way, which I hope I can continue to do.'

Other student voices on the same programme were as follows:

'I am a lot more independent now.'

'I am more flexible now and more willing to take a job in a foreign country because of this trip.'

'I am much more aware and interested in news from around the world now.'

'People are similar around the world but we just do things differently.'

'I was able to better understand how people from the US are perceived around the world.'

'I am much more open-minded now and intend to seek out opportunities to talk and learn about exchange students and faculty.'

'I am more flexible with people and have learned that plans change and there are times that going with the flow not only makes life easier but is more effective.'

'I have learned the value of listening to others' thoughts more carefully will help me serve others.'

'I learned a lot about working with others and how we can learn something for everyone.'

'I most benefited by working on my people and small group skills and how to work with a diversity of people. It made me take a step back and work on my open-mindedness and acceptance of others.'

Service Learning in Remote Villages in Ecuador

Examples from this programme were more specific to course objectives. Here students lived and worked with indigenous and Afro-Ecuadorian underserved people. The faculty team brought in an expert from the Purdue Center for Instructional Excellence who travelled with the class in 2006 and then drafted questions around the stated learning objectives. Examples include:

- How do you view the gender roles in Ecuador?
- How receptive do you feel the people here are to our efforts?
- How do you view the effectiveness of our group now?
- Give three examples of uncertainty and how you are coping.
- Describe a time when you and/or your team weren't sure what you were going to do or how you were going to handle a situation: what did you learn about yourself and how you deal with uncertain situations?
- How are you communicating with our hosts?
- Describe how you felt that we were welcomed by our partners in Quito?
- How did you react to the way the community partners live?
- How work in the community is organized: discuss how your impressions of the culture and customs are similar to and different from your expectations prior to coming to Ecuador.
- Do you think it is important be able to accept the community as it is, even when aspects of its culture and customs may challenge your own world view or values? Why/why not?
- Think back across your time in Ecuador to date. Describe your two most rewarding or meaningful experiences. Discuss what made those experiences rewarding or meaningful for you.
- How has your experience in Ecuador increased your understanding of your own discipline? Describe specifically what you have learned about your own discipline/profession based on your interaction with your team and community partners in Ecuador.

- Identify and describe the approach you or others took or, looking back on it, could have taken, toward meeting the objectives you and your community partner jointly decided on. What alternative approaches could have been taken to meet these objectives (e.g., directing action toward an individual rather than a group, toward a short-term rather than long-term solution)?

Student voices from this programme included:

'I've become more aware of myself and know what I can do and what I can't. However, I also learned that the things that I thought I couldn't do I actually can.'

'I learned to accept help from others as not a statement that I am incompetent but an expression of sincere desire to assist and I have gotten better at realizing this.'

'I really learned a lot about using my communication skills to interact with and develop relationships with (Ecuadorian) people. When you come to work beside others, you can find a way to communicate.'

'I am a lot more adventurous than I thought I was. I had never used a machete, never harvested pineapple and cocoa, or ridden a horse down a mountainside but if I let myself try, I now know that I can do more than I thought possible.'

'When you are put in a totally foreign place (with no electricity, roads, or running water) to live with people you don't know anything about you have to be willing to communicate and find out what their needs are and how you must live. I don't think I could ever grow so much sensitivity in a place where I am already comfortable.'

'I now realize how fortunate I am to have the opportunities I have and getting a Frisbee out to play with the village kids and realizing they had never seen one was a reality check for me. I learned most about my self on this trip.'

'I have learned that even though people see me as a quiet girl, I see when it is needed to step up and lead a work team. I learned that I am a leader.'

Summary

This chapter serves as a case study of one college's attempts to demonstrate and document the impacts of two short-term international experiences on undergraduate students. As teachers and administrators we will continue to find it challenging to measure that which we have difficulty defining such as intercultural skills, global mindedness, a worldview, etc. We need to be more specific in our expected learning outcomes – open mindedness, flexibility, intercultural sensitivity, etc. and not expect every international experience to result in the same outcomes.

There is no doubt that students involved in international experiences are changed through these experiences but we have not yet found an effective quantitative method to measure changes in these rather subjective skills and attributes. Rather, we suggest it is possible to develop qualitative measures through reflective journalling to demonstrate change. Moreover, when similar guiding prompts are used sequentially throughout the course it is possible to measure growth or change in individual student responses. We have noted that more change appears to occur in students when the guided reflections are consistently part of the learning experience rather than only used at the beginning and at the end. We also believe that learning from experiences is enhanced when the learner is forced to reflect on the experiences while simultaneously engaged in the experience itself.

References

Ashwill, M. A. (2004). Developing intercultural competence for the masses. *International Education Journal*, Spring, 16-25.

Boyd, B., Felton, S., & Dooley, K. (2004). Providing virtual international experiences for undergraduates. *Journal of International Agricultural and Extension Education, 11*(3), 63–68.

College of Agriculture, Educational Outcomes of the Purdue University (2007). Available from: http://www.ag.purdue.edu/oap [Accessed April 2009].

Deardorff, D. K. (2004). Internationalization: In search of intercultural competence. *International Education*, Spring, 13–15.

Denzin, N. K., & Lincoln, Y. S. (Eds.). (1994). *Handbook of qualitative research.* Thousand Oaks, CA: Sage.

Green, M. F. (2003). The internationalized campus: A strategic approach. *International Education*, Winter, 13–21.

Green, M. F., & Olson, C. (2003). *Internationalizing the campus: A user's guide.* Washington, DC: American Council on Education. Available from: http://www.acenet.edu/AM/Template.cfmSection=Leadership&Template=/CM/ContentDisplay.cfm&ContentFileID=1350 [Accessed September 2008].

Jones, L. (2005). Personal correspondence.

Jones, E., & Brown, S. (Eds.). (2007). *Internationalising higher education.* London: Routledge.

Leggott, D., & Stapleford, J. (2007). Internationalisation and employability. In Jones & Brown (2007), pp. 120–134.

McMillan, J. H., & Schumacher, S. (1997). *Research education: A conceptual introduction.* New York: Longman.

Moustakas, C. (1994). *Phenomenological research methods.* Thousand Oaks, CA: Sage.

Nicodemus, N. A. (2006). *The travel journal: An assessment tool for overseas study.* New York: Council on International Education Exchange, pp. 2–3.

Patton, M. Q. (2002). *Qualitative research & evaluation methods.* Thousand Oaks, CA: Sage.

Purdue University facts. (2008). Available from: http://www.purdue.edu/ [Accessed April 2009].

Purdue University. New synergies strategic plan 2008–2014. Available from: http://www.purdue.edu/strategic_plan/documents/StrategicPlanBrochure.pdf [Accessed April 2009].

III
Student Learning in the Cross-Cultural Classroom

9

Sometimes It Means More Work...
Student Perceptions of Group Work in a Mixed Cultural Setting

JANE OSMOND AND JANNIE ROED

Introduction

As described by Betty Leask elsewhere in this volume, immersion in an internationalised curriculum is seen as a positive force for students in that it exposes them to different cultural experiences during the course of their university education. From this, it is intended that students begin their preparation for life in a 'global society'. In the United Kingdom, group work is an integral part of a university education, which, on the surface, would seem an obvious way in which to promote cultural awareness and collaboration between international and home students. Indeed, Doyle, Beatty and Shaw (1999) argue that mixed cultural groups help students learn about multicultural issues that they would not otherwise have done. However, as a learning method it is not unproblematic; Mills (1997) found that although international students passed required language proficiency exams, the speaking pace of domestic students could negatively affect classroom interactions; international students would often misunderstand the examples given to clarify issues due to specific cultural (usually Western) contexts. Also, allocation of group members, maintaining group motivation and ensuring fair distribution of final marks are just some difficulties facing lecturers and students alike (McAllister & Alexander, 2003; Volet & Mansfield, 2006). Further, Barron's study (2006) of the impact that international students have on domestic students' educational experience at an Australian university found that around a quarter of respondents claimed that the quality of their educational experience had been negatively affected by the number of international students on their courses, with 72 per cent mentioning key issues relating to communication and group work. For domestic students in particular, resentment was expressed at what they perceived as a negative effect on their final marks caused by international student interactions.

Nevertheless, working in groups is generally accepted as constituting an important part of students' intellectual development as it fosters higher-level critical thinking if applied appropriately (Payne, Monk-Turner, Smith & Sumter, 2006). Working in groups can also encourage a better 'performance': in a study conducted amongst university geography students, Knight (2004) found that although students preferred individual assessments, they performed better when assessed in small groups, which also fostered the development of good communication and teamwork – desirable skills from employers' point of view throughout the world (Lordan, 1996). With this dichotomy in mind, this study attempts to explore domestic and international students' views of group work and the extent to which group work may, or may not, promote cross-cultural understanding.

Method

This study was carried out at Coventry University, which has over 2,300 international students from 146 different countries on campus. The aim was twofold: first, to capture both international and domestic students' views on group working, in particular, working in culturally mixed groups; second, we wished to explore the benefits and problems working in groups entailed. It was paramount that students could discuss issues in an informal, non-threatening environment, so two existing students were employed to carry out several focus groups, to 'draw out the feelings, ideas, attitudes and perceptions of participants' (Ottewill & Brown, 1999, p. 373).

Participation invites were posted on both the Students' Union website and the University's 'message of the day' website. Over 100 students volunteered, and 25 were selected based on gender, age, year of study, discipline and ethnicity. Twenty-three participated: 11 males and 12 females; 10 home and 13 international students, including 7 from the EU. Nine were year-one students; 4 were year-two; 7 were year-three; 2 were master's students; and 1 was on a short exchange. Ages ranged from 19 to 37. International students were from China, Denmark, France, Germany, India, Latvia, Nigeria, Pakistan, Poland, Spain, the United States and Uzbekistan. The home students' ethnicities comprised 5 white British, 2 African, 2 Indian and 1 Caribbean.

The discussions were taped, transcribed and analysed to draw out common themes. Six main themes emer ged: how groups were formed, language barriers, educational/cultural differences, study commitment, cross-cultural friendships and 'value-added' benefits.

Findings

International Students

Group Selection

International students preferred to choose their own groups and would often choose people with the same ethnic background because they felt comfortable, were able to 'communicate well' and thus make themselves understood. But they also recognised that such groupings could be problematic for others, based upon their own experience of having to join groups composed of ethnic groups that were not their own:

'I got into a group with three Polish people ... you feel an outsider ... because they have the same background, even if they are from different parts of Poland.'

'It is kind of natural thing, whenever a culture gets dominant then it gets hard to do group work, because I experienced the same ... the Chinese sit there, English there and the rest of us here.'

To avoid this, some students felt that tutors should form the groups to ensure a cultural mix as this left no option but to work together. However, one student expressed concern that he could end up in a group that did not play to his strengths:

'I feel comfortable working with a person who knows my strengths and weaknesses – at the end we should not forget that ... we have to get good results, that is why we are a group project, so if you are paired with a group that doesn't appreciate your strengths.'

Language Barriers

International students also found that their poor command of English, caused interaction problems. One student was told by a group of mostly UK students that they didn't want to work with him because of this. Another student mentioned she felt too shy to participate: '[L]anguage is a big problem ... I am shy in the discuss – most of the time I will be quiet and prefer to do some writing.'

Another found that unfamiliarity with discipline-specific vocabulary intensified language difficulties:

'[W]hen you want to express your ideas you know what you want to say – but you don't find – in Business there is a lot of vocabulary that I don't know yet, so don't know how to express – sounds not as good as the other [people], so you cannot explain it properly – so before coming to group meeting I have to know what I want to say.'

This feeling of 'not being as good' was expressed by another student: '[They] cannot know that if you have difficulty to express yourself ... sometimes i feel very stupid when i am working with British [students].'

Educational Differences

However, international students did feel that working with home students in groups was, overall, of benefit, in particular in terms of coping with the challenge of an unfamiliar style of teaching and learning:

'[H]ome students are good in doing coursework ... but ... international students they have been taught more to achieve well in final exams rather than coursework ... home students could help you with actually going about coursework.'

'UK has one of the best academic standards in the whole world, it is really appreciated in my country we believe that a UK certificate is the best, so it would be good for me to work with home students – the home students will pose me with a challenge – being from an educationally disadvantaged country ... so this challenge make me do something great.'

This unfamiliarity was expanded upon by a Chinese student, who had not come across group work in her home country and faced an added cultural barrier in relation to group dynamics:

'[G]roup work – we will discuss and say I don't agree with you, no one would do that because it is very rude and it is horrible to say your ideas are wrong ... in China ... individual work is better than group work – there is no group work in my college because the teachers they prefer to choose individual work – in the discuss people don't like to show they had the best idea, they will hide it, they don't want to share the best idea to share with each other, so I think culture is a big problem during the group work ... it would be rude to interrupt somebody talking.'

Commitment to Study

When international students were asked if they felt they were more motivated and worked harder than home students, the overall response was yes, mainly due to needing to justify the higher fees they had to pay:

'Yes – I could do a masters degree spending not more than £500 in my country, but here it is £9000 – you can see the investment on studies – so I really need to work hard not to disappoint myself or my sponsors.'

'I could buy three incredible cars for what I have spent on my education ... so I want the most out of it.'

One went as far as to say that home students were lazy: 'I think some home students are kind of lazy ... they discuss the group work and don't do the work.'

Cross-Cultural Friendships as a Result of Group Work

When asked if group work encouraged friendships, some agreed and socialised with friends made during projects, but others, although they did make friends, did not feel the friendships were deep enough for socialising:

'[M]y coursework group are my friends ... and are better friends than the previous friends I had before starting group work.'

'Most people who I worked with – were people who communicated after – meet for group discussions for drink or dinner and we talk a lot, so we relate it is really good.'

'I am just the opposite – the last group I worked in I liked everybody in the group but they are not the people I go out and do things with.'

Value-Added Benefits

Beyond their academic experience, most also looked to their university experience to broaden their exposure to different cultural groups:

'I believe ... working in groups and meeting people is the greatest thing anyone can do – even religion – if you are a Christian you must be working with people ... if you are Muslim – you really relate people even in hospital you might be a doctor you interact with people – the whole life is all about people and meeting different people is the greatest achievement you can make.'

'[I want to] learn about [other] cultures and how I can understand them and make myself understand.'

Most international students could clearly see the link between what they learned through group work and their subsequent career plans:

'[I]t is just like the companies, society – when you finish your studies if you are going to work you cannot say this person is Chinese I won't work with him or this person is Indian and I can't work with him – you can't say that in organisations.'

'[W]orking for a corporation or multinational company ... you will find out that you will have probably 7 or 15 different engineers that you work with, you have different capability/capacity, different motives and abilities, so that means you might be better.'

Again, reflecting their outward focus, they felt that friends made at University would be useful contacts when they entered employment:

'I try to leave on agreeable terms so you can contact later – like business connections – it's a kind of networking so you can always call back, so I try to leave on agreeable terms and then in future might contact for business, or visits, call them up.'

Home Students

Group Selection

In contrast to international students, home students preferred to be part of mixed cultural groups from the outset feeling that this helped them break out of a 'comfort zone', often fostered by their previous educational experience:

'Education – like secondary and college education before we come here – at high school a lot of courses, go into your own group – hang with your mates, don't really ever go outside ... but now, there is a chance to meet other people.'

'I think a lot of people are stuck in their ways from secondary schools, then they come to uni, so used to having people who are exactly like them.'

They also recognised that working in mixed cultural groups brought a breadth of opinion and variation that they otherwise would not be exposed to:

'A good thing if people attack things from a different angle, gives different variations, there is a lot more different angles to take, cover all the angles, more ways to get the final answer.'

'Yes I think [mixed groups work well] because you get ideas from them as well – it is always nice to hear someone else's opinion, someone from outside, hear what they have to say.'

Asked if they felt international students tended to form groups based upon ethnicity, they agreed putting this down to the need for ease of communication:

'I think they stick together because they are probably embarrassed about the fact that they can't communicate well with home students properly, they would rather stay with people that they know, that they can interact with properly – I think it creates a divide between home and international students.'

Language

The issue of language barriers was extensively discussed by home students: in some cases, this meant international students were excluded from groups:

'[Y]ou don't want to offend them ... but it can be frustrating when trying to say something and the person just doesn't understand what you are saying – I think that is why sometimes we exclude them just because you don't know how to talk to them.'

Added to this frustration was a worry about offending international students and having to walk 'on eggshells':

'[Y]ou kind of have to walk on eggshells around them and sometimes that can be frustrating because ... we have all grown up here and we all have our own colloquial way of talking and so on and so forth, and they don't necessarily pick up on that and they think "Oh they are all taking the mick out of me" ... they exclude themselves from the group and ... there is so much tension and you can't actually get anything through to them because they are just like "Wow, you guys don't put me in your group so I am just not going to bother".

One student also mentioned that sometimes international students could be quite aggressive as a result of the length of time they took to understand what was expected of them: '[S]ome of them are quite aggressive ... you haven't got much time, and that is when it gets frustrating – and that is when they get aggressive.'

The students also were frustrated by the need for a 'translation phase' which resulted in both sides having to repeat themselves in order to be understood, and this could increase the length of time added to a project. In addition, it proved to be a barrier to assessing the international students' skill levels:

'[S]ometimes it takes so long just to get a single point across ... obviously we all wait, but it can be quite frustrating if you don't understand what they are saying once they have said it.'

'[I]t wasn't actually until we did the skills set that we realised how good [an international student was] at finance. It is difficult to identify people's skills ... because of the language barrier thing.'

Another issue was communication difficulties increasing the workload for home students, in one case leading to a home student having to do the work of an international student to meet the project deadline:

'Sometimes it means more work – my first year I was working with a chap from Japan and we had to do a report ... and I pretty much wrote his side of the project as well because his grammar – couldn't read it ... it is not that he didn't try but he just didn't have the knowledge to write it so I think it can add to workload for some students.'

Despite this frustration, home students were not reluctant to help international students, but time constraints meant they could be perceived as being unfriendly:

'You want to help but if you got two weeks to hand this assignment in there is no time for help. Which is really unfortunate. That is why some international students think that as a nation we are really unfriendly. It is just that we are always on the move. Always got things to do and there is not enough hours in the day.'

Educational Differences

Home students did not seem aware of the fact that some international students are unfamiliar with group work, but they did mention unfamiliarity with class presentations: 'We have got modules and we have to do presentations and three international students who are working with me are quite nervous about standing up in front of people.'

Commitment to Study

Home students also felt that there was a difference in terms of routines and lifestyles, with the resulting perception that international students work harder:

'[M]ore of a regime like you wake up this time or that time and so on and so forth. … [G]ot to be here at that time and that time. Whereas over here we are all over the place we go here, get something to eat go and have a little nap go to the library.'

'Home students live this lifestyle – we go out and get wasted, wake up the next day and do it again, whereas … [this international student] lives with his uncle who keeps him, he is not allowed to go out … they live different lifestyles – he goes home does his work, he works in a factory as well, so he has to be very efficient with his time.'

They also acknowledged that international students were more outward focused in that they tended to have a 'game plan':

'[I]nternational students have a … longer game plan – they know what they want to do, start working straight away in a quite a good job, carry on studying and try to get citizenship in Britain … got more or less 5 or 6 years planned out ahead.'

The difference in financial commitment was also recognised, as was motivation, with one student saying he felt this 'upped' everyone else's motivation:

'[F]inancially they are investing a lot more, and also because they have got to be that much better, they are fantastic to work with, because they are high standard themselves, it ups everyone else's game as well.'

'[If] they go back home and they have failed and they haven't got a degree or qualification they came here to get, their families will be disappointed and they will be disappointed in themselves – so they have a lot more to lose, so they don't necessarily work harder, they have more motivation to work.'

Cross-Cultural Friendships as a Result of Group Work

In terms of group work fostering friendships, home students did not feel that this happened, in some cases because they were local students and already had friendship groups: 'Because this is my home town, I have my own social group of people I have grown up with and … I tend to go out with them.'

Another felt she 'didn't have time' to make friends this way because 'everyone is out here for themselves', whilst another said: 'It just depends on … if someone makes themselves as difficult and unapproachable as possible – nothing to do with the group work.'

Value-Added Benefits

However, home students did think that working with international students enhanced their cultural understanding and future employment prospects:

'[It] does increase my understanding of different cultures and I have always wanted to learn not just academically but about different cultures … I am thinking of doing a 6 week placement abroad … and if I do get it I will be on the other side … I will have language boundaries that I need to get across and I just hope that people are as friendly as I am to them.'

'A lot of my work is design so when we are designing we want to make our potential products or vehicles as successful as possible, which might well mean making a global product or vehicle, so in order to make it global it is fantastic to get the input of various cultures around the world.'

Discussion

That international students in this study tended to prefer working in groups which contained people of a similar ethnic background was not surprising, considering the language problems mentioned by both groups. In particular, home students expressed frustration with the amount of time it took to communicate and in one case an international student was excluded from a group for this reason. This echoes Grey's findings that Asian students 'generally prefer to work in the same ethnic group or with other Asians because they feel "equal" and 'there are no barriers between us' (2002, p. 106).

It is likely, therefore, that working in a group with students for whom English is a second language may seem less intimidating to some international students. Kondo and Ying-Ling (2004) suggest that checking with peers if they have understood what is happening in an educational context is a significant factor in reducing language anxiety for international students. Language anxiety has been defined as a situation-specific personality trait with two psychological components, emotional arousal and negative self-related cognition (MacIntyre, 1995, p. 91): consequently, for those with English as a second language, forming a group with other international students will give the group as a whole an emotional safety blanket.

Further in terms of language difficulties, home students expressed concern about causing offence if they used colloquialisms, a finding that resonates with Allen and Higgins' (1994) national study into the experiences of international students in higher education, finding that they had problems with understanding local accents, the speed at which people spoke and local slang. This worry about causing offence is perhaps linked to another comment made by home students about how they had experienced aggression from international students when they got frustrated with trying to understand set tasks. The 'fear of causing offence' is also an emerging theme in the study reported by Harrison and Peacock in this volume, referred to as 'passive xenophobia'.

Educational differences were highlighted, in particular, written skills, which Allen and Higgins (1994) found were a problem with regard to essay and report writing, reflected in this study in comments from home students about resenting the increased workloads caused by having to complete work for international students to meet project requirements. Indeed, Barron's (2006) study included comments from home students indicating that working with international students resulted in more work and might negatively affect their final mark.

In addition, there was unfamiliarity with course work and presentations for some international students. The fact that teaching traditions and methods vary from country to country is well known, and as pointed out by Chen (1999) in a study of Chinese students, the UK experience encourages students to reformulate their ideas about teaching and learning and place greater value on peer learning. This can be in contrast to the international educational experience, in particular the experience of the Chinese student who felt that interrupting and putting forward her opinion in group work interactions would be seen as rude in her home country.

Another difference between international and home study concerned the commitment to study: both groups recognised that international students seemed more committed, or at least, more organised, and a review by Ward (2001) found that one of the benefits of international students in New Zealand was the impact of their 'good work habits' on home students. This commitment was recognised as being mainly due to the larger financial cost of their education and also to expectations of their families. Given this higher commitment it is perhaps unsurprising that international students seem to have a clearer long-term view of their future with several linking the experience of group work with what would be expected of them once employed. They also saw their UK higher-educational experience as being about more than their education, in particular the potential exposure to different cultural groups.

Regarding friendship, international students felt that group work enabled them to make a variety of friends – some of whom were home students. In contrast, home students tended to stick to ready-made friendship groups, often due to having limited time to pursue new friendships. This may be why some home students are reluctant to socialise with students from overseas. Other studies have shown similar findings: Al-Harthi's (1997) study of a group of Omani students found English students to be 'unsociable' and a study of Spanish and Greek students by Katsara and Gil (1999) showed that they made very few relationships with home students.

Finally, there appeared to be some differences in terms of an 'outward focus' between the two groups. International students were much clearer about how studying abroad could enhance their understanding of different cultures and future employment prospects and this was factored into their decision to study abroad. In contrast, whilst home students recognised the potential impact of exposure to different cultural interactions and ideas on their employment prospects, they seemed to view these interactions as an 'unlooked for' benefit of their studies. However, although home students felt that there were problems with working in mixed cultural groups, they indicated a preference for doing so, because they could see the benefits of exposure to new ideas and cultures. One particular student felt that inclusion of international students in a group work project 'raised the game' for all due to a higher motivational level and also, in one case, due to a 'good skill set' that emerged from a specific tutor set exercise. This is reflected in Trice's (2003) study which found that international students' mathematics acumen helped to improve home students' own levels and hence raise standards. On a further positive note, home students did not express lack of motivation in terms of helping international students overcome language barriers and other difficulties, but felt that a lack of available time in the curriculum precluded this.

Conclusion and Recommendations

This small-scale study has explored domestic and international student perceptions of group work in a UK university and the extent to which this promotes cross-cultural understanding. The findings indicate that students found working in mixed-cultural groups is, overall, a positive experience and does indeed promote cross-cultural understanding. However, the findings also indicate that a fuller understanding is precluded by language barriers and, in some cases, unfamiliarity with group work on the part of international students. Based on our findings from this study we suggest the following recommendations to enable a smoother interaction between domestic and international students, thus enriching the experience for both groups:

- Institutions should provide English language, study and presentation classes throughout the first year of study for international students with poor language skills.
- Institutions should outline the benefits of cross-cultural interactions to both domestic and international students upon entry to university.
- Lecturers should prepare international students for working in groups by outlining the rules and expectations relating to group work. This may also be useful information for some home students.
- Lecturers should ensure that there is enough time for groups to 'gel' and work through tasks, supported by regular tutorials to ensure that all students benefit from the experience.
- If possible, intercultural content should be included in group tasks so all students can make some unique contribution to the final outcome.

Acknowledgements

We would like to thank the Higher Education Academy for funding this project and Glynis Cousin for her support. Also thanks to Nicola Ayres, Emma Jackson (third-year psychology students who conducted the focus groups), Rahul Timilsina, Phil Pilkinton, Juhi Aggarwal, Susan Amos, Kirsty Bate, Ashia Bibi, Jilo Katter, Katherine Maryon, Paul Massiah, Maciej Pawlikiewicz, Christian Jacobsen Petersen, Laura Pibworth, Laura Raynal, Kaytlyn Reese, Mohammed Ribady, Chen Yiliang and others who contributed but did not wish to be mentioned by name.

References

Al-Harthi, H. L. (1997). Overseas students' reaction to interculturality: A study of the experience of Omani students in England. Unpublished MA dissertation. Institute of Education, University of London.

Allen, A., & Higgins, T. (1994). *Higher education: The international student experience.* Leeds, UK: HEIST in association with UCAS.

Barron, P. (2006). Stormy outlook? Domestic students' impressions of international students at an Australian university. *Journal of Teaching in Travel and Tourism, 2*(2), 5–22.

Chen, L. (1999). Chinese students at a UK HE institution: An evaluation of their educational experience. Unpublished MA dissertation. University of Bristol, UK.

Doyle, E., Beatty, C., & Shaw, M. (1999). Using cooperative learning groups to develop healthy cultural awareness. *Journal of Social Health, 69*(2), 73–80.

Grey, M. (2002). Drawing with difference: Challenges faced by international students in an undergraduate business degree. *Teaching in Higher Education, 7*(2), 153–166.

Katsara, R., & Gil, M. C. (1999). The experiences of Spanish and Greek students in adapting to UK higher education: The creation of new support strategies. Paper presented to the British Educational Research Association Annual Conference. University of Sussex, UK.

Knight, J (2004). Comparison of student perception and performance in individual and group assessments in practical classes. *Journal of Geography in Higher Education, 28*(1), 63–81.

Kondo, D. S., & Ying-Ling, Y. (2004). Strategies for coping with language anxiety: The case of students of English in Japan. *ELT Journal, 58*(3), 258–265.

Lordan, E. (1996). Using group projects to sharpen students' PR skills. *Public Relations Quarterly, 41*(2), 43–47.

MacIntyre, P. D. (1995). How does anxiety affect second language learning? A reply to Sparks and Ganschow. *The Modern Language Journal, 79*, 90–99.

McAllister, G., & Alexander, S. (2003). Key aspects of teaching and learning in information and computer science. In H. Fry, S. Ketteridge & S. Marshall (Eds.), *A handbook for teaching and learning in higher education: Enhancing academic practice* (pp. 278–300). London and New York: Routledge Falmer.

Mills, C. (1997). Interaction in classes at a New Zealand university: Some international students' experiences. *New Zealand Journal of Adult Learning, 25*(1), 54–70.

Ottewill, R., & Brown, D. (1999). Student participation in educational research: Experimenting with a focus group. *Journal of Further and Higher Education, 23*(3), 373–380.

Payne, B. K., Monk-Turner, E., Smith, D., & Sumter, M. (2006). Improving group work: Voices of students. *Education, 126*(3), 441–448.

Trice, A. (2003). Faulty perceptions of graduate international students: The benefits and challenges. *Journal of Studies in International Education, 7*(4), 379–403.

Volet, S. E., & Mansfield, C. (2006). Groups work at university: Significance of personal goals in the regulation strategies of students with positive and negative appraisals. *Higher Education Research & Development, 25*(4), 341–356.

Ward, C. (2001). The impact of international students on domestic students and host institutions: A literature review. Prepared for the New Zealand Ministry of Education, 5 March.

10
Interactions in the International Classroom
The UK Perspective

NEIL HARRISON AND NICOLA PEACOCK

Internationalisation in UK Higher Education

In response to the changing landscape of global higher education, there has been a growing emphasis in the United Kingdom on the role of higher education in developing global citizens for global employability and global responsibility (Fielden, 2007). Such trends find expression in the internationalisation strategies of UK universities, as documented by Middlehurst and Woodfield (2007) and Caruana and Spurling (2007) and explored further by Jones and Brown (2007). These strategies place an increasingly high academic premium on intercultural learning, an appreciation of cultural diversity, the development of cross-cultural communication skills and the fostering of a global perspective across all subject areas. Meanwhile, the second of the 'Prime Minister's Initiatives' in 2006 has supported these trends at national level with resources allocated to improving the international student experience.

While staff and student mobility programmes have traditionally been the main means of achieving these outcomes, there is now significant attention given across Europe to the process of 'internationalisation at home' (Crowther et al., 2000). This term refers to the acquisition of certain globally relevant knowledge, skills and perspectives by students on university campuses in the home country, based on the assumption that the vast majority of students will not be internationally mobile. To achieve this, it is widely proposed in the literature (Fielden, 2007; UKCOSA, 2004) that institutions radically review their academic, social, support and housing policies in order to create situations in which positive and rewarding intercultural dialogue may occur. Increasingly the 'international classroom' is considered key to the process (Leask, 2007).

The success of 'internationalisation at home' strategies, however, is not achieved through the mere presence of international students. Significant culture change is demanded, not least a reassessment of the relationship between institution and student; a shift in perception from international student as academic tourist or consumer, to fully integrated partner and active agent in the intercultural learning process 'at the heart of the university as a source of cultural capital and intentional diversity' (Brown & Jones, 2007, p. 2). Despite developments in internationalisation of the curricula and inclusive pedagogical approaches to this end, there is still little evidence of significant change.

For example, we continue to hear in the press that international students feel isolated and alienated on our campuses (e.g., Asthana, 2007; Hodges, 2007; Lipsett, 2007). Middlehurst and Woodfield (2007) report that international students wish for more cross-cultural experiences but are often dissatisfied, reporting in particular a lack of social integration with UK students, reflecting findings in previous research (UKCOSA, 2004; UNITE, 2006). This is likely to impact on their overall experience (Ward, Bochner & Furnham, 2001). Ward et al.'s (2005) large-scale work in New Zealand draws a correlation between better integration into the host culture with overall levels of academic satisfaction and general wellbeing. It also suggests that home student populations are not experiencing the benefits of living, working and studying in the sort of international environment on which the 'internationalisation at home' agenda is predicated. One of the participants in our focus groups told us, 'You gain like a minimal amount of cultural understanding or anything because they don't communicate and stuff. I would hardly say that it's changed my education or helped a great deal 'cos I've had foreign students in my class'.

In De Vita's words, 'the ideal of transforming a culturally diverse student population into a valued resource for activating processes of international connectivity, social cohesion and intercultural learning is still very much that, an ideal' (2005, p. 75). Leask (in this volume) identifies a gulf between the policies of internationalisation and the lived realities for both home and international students.

The 'International Classroom'

'International classrooms' vary greatly in their constitution (Leask, 2007). The classrooms discussed in this chapter are 'international' in so far as they include students from a range of nationalities and cultures who meet and learn in English from staff who, in the majority of cases, are UK nationals with English as a first language. The 'international classroom' is thus composed of three interacting agents – home students, international students and academic staff (Figure 10.1).

As one of the only structural spaces in which international and home students[1] are formally brought together, there are great hopes for the *international classroom* as a place for intercultural learning. Jones and Killick (2007, p. 113) suggest, 'Within the range of tools, techniques and resources available to help pursue effective learning and teaching within an internationalised curriculum the most obvious, and perhaps least utilised, is the diversity of the student body itself'. In an effective cross-cultural learning environment, which for the purposes of this chapter, the authors have defined as an 'internationalised classroom', students might be expected to:

- gain knowledge of other cultures and appreciation of cultural diversity;
- gain international perspectives on the field of study;

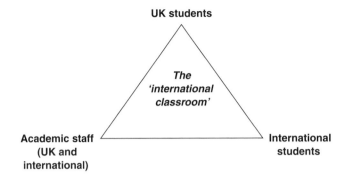

Figure 10.1 The Intercultural Dynamic of the International Classroom

- develop the ability to work effectively in settings of social and cultural diversity;
- develop the ability to think globally and consider issues from a variety of perspectives;
- develop the ability to communicate across cultures;
- develop the ability to engage positively with cultural others in both their professional and private lives;
- be responsive to international communities;
- gain awareness of their own culture and its perspectives and how and why those are similar to and different from other cultures and their perspectives.

(Adapted from Leask, 2007, p. 91)

The Missing Third Perspective: A Review of the Literature

We frequently hear from the international student and the practitioner, but what of the other perspective? What are the home students' experiences and perceptions of international students in the classroom and intercultural learning? How does internationalisation impact on their student experience and how might this knowledge influence our attempts to address the issue of integration?

It was recognised by the authors that there was a significant body of literature concerning the international classroom experiences of international students and, to a lesser extent, of academic staff (e.g. Carroll & Ryan, 2005; Trahar, 2007; Turner & Robson, 2006; Ward et al., 2005). However, there is very little previous research undertaken into the role of the third interacting component in the dynamic; namely, the home student.

Based on small-scale studies in the United Kingdom, various recent authors (Cathcart, Dixon-Dawson & Hall, 2006; De Vita, 2005; Ippolito, 2007; Osmond & Roed, this volume; Phillips, 2005) report a broadly similar picture, with limited classroom interaction between home and international students, coupled with a degree of indifference or avoidance. Common themes are a preference for monocultural workgroups and fears about academic marks being compromised. Peacock and Harrison (forthcoming) report similar findings, describing the majority culture within the home student population as one of 'passive xenophobia', where cross-cultural encounters are generally low-level, incidental and unconnected to wider learning. In all these studies interaction is exacerbated by language barriers (real and perceived) and anxiety about cross-cultural communication with its associated risks and demands.

There is growing evidence to suggest that these issues are endemic in any country which attracts a significant population of international students, with similar findings emerging from earlier and more recent studies in Australia (Leask, this volume; Summers & Volet, 2008; Volet & Ang, 1998; Wright & Lander, 2003), the United States (Spencer-Rodgers, 2001; Spencer-Rodgers & McGovern, 2002) and New Zealand (Li & Campbell, 2008; Ward et al., 2005).

Placing this limited literature in the context of social psychology theory, it would appear that for international students, 'prejudice comes in the form of relative indifference and exclusion from the benefits of positive affect and leniency accorded to ingroup members' (Brewer, 2003, p. 84).

Methodology

This chapter is based on the provisional results of ongoing research at two mid-ranked teaching-intensive universities in the southwest of England. The research subjects are UK full-time undergraduate students in their second or final year; it is recognised that the experience of postgraduate students may differ significantly (Neame, Odedra & Lloyd-Jones, 2007; Phillips, 2005) or in more subtle ways (Trahar, 2007). In particular, undergraduate students are less likely on average to have previous experience of working alongside people from other cultures and are less likely to have stable learner identities. Both have a range of recruiting and selecting programmes.

Two main forms of data collection have been used, in both cases with mirrored methodology and data collection tools between the two universities:

1. *Focus groups.* Sixty students attended one of eight focus groups, each lasting around one hour. Students were drawn from 'business studies' and 'creative arts' course on the basis that they these were offered in both universities and had contrasting proportions of international students – very high (around 30 per cent) in the former and relatively low (around 10 per cent) in the latter. There were thus two focus groups held per subject area per university. The focus groups aimed to gather information across the range of social and academic interactions between home and international students.

2. *Semi-structured interviews.* Forty students attended a semi-structured one-to-one interview lasting around one hour. These comprised 20 students from each university drawn exclusively from 'business studies' courses where proportions of international students were relatively high. These interviews focused specifically on groupwork experiences and night-time socialising.

In both cases, the participants self-selected in response to e-mails sent to all students in the cohort and were paid for their involvement. In order to minimise bias, the invitations did not state the purpose of the research beyond that it was concerned with aspects of 'the student experience'. The make-up of the participant group broadly echoed the populations from which they were drawn, including students from black and minority ethnic groups and mature students. There were no identifiable differences between the data from the two universities.

Limitations and Challenges

In attempting to redress the imbalance in student response through researching the home student perspective, we nevertheless recognise the limitations of our methodology, particularly in the crude distinction made between international and home student groups. Our approach is perhaps in danger of reinforcing the concept of segregation and undermining the inclusive premise upon which intercultural learning depends. Indeed by creating false divisions we are in danger of contradicting the proposition that 'responding to the diversity of international students and referring to the diversity of home students are in fact not two agendas but one' (Jones & Killick, 2007, p. 110). On occasion, it has prevented us from reflecting fully the range of perceptions of, and attitudes towards, culturally very diverse individuals and groups of students.

In defence, our study is no less flawed than the majority of existing studies which assume homogeneity among the international student population, ignoring important differences in culture, faith and ethnicity which in fact exist across the home/international divide. The next stage of the research being planned, however, will be to explore issues of diversity within the total student population, the complex nature of perception and the rich web of relationships that exist and defy simple categorisation and understanding.

A further challenge presented itself early in the research. As outsiders possessing a degree of objectivity, international students are well-placed to identify and analyse the influence of culture on behaviour. Discussing cultural difference with home students is more challenging. As members of the majority culture, with the privileges that that entails, blindness to the existence of 'other' is not uncommon. Several of our participants struggled to comment on international students' behaviour in class because they were unused to observing the invisible minority. Where international student commentary is often perceptive, detailed and contextualised, much of the data collected from home undergraduates was quite general and unreflective. The authors noted that there was a rich paralinguistic discourse which gave further clues about students' affective anxiety.

Further, students evidently felt high levels of anxiety in both focus groups and one-to-one interviews when discussing their attitudes to and perceptions of international students; many described a pressure to self-monitor and 'watch their words'. A number commented that they did not have the language to discuss difference and felt uncomfortable in expressing their views for fear of being perceived as racist by their peers. We have considered that self-censorship might compromise the validity of the data, a concern raised in other research (e.g. Hyde & Ruth, 2002; Le Roux, 2001; Osmond & Roed, this volume; Spencer-Rodgers & McGovern, 2002; Ward et al., 2005).

Patterns of Spatial Interaction

One of the most immediately obvious features of the 'international classroom' as described by the participants in the study was with regard to seating arrangements in lecture theatres, seminar rooms and other spaces: 'The international students are sat there and the English students are sat there and they don't really talk much'.

A further observation was the tendency for 'large groups of foreign students' to sit at the front of the lecture theatre, often in the 'front two rows'. Sitting at the front was ascribed to either demonstrating a strong work orientation or an inability to follow lectures at the same pace as their home counterparts. Proximity would, the students concluded, facilitate better listening and comprehension for speakers of English as a second language: 'It made me realise they probably sit at the front of lectures 'cos they may not understand the language. They sit and listen, whereas people in the middle, back, are talking about other stuff rather than the lecture'.

In either case, the seating pattern visibly differentiates international students from their home peers, and their choice of seat brands them as either overly keen or deficient learners. As a result, spontaneous interaction between the two groups was rare, an observation which is supported in the wider research (e.g. Li & Campbell, 2008, UKCOSA, 2004; Ward et al., 2005).

Patterns of Interaction Through Groupwork

De Vita (2005, p. 76) claims that intercultural learning 'involves the discovery and transcendence of difference through authentic experiences of cross cultural interaction that involve real tasks and emotional as well as intellectual participation' and that this can be achieved through multicultural groupwork. Groupwork has, for many years, been a key component in most areas of study in UK higher education and is often negatively perceived by students. Carroll (2005, p. 84) suggests that 'difficulties with group work arise from the complexity of the method itself' and not from the cultural diversity of the students. The presence of international students does, however, add another layer to the process wherein home students are exposed to viewpoints, knowledge, pedagogic approaches and ideologies which are perhaps beyond their previous experience and will be communicating with students for whom English may not be a first or even second language.

Participants in this study described a wide range of methods by which workgroups were constructed. The main categories in decreasing apparent order of frequency were:

1. *Self-selection.* Students were told which size of group to form and allowed to select their own team members. This process typically created monocultural groups (Carroll, 2005; Cathcart et al., 2006; De Vita, 2002), often based around existing friendship circles.
2. *Random allocation.* Here students were allocated by staff using the class register or numbering methods. This tended to yield multicultural groups, but it appeared that difficulties with group dynamics were most likely to occur under this system.
3. *Pseudo-random allocation.* Here some attempt at random allocation was made, but this didn't achieve a random grouping. For example, groups were decided by seating, order of arrival or alphabetical order (which were often determined by friendship group or nationality).
4. *Planned allocation.* In a small minority of cases, students were allocated to groups by staff who made some effort to make individuals work with people they had not worked with before or where there were different skill sets. This approach often generated successful multicultural groups, although Wright and Lander's (2003) experimental study found that international students tended to contribute less in these situations.

Students generally recognised that groupwork in class is often their only experience of interacting across culture. One described how it was a starting point for getting to know the international students on his course a bit better: 'You are not necessarily going to go up to somebody and just start chatting to them because you think they are an international student. But I think you can find similarities when you are working with them'.

Another reported that an initial shared groupwork exercise with an international student led to a fulfilling social relationship which continued on outside of the classroom:

'So Jason [a Chinese student] came up to me one day and said, "have you got a group yet" – I didn't know him at the time […] They're all my friends now – all three of the Chinese students are now my friends.'

However, this experience was atypical, with the vast majority of interactions between home and international students terminating at the end of the formal exercise.

Intercultural Learning and Intercultural Anxiety

When asked to describe the impact of international students on their overall learning experience, some home students were able to discuss the very benefits sought by policy-makers. For example, in terms of global perspectives:

'I think in a way it's good, like with advertising you've got to be constantly thinking of new ideas, being a bit creative, having somebody from another culture just gives it another angle. It's different ways of thinking. Different ways of approaching the same thing.'

Similarly, in terms of cross-cultural communication skills: 'I think it sort of pre-pares you for the working world as well, because you are going to come across different people, different cultures – the way they do things when you get into groups in the working world.'

However, the reality did not always meet these aims. In interviews, students were asked to discuss a significant piece of summative groupwork they had undertaken with international students and to explore their feelings around this experience. For the majority of participants in this study, the perception of the experience had, in reality, been a neutral or negative one. Many were simply indifferent to the presence of international students in the group – they were 'not a problem' and 'just the same as anyone else'. Others found the experience more actively divisive, unproductive or frustrating: 'We tried to include [the international students] as well. They didn't come to all the group meetings. There was a kind of separation; not a horrible one but you could just tell.'

At the extreme, a small minority of participants described situations where they felt that their classroom interactions with international students had been damaging to them:

'Me and my friend were doing all the work […] They just went off and did their own thing. They didn't take anything in from what the lectures and tutorials were teaching us […] Only a few days before the actual hand-in date, we split into two groups. It was partly because if you do stay in the same group and they've done no work, you are committing an assessment offence to submit it as their work as well.'

Ward et al. (2005) assert that where international student numbers reach a critical mass of around 15 per cent, perception turns from positive to negative among the host student population. Findings from this study broadly support this hypothesis. Anxiety and irritation was frequently acknowledged in class-rooms with a large proportion of visibly international students:

'[My friend] used to get irritated with all the international students, but I think it was 'cos she was sort of surrounded by them a lot of the time […] I'm not always working with them so I don't see it as too much of an issue. She's sort of surrounded by them because there happen to be a lot of them on her course and I think that frustrated her a bit.'

The conceptualisation of threat felt among the home student population is explored in more detail in Harrison and Peacock (2007). The remainder of this chapter will focus on attempting to understand some of the particular anxieties which home students feel about their role in the 'international classroom'.

English Language: Barriers and Difference

It is no surprise that English language competency was perceived to be a fundamental barrier to both interaction and learning and a major source of anxiety for home students when faced with working with international students in groups. Language is central to the communication process and the balance of power in any relationship and particularly in a learning environment when 'language skills and intellectual ability are often conflated in people's minds' (Trahar, 2007, p. 17). One participant explained, 'Thinking about the first year – this sounds really horrible. When we got put into groups there were people I didn't want to work with because of their level of English.'

In particular, home students focused on the individual effort involved in communicating with somebody for whom English is not a first language: 'Obviously you can communicate in other ways and stuff, but sometimes […] meaning and terms are sometimes quite different and so when you are doing a project with that person it's not straightforward.'

In the minds of the majority of participants, language functioned both as a barrier to personal interaction and to academic understanding. Conversations were more difficult where the international student's level of spoken English was less strong, while ensuring that meaning was shared made the groupwork dynamics slower and more fraught, relying heavily on forms of 'Global English' (Graddol, 2006). Indeed, Volet and Ang (1998) identify a lack of goodwill and unwillingness to make the effort was at the root of conflict and a breakdown in communication rather than the issue of language itself.

There was evidence that some students used language as a marker for an unspoken power relationship between the home student as 'expert' and the international student as 'deficient', although the more reflective and egalitarian-minded students rejected this. Instead, they could identify with the difference between language and ability and occasionally took responsibility for assisting their international peers in the classroom, taking on the role of 'cultural host' (Cathcart et al., 2006): 'I sat with them and helped them and made sure that they understood the task and made sure their English was grammatically correct. Really – it wasn't a problem or anything'.

Though our participants consistently identified language as a significant barrier, it is important to question the assumption that language is *always* the issue. A willingness to discuss language ability in focus groups contrasted heavily with reticence around discussing other aspects of culture. It is possible then that the language barrier is easily identifiable and a comfortable indicator of difference, which can be publicly discussed, while deeper cultural differences such as conflicting value systems or educational backgrounds cannot. One participant noted, in describing a group of American students and echoing George Bernard Shaw's famous phrase,[2] 'We may speak the same language, but we don't understand them!'

Work-Orientation and Commitment

In around half the interviews, home students commented on international students' perceived lack of commitment or contribution to the workgroup, whether that was during group meetings,

'I've done a presentation with somebody similar to me and a boy from China, I think it was, and he was very quiet – didn't contribute much. He probably had less confidence because we all knew what we were doing more so and I think also obviously with the language.'

or their actual attendance at meetings:

'[My friends] just had problems with her turning up … she doesn't have a problem communicating in English, but they just had problems with her not putting the effort in.'

This contrasts interestingly with data collected, particularly from the focus groups, where international students were often portrayed as having a much more positive work-orientation, with their primary focus being on study. As home one student explained, 'I guess because they make more of an effort to get here, they've come all the way especially for their education, so a lot of them are more really hard-working – some more hard-working than the British students here'.

In many cases this was attributed to the fact that international students tended to be a little older than average, exhibiting more mature attitudes and having real-life work experience on which they could draw: 'A lot of them have worked in industry … whereas not very many of the English students have, so it gives them a different mentality to the work they're approaching than we have.'

It was noted from the interviews that instances of negative assessment of work-orientation came from home students who showed very strong work-orientation or instrumentalism towards grades themselves. These participants expressed a strong desire to maximize their own academic outcomes (but not necessarily learning) and were concerned if international students had the opportunity to jeopardise this. We will return to this observation below when considering risk in the context of multicultural workgroups.

At the other end of the spectrum, some participants did describe intimidating and domineering international colleagues who presented an issue in the group, but not through deficit. There was a fear of them 'taking over' the control of the group due to their confidence or the strength of their academic ability:

'I hate talking in front of people and some of [the international students] have got more confidence in that respect … Like they've done the group-work and the presentations and they're just used to talking in front of people.'

This 'hard working' versus 'poor attendee-contributor' dichotomy is an inter-esting tension that calls for further exploration, including with the international students themselves. It may be due to the difficulty of meeting up outside the classroom when students have different social or study patterns. Perhaps the group dynamic demotivated international students where they were in the minority and were perceived as deficient (Wright & Lander, 2003). Further, different approaches to groupwork and understanding of what makes a good group member are culturally determined. Lastly the data would suggest that anxiety and expectation on occasion clouded the home students' perceptions of their international colleagues.

'Mindfulness', Racism and Fear of Causing Offence

The concept of 'mindfulness' (Langer, 1989) with regard to cross-cultural encounters has been touched on above and is explored in more detail in Harrison and Peacock (2007) and Peacock and Harrison (forthcoming). Home students experience significant anxiety when interacting with their international peers. In the social sphere, this often leads to the active or *de facto* avoidance of the company of international students, which the authors have dubbed 'passive xenophobia'. In the context of the international classroom, especially where workgroups are cross-cultural, this is not usually possible and home students are required to interact to varying degrees.

Many participants expressed a deep-rooted tendency to seek out like-minded individuals for work and pleasure, explaining, 'People just tend to flock together if they have things in common'.

There was active effort involved in cross-cultural encounters; trying to understand another point of view, accent, educational background or sense of humour:

> 'So if you get on really well with other people that aren't [international], it's much easier, especially if you're tired and you're working hard. You don't want to have to spend time trying really hard to get on with people you don't really get on with.'

Some participants hinted at the need for constant vigilance and self-monitoring in intercultural encounters, for fear of 'saying the wrong thing' or causing offence. This was particularly in relation to the British culture of so-called 'political correctness' which, in expounding egalitarian values and terminology, can frustrate attempts at finding acceptable words. One student described the anxiety and the communication paralysis that can result:

> 'You have to watch what you say … There's this Nigerian boy and [my friend] is scared 'cos she's worried she's going to say the wrong thing. She's not racist, but she's worried she's gonna say something and that worry has stopped her from talking to him.'

In other interviews, students discussed their own feelings of fear at not knowing the 'correct' words to use when discussing diversity, especially in the context of race. In many ways, a more powerful fear was that of being perceived by one's British peers to be holding racist values expressed through morally ambiguous language. Participants were concerned about the moral condemnation which could ensue, along with fears of being branded as 'stupid' as a result of making a cultural *faux pas*. A number of the focus groups were particularly marked by 'response amplification' (Stephan & Stephan, 1996); a tendency to describe 'other' in excessively positive tones. International students were described variously as 'really, really clever' or 'really, really hard working', in attempts to establish a sympathetic or egalitarian position.

Similarly, the participants were generally very aware of the dangers of stereotyping and made active efforts to avoid doing so and to be seen to be avoiding doing so. Some were keen to tell us that they didn't identify physical or cultural difference. They considered international students to be 'just like us', avoiding discussion of the unique characteristics of other cultures for fear of muddling difference with discrimination. This 'stereotype suppression' (Bodenhausen & Macrae, 1996), was, however, balanced by the frequent use of subconscious stereotypes relating to particular ethno-national groups. For example, there was generally little evidence of individuation of 'Chinese' students; personal details like names or countries of origin were unknown (Ippolito, 2007). In fact, the very label of 'Chinese' was used indiscriminately to describe people from a range of South and East Asian countries, including Japan, Malaysia, Thailand and Vietnam. These 'Chinese' students were most usually referred to through group memberships and typified as 'unfriendly' or, as noted above, 'sticking together', thereby falling neatly into the Western stereotype of the 'inscrutable oriental' (Said, 1978).

Fears About Academic Outcomes

One finding from the focus group component of this study was consistent fears and anecdotes about international students compromising the performance of workgroups or the wider student cohort. This was explored in more detail through the interviews, where a sizable proportion of the participants were able to discuss instances where they felt that international students had jeopardised their marks or learning – or were able to recount 'friend of a friend' stories. While De Vita (2002) discounts this hypothesis, other writers are less certain (e.g. Summers & Volet, 2008) and this form of 'realistic threat' (Stephan & Stephan, 2000) appears to be a strong and present theme within the home student psyche (Spencer-Rodgers, 2001) which bears further investigation. For example,

> '[This international student] has got one of the poorest levels of English and obviously work gets marked on what they've done as a group and [my friend] doesn't think that it's fair. She says he is trying his best, but it's not to their sort of standard.'

The most common manifestation is the perception that intercultural workgroups achieve lower marks than those which comprise only home students. Various explanations for this are proffered. The most common are that the international student is unable to engage in the task at the appropriate level, either due to their language skills or educational history, or that their work-orientation is low and that they effectively absent themselves from the group. At the lower levels, this tension expresses itself in terms of annoyance about the limited, irrelevant or unusable contribution of an individual. At a more serious level, a minority of students described in detail how workgroups broke down and required intervention from academic staff, or how they colluded to cover up the perceived shortcomings of an international member of the group. By way of illustration the following extract is drawn from a lengthy dialogue between three students:

'This is gonna make us sound really bad. Sven was in our group and I wrote his section for him because … we were like, "this doesn't make sense, this doesn't fit in with the rest of the report" and I dictated it.'

Outside of the workgroup environment, participants identified two other situations in which international students posed a potential risk to their education. The first related to the practice on some courses of using students as peer educators, for example, by asking students to present core content to the rest of the class: 'They are all Chinese and … it was very hard to actually understand what they were getting at and to actually understand what they were trying to teach.'

Here a relationship was created in which students perceived their progress, defined in terms of knowledge acquisition, to be dependent on the English language competence of the Chinese students, resulting in resentment and frustration and compounding negative perceptions of other.

The second related to instances where a disproportionate amount of academic staff time was perceived as being used by international students in order to support their learning (Spencer-Rodgers, 2001). This might occur within the 'international classroom' or during tutorial or open-door time. The participants felt that their own learning was slowed down or that they were unable to procure individual access to academic staff when needed:

'We ended up spending the whole tutorial discussing what a certain word meant in English. We missed out of an hour of teaching on the module when we knew what those words meant. We were a bit disheartened by it really because we were paying for that tutorial and yet we're not getting the teaching.'

Discussion: A Risky Proposition

Though responses from our participants varied and there were many examples of positive perceptions of, and attitudes towards, international students and intercultural interaction, many home students in our study perceived a high level of risk associated with intercultural communication combined with a significant amount of effort required to understand, be understood and not offend. Many lacked the courage, motivation or skills to successfully communicate across culture, yet were not averse to the idea in principle and not blind to the associated benefits for personal development and global employability. These risks can be categorised in three main ways:

- the risk of an *unsatisfying interaction*, due to language barriers which make conversation and collaboration more time-consuming, more mentally challenging and more prone to misunderstanding;
- the risk of *causing offence or political incorrectness*, either by making a cultural *faux pas* directly with an international student or by being thought by one's peers to be 'stupid' or 'racist';
- the risk to *academic performance*, especially due to language barriers and differences in work-orientation or pedagogic background, although this appeared to be more a well-entrenched fear than an evidenced reality.

The feeling of risk was not directed solely towards international students. It was appreciated that there were other sources of risk within the classroom setting, including through other forms of cross-cultural interactions, e.g. by social class, ethnicity or age. While most students, for example, self-selected into friendship-based workgroups, a minority explained that they preferred not to work with their friends as they were afraid that group conflict could jeopardise their existing relationship, felt they did not work hard enough or were not the most able members of the class.

The contrast between the work-orientations of the home and international students (Figure 10.2) appeared to have a strong role in defining the risk levels and therefore the likelihood that the home student would choose to work with an international student (and the predicted likelihood of success if they were allocated to the same workgroup).

Where there was a dissonance between the work-orientations, the home student was likely to see the interaction as 'risky' to either their marks or their

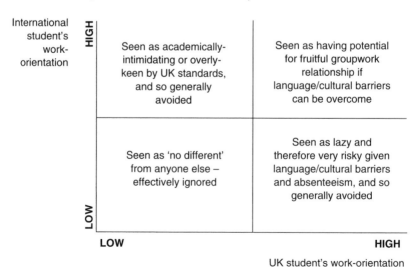

Figure 10.2 The Interaction Between the Work Orientations of Home and International Students

self-esteem. In contrast, similar work-orientations posed less risk and could be very rewarding where both were high. Clearly a similar analysis could be posited for any two students, but the key distinction in this case is that a student's status as international heightened the tensions, especially where their behaviour or perspectives were seen as being outside British academic norms. In some cases participants appeared to use the international status of another student to explain their perceived deficiencies in ability – a form of cultural scapegoating.

Several of our participants commented that they had never previously considered issues of diversity or reflected upon their interactions with diverse student groups. The majority welcomed the opportunity and said it had raised their awareness of international students and led them to question the ways in which they perceived them. Several said that this would impact on their future behaviour. This suggests that students would welcome more opportunities to explore dissonance, discomfort and difference, ideally in mixed groups, and that creative ways of approaching the topic are called for.

Intercultural interaction can facilitate intercultural learning but this is dependent upon both staff and students having the motivation and skills to make this happen successfully (Leask, 2007). It has been understood by social psychologists for many decades (e.g. Allport, 1954) that simple proximity does not predict rewarding cross-cultural outcomes. Shared goals and managed positive intergroup interactions are also necessary, alongside equality of status and the promotion of egalitarian attitudes. Indeed, it is the role of the international teacher to create motivation in the students and manage the risk associated with intercultural interactions through:

- incorporating a range of international content and perspectives in the programme;
- seeking, evaluating and responding to feedback of different kinds;
- changing teaching approaches to achieve different course objectives in different ways, depending on the needs of students;
- reflecting on and learning from teaching experiences.
  (Adapted from Leask, 2007, p. 88.)

The last of these steps may be particularly important as Summers and Volet (2008) find that students are no more positive about intercultural groupwork *after* having an experience, while Pritchard and Skinner (2002) found that encounters with international students can act to reduce home students' enjoyment and confidence as the shortcomings in their intercultural skillsets are revealed.

Conclusion

Academic staff must also have an awareness of how culture impacts on their own behaviour and knowledge of the cultural background and motivations of their students. As such, they become key agents of transformation within the internationalisation agenda, transforming 'international classrooms' (a place where different cultures meet) into 'internationalised classrooms' (a place where different cultures meet *and learn from each other*). A key finding that emerges from the study and a vital development in the formation of the 'internationalised classroom' is the need for proactive management of the groupwork component. In the words of one participant, 'I think in maybe the first year, where it's not academically kind of dependent, then interaction with other international students should be more encouraged. It should be almost forced gently when it comes to groupwork.'

Le Roux (2001) concluded that 'Intercultural relations in the classroom may be a source of knowledge and mutual enrichment between culturally diverse learners if managed proactively by teachers, or a source of frustration, misapprehension and intercultural conflict if not dealt with appropriately' (p. 286). In his work on group allocation, Kelly (2008) agreed that classroom diversity was a major challenge: 'a double-edged sword, increasing the opportunity for creativity as well as the likelihood that group members will be dissatisfied and fail to identify with the group' (p. 31). However, in many universities, much of the frontline teaching of first-year students is undertaken by part-time or visiting lecturers and postgraduate teaching assistants. More generally, Cathcart et al. (2006) and Li and Campbell (2008) found that staff were under-equipped to deal with the international classroom, while Ippolito (2007) and Kelly (2008) note that there is often too little time or academic 'space' for groups to effectively form and negotiate the barriers to successful teamwork. One challenge therefore is how to equip all our staff with an understanding of the issues and the necessary skills to create, support and sustain successful workgroups. There are clear lessons to be learned from the field of group theory.

Developments in curriculum and pedagogy cannot, however, be dissociated from the wider process of institutional internationalisation. Students in our study repeatedly commented on housing policy and how it impacts on friendship networks, which in turn have implications for intercultural interaction in and out of the classroom. They also confirmed that some of the traditional approaches to support, orientation and social provision, by focusing on the 'special' needs of international students, can further serve to segregate the student community at the early stages when friendship groups are being formed and social norms are settling. Institutions therefore need to give serious consideration to how these practical aspects of the international campus are managed to best effect. In particular, a number of our participants and other writers (e.g. Pritchard & Skinner, 2002; Summers & Volet, 2008) have stressed the need for positive engagement between home and international students at an early point in their academic careers.

Notes

1 It should be noted that the authors are keenly aware that this is often an artificial distinction, with, for example, some UK students displaying characteristics generally associated with international students (e.g. those with English as a second language and those recently naturalised in the United Kingdom after an asylum application),

while some international students may have been resident in the United Kingdom for long periods and/or have English as a first language.

2   Shaw once described the United Kingdom and the United States as being 'divided by a common language'.

References

Allport, G. (1954). *The nature of prejudice.* Cambridge, MA: Addison-Wesley.

Asthana, A. (2007). Costs deter foreign students. *The Observer,* 16 September.

Bodenhausen, G., & Macrae, C. (1996). The self-regulation of intergroup perception: Mechanisms and consequences of stereotype suppression. In C. Macrae, C. Stangor & M. Hewstone (Eds.), *Stereotypes and stereotyping.* New York: Guilford Press.

Brewer, M. (2003). *Intergroup relations* (2nd ed.). Buckingham, UK: Open University Press.

Brown, S., & Jones, E. (2007). Introduction: Values, valuing and value in an internationalised higher education context. In Jones & Brown (2007), pp. 1–6.

Carroll, J. (2005). Multicultural groups for discipline-specific tasks: Can new approaches be more effective? In Carroll & Ryan (2005), pp. 84–91.

Carroll, J., & Ryan, J. (Eds.). (2005). *Teaching international students: Improving learning for all.* London: Routledge.

Caruana, V., & Spurling, N. (2007). The internationalisation of UK higher education: A review of selected material. Available from: www.heacademy.ac.uk/assets/York/documents/ourwork/tla/lit_review_internationalisation_of_uk_he.pdf [Accessed April 2009].

Cathcart, A., Dixon-Dawson, J., & Hall, R. (2006). Reluctant hosts and disappointed guests? Examining expectations and enhancing experience of cross cultural group work on postgraduate business programmes. *International Journal of Management Education,* 5(1), 13–22.

Crowther, P., Joris, M., Otten, M., Nilsson, B., Teekens, H., & Wächter, B. (2000). *Internationalisation at home: A position paper.* Amsterdam: European Association for International Education.

De Vita, G. (2002). Does assessed multicultural group work really pull UK students' average down? *Assessment and Evaluation in Higher Education,* 27(2), 153–161.

De Vita, G. (2005). Fostering intercultural learning through multicultural group work. In Carroll & Ryan (2005), pp. 75–83.

Fielden, J. (2007). *Global horizons for UK universities.* London: Council for Industry and Higher Education.

Graddol, D. (2006). English next. Available from: www.britishcouncil.org/learning-research-english-next.pdf. [Accessed April 2009].

Harrison, N., & Peacock, N. (2007). Internationalisation, 'mindfulness' and the cross-cultural discourse between UK and international students. Paper delivered at Society for Research into Higher Education Annual Conference, Brighton, UK, December 2007.

Hodges, L. (2007). Foreign students: Overlooked and over here. *The Independent,* 27 September.

Hyde, C., & Ruth, B. (2002). Multicultural content and class participation: Do students self-censor? *Journal of Social Work Education,* 38(2), 241–256.

Ippolito, K. (2007). Promoting intercultural learning in a multicultural university: Ideals and realities. *Teaching in Higher Education,* 12(5), 749–763.

Jones, E., & Brown, S. (Eds.). (2007). *Internationalising higher education.* London: Routledge.

Jones, E., & Killick, D. (2007). Internationalisation of the curriculum. In Jones & Brown (2007), pp. 109–119.

Kelly, P. (2008). Achieving desirable group-work outcomes through the group allocation process: *Team Performance Management,* 14(1/2), 22–38.

Langer, E. (1989). *Mindfulness.* Cambridge, MA: De Capo Books.

Le Roux, J. (2001). Social dynamics in the multicultural classroom. *Intercultural Education,* 12(3), 273–288.

Leask, B. (2007). International teachers and international learners. In Jones & Brown (2007), pp. 86–94.

Li, M., & Campbell, J. (2008). Asian students' perceptions of group work and group assignments in a New Zealand tertiary institution. *Intercultural Education, 19*(3), 203–216.

Lipsett, L. (2007). Overseas student talent 'is wasted in UK'. *Guardian Education Supplement,* 4 October.

Middlehurst, R., & Woodfield, S. (2007). *Responding to the internationalisation agenda: Implications for institutional strategy.* York, UK: HE Academy.

Neame, C., Odedra, H., & Lloyd-Jones, G. (2007). An exploration of diversity in a UK postgraduate university. Paper delivered at the Education in a Changing Environment Conference, Salford University, UK, September 2007.

Peacock, N., & Harrison, N. (forthcoming). "It's so much easier to go with what's easy": 'Mindfulness' and the discourse between home and international students in the UK. Accepted for 2009 publication in *Journal of Studies in International Education.* Available from: http://jsi.sagepub.com/cgi/content/abstract/1028315308319508v1 [Accessed April 2009].

Phillips, A. (2005). Working in groups in an international publishing class. *Art, Design & Communication in Higher Education, 4*(3), 173–187.

Pritchard, R., & Skinner, B. (2002). Cross-cultural partnerships between home and international students. *Journal of Studies in International Education, 6*(4), 323–354.

Said, E. (1978). *Orientalism.* London: Penguin.

Spencer-Rodgers, J. (2001). Consensual and individual stereotypic beliefs about international students among American host nationals. *International Journal of Intercultural Relations, 25*(6), 639–657.

Spencer-Rodgers, J., & McGovern, T. (2002). Attitudes towards the culturally different: The role of intercultural communication barriers, affective responses, consensual stereotypes, and perceived threat. *International Journal of Intercultural Relations, 26*(6), 609–631.

Stephan, W., & Stephan, C. (1996). *Intergroup relations.* Boulder, CO: Westview Press.

Stephan, W., & Stephan, C. (2000). An integrated threat theory of prejudice. In S. Oskamp (Ed.), *Reducing prejudice and discrimination,* pp. 23–45. Mahwah, NJ: Lawrence Erlbaum Associates.

Summers, M., & Volet, S. E. (2008). Students' attitudes towards culturally mixed groups on international campuses: Impact of participation in diverse and non-diverse groups. *Studies in Higher Education, 33*(4), 357–370.

Trahar, S. (2007). Teaching and learning: The international higher education landscape – some theories and working practices. Available from: http://escalate.ac.uk/3559 [Accessed April 2009].

Turner, Y., & Robson, S. (2006). Beleaguered, bothered and bewildered: A story of academics and internationalisation. Paper delivered the Supporting the Chinese Learner Conference, University of Portsmouth, UK, July 2006.

UKCOSA (2004). *Broadening our horizons: International students in UK universities and colleges.* London: UKCOSA.

UNITE, & UKCOSA. UNITE international student experience report 2006. Available from: http://www.unitegroup.co.uk/data/Research/default.aspx [Accessed September 2008].

Volet, S. E., & Ang, G. (1998). Culturally mixed groups on international campuses: An opportunity for inter-cultural learning. *Higher Education Research & Development, 17*(1), 5–23.

Ward, C., Bochner, S., & Furnham, A. (2001). *The psychology of culture shock.* Abingdon, UK: Routledge.

Ward, C., Masgoret, A-M., Ho, E., Holmes, P., Newton, J., & Crabbe, D. (2005). *Interactions with international students: Report prepared for Education New Zealand.* Center for Applied Cross-Cultural Research, Victoria University of Wellington.

Wright, S., & Lander, D. (2003). Collaborative group interactions of students from two ethnic backgrounds. *Higher Education Research & Development, 22*(3), 237–252.

11

Has Everybody Seen a Swan?
Stories from the Internationalised Classroom

SHEILA TRAHAR

Introduction

One night in November 2007 I sat in a lecture theatre listening to a colleague talk to Master of Education (M.Ed.) students about quantitative methodological approaches to educational research. In introducing Karl Popper and his theory of falsification, she used the well-known example of white swans. We may claim that all swans are white but we need to see only one black swan in order to refute or 'falsify' that claim. Quite appropriately in a lecture theatre of more than 100 students, from almost as many countries, she asked whether everybody had seen a swan. Giggles reverberated around the room. 'Why is she asking such a question?' 'Surely everyone knows what a swan is and has seen one?' But swans are not seen in all parts of the world – there are no swans in parts of sub-Saharan Africa for example. Yet more chuckles broke out when she revealed that some swans are black and native to Australia. Being married to an Australian and having lived and travelled there many times, it was no surprise to hear her speak of black swans, yet there were those in the room who had never heard of black swans, let alone seen one.

This story may seem light hearted and anecdotal but it is an illustration of an event that occurs all too often in the so-called 'internationalised classroom'. The majority of people – students and academic staff – will claim that they are tolerant of diversity; indeed, in the case of my own department, the 'international' nature of it is what attracts very many of the students, but 'the degree of tolerance to otherness and different styles can dwindle quickly when teaching and learning demand more time, energy and patience' (Otten, 2003, p. 14) and when we realise that our differently situated knowledges give rise to exclusion rather than inclusion (Minnich, 2005).

In this chapter, I draw on my experiences as a lecturer in a postgraduate university department together with research conducted for my doctorate and subsequent research projects, including a project funded by the United Kingdom's Higher Education Academy, 'Perspectives on Internationalising the Curriculum' to consider the following questions:

- What is it like to learn and to teach in an environment that is extremely diverse culturally, where people bring a range of different academic experiences and traditions?
- What is the role of the lecturer in the process of intercultural communication?
- What is the role of the student?
- What occurs when each is interacting with the other?
- Are there ways that such complex learning environments can be managed so that everyone, all of the 'players in the process' (Teekens, 2000, p. 26) benefit?
- To what extent are we all, academics and students, perpetuating a form of neo-colonialism if we do not reflect critically on our approaches to learning and teaching when working alongside people from different academic traditions?

Research conversations with postgraduates at master's and doctoral level will be integrated with my own reflections and observations. Critical consideration of learning and teaching experiences of research methodology and counselling will be used as illustration. I acknowledge that my insight is gained from one university and derived from being a white British woman working with postgraduate students whose backgrounds also inform their insights. Readers should consider these elements when reading the chapter; however, I believe that the experiences recounted here will resonate with many others, whatever their discipline and context; core principles of working sensitively with diversity obtain across the disciplines and academic levels.

Culture, Internationalisation and Globalisation

Culture is one of those words bandied about in the literature, often without a working definition (Laungani, 1999). For the purposes of this chapter, I am defining culture as the knowledge that we use to interpret behaviours. In a context where people are drawing on a range of knowledges, be they academic, social or professional, to inform their learning and teaching approaches, the outcome is an environment that is multi-layered in its complexity.

Internationalisation and globalisation are terms often used interchangeably – 'different but dynamically linked concepts' (OECD, 1999, p. 14) – yet inadequately understood, defying simple explanation (Sanderson, 2004). Altbach and Knight (2007, pp. 290–291) offer a simple and plausible distinction:

Globalization is the context of economic and academic trends that are part of the reality of the 21st century. Internationalization includes the policies and practices undertaken by academic systems and institutions – and even individuals – to cope with the global academic environment. Globalization may be unalterable but internationalisation involves many choices.

Their words 'and even individuals' imply that 'individuals' somehow are not actors in the drama of the changing nature of higher education and yet it is we, the individual students and academics, who constitute the 'deeply embedded values, cultures and traditions' (Stenasker, Frolich, Gormitzka & Maassen, 2008, p. 2) of higher education, the values, cultures and traditions that are rarely articulated and exposed to critical scrutiny (Trahar, 2007; Turner & Robson, 2008).

'You know if the module is geared towards what is happening in the UK, what is happening in the US or perhaps Japan, so you follow that line. There was no room to discuss what is happening in my country.'
(Participant in HEA project, 2008)

One aim of this chapter is to challenge the above comment and make transparent those values, cultures and traditions.

'International Students'?

In the United Kingdom, although this may not be so in other contexts, the meaning of internationalisation is often elided with increasing numbers of international students. Discussions of internationalisation tend, therefore, to focus more on income generation for cash-strapped higher education institutions (HEIs) (Haigh, 2007) rather than on the internationalised curricula that might prepare learners – and academics – for a multicultural world that is interdependent (OECD, 2004). Many academics sense a paucity of support, resources and recognition for innovative teaching practices in environments that are culturally complex, yet the attitude of the academic is crucial in determining possibilities for intercultural dialogue. It is our beliefs about learning and teaching that guide the way we work, that influence whether we position 'international students' as needing to acquire a set of skills to assimilate with the dominant pedagogical approaches or whether we position ourselves as local academics and students as needing to learn and be open to change. International students are no more a homogeneous group than any other group of people or students, for example, home students, yet the terms are often used as if they were descriptors of homogeneity.

Internationalisation at Home

Internationalisation at Home is a concept gaining prominence. It recognises that the majority of students and academics in higher education are not mobile and therefore the opportunities for cultural capability will not be gained by travelling to other countries for study or work; they can be developed 'at home'. In many ways Internationalisation at Home is much more inclusive than 'internationalisation' as it focuses our attention on 'academic learning that blends the concepts of self, strange foreign and otherness' (Teekens, 2006, p. 7, original emphasis) and is congruent with the perspectives of those such as Appadurai (2001), Haigh (2007) and Sanderson (2007) who foreground the importance and value of personal awareness in intercultural encounters in higher education.

Appadurai (2001) speaks of the personal journey of internationalisation, Sanderson (2007) calls for the 'internationalisation of the academic Self', while Haigh (2007, p. 7) asserts that the 'best approach is to assume that all students are "international"'. Such calls for greater personal responsibility for intercultural learning and communication were reflected in my own doctoral research (Trahar, 2006b) where I interrogated my own values, beliefs and behaviours in order to exemplify the knowledge that underpinned my pedagogical approach. My interactions with people from very different cultural backgrounds from mine challenged me to engage more rigorously and fully with my own (Trahar, 2006a, 2006b, 2008). In spite of those such as Teekens (2000) and Ippolito (2007) who position educators as holding clear responsibilities to effect intercultural communication in the international classroom, this is something that does not just happen (Otten, 2000). Indeed there can be resistance to 'difference' from many corners and 'international students' scapegoated as the source of academics' frustrations (Devos, 2003) yet:

> Addressing fears about change in a positive and constructive manner and assisting established and new participants to explore and optimise the match between their theories of teaching and learning and those required in an internationalised institution can help to foster an overall positive climate.
>
> (Turner & Robson, 2008, p. 68)

Learning and Teaching Research Methodology

One of the delightful challenges of teaching research methodology in a postgraduate education department is that the majority of students do not have a social science background. This means that for many of them the language of the subject is completely alien. In addition, many students are working in a language that is not their first. I am a member of a team teaching this course, Introduction to Educational Inquiry and, as a team, we have developed a pedagogical approach that allows for the diversity of knowledge and linguistic fluency to be celebrated rather than seen as problematic (Stier, 2003). The course is presented, currently, via a weekly 'lecture' when all of the students are introduced to a particular topic such as 'Issues for Researchers', 'What is Knowledge'? 'A Critical Reading of Research Literature'. These lectures are then followed up with a seminar within which students are grouped according to their particular 'Pathway' on the M.Ed. programme, for example, Educational Leadership and Development, Psychology of Education or Counselling in Education, the Pathway that I teach on. The purpose of these seminars is to facilitate students' developing understanding of the whole research process by providing space for creative activities that deepen understanding of the week's topic or concept, to raise questions or problems from the lecture and its associated readings and to work together in groups to conduct a small piece of research. The intention is that students apply the concept addressed each week to their research project. This approach receives excellent feedback from students who attest to the value of being able to apply complex and unfamiliar concepts to a small research study of personal interest.

Given that, as indicated earlier, the majority of students do not have English as their first language, are from outside the United Kingdom and are encountering many differences in the way of life, it is perhaps not surprising that it is quite common for them to conduct research on 'international students' – their stressors, how they manage them and their relationships with 'home' students. Through conducting a small research study with a group of peers, students take great comfort from learning that they are not the only ones feeling lonely, homesick and struggling with this strange 'culture' that they are encountering. In addition, we as facilitators have the opportunity, through the learning and teaching process, to understand how and why what is familiar to us is strange to others, thus providing us with rich insights.

In 2007–08, the topic chosen by one group was 'How students make relationships with each other and the extent to which these impact on their learning'. This group consisted of five students from Saudi Arabia, Taiwan and the Caribbean, only one of whom was a first-language English speaker. They decided to research their own experiences as a group, filming their conversations as they struggled to grapple with the many differences between them. In this group of students I witnessed exemplification of the layers of complexity that are intrinsic to the international classroom. I was called upon frequently to offer advice and even to mediate when it seemed as if their differences could not be resolved. I suggested material on group dynamic theory, and research on international higher education, yet I was unaware until I read their assignments of how complex their relationships had become. In these assignments, which took the form of research reports, I was privileged to read how each one of them experienced conducting this research, how each one grappled with the range of differences, and how gradually they found a way of working that enabled them to address, openly and robustly, their different world views.

Volet and Ang (1998) highlighted the apparent reluctance of students in multicultural higher education settings to move from their 'comfort zones' to make relationships with each other. The authors concluded that when students did move from their 'comfort zones', their experiences were positive, but left to their own devices, they would remain with students who shared a similar cultural background. In my experiences of working in international classrooms, I have been influenced by this research and have challenged its findings by putting students into multicultural groups to work on set tasks between sessions. Such an activity encourages them to work together and to get to know each other, and provides space for the more reticent students to express their ideas. I have had interesting feedback on this kind of activity such as:

'But here, I don't know, maybe it's because I'm alone, away from home …
I feel that we have the intense relationship. I think it's because all the activities. You know we enjoyed very much. We will discuss it, about the material, you know think about idea. We liked it very much.'
(Conversation with Ying, a Chinese student)

In addition, it often leads to students socialising together outside sessions; for example, I learned that several students taking courses with me this year were attending ballroom dancing classes together.

Yuan's Story

Yuan is from Taiwan, a woman in her early forties. With a background in restaurant management and a Master's degree in hospitality management from the USA, her reasons for choosing to undertake the M.Ed. programme are not immediately obvious. She is one of the students therefore for whom research methodology is a completely new topic – Yuan was a member of the group whose experiences were discussed earlier in the chapter. Yuan participated in a research conversation with me about her experiences as a learner. Below is my synthesis of her story, using her own words:

'I found that doing a Master's degree in the USA was very similar to my experiences as an undergraduate in Taiwan and so this time I decided that I wanted to study in Europe. The first thing I noticed was that on the very first day, I felt that the lecturers wanted to help us. Everything was made very clear although the emphasis on how difficult the coming year was going to be made me rather anxious.'

Unlike many other people, I enjoyed the Introduction to Educational Inquiry lectures. I could be quite anonymous in the lecture theatre – I found it intimidating being in such a large group and certainly did not have the confidence to speak out. I had never encountered social science research methodology – the subject was completely new to me – and so the lecture was good for me as it gave me the basic ideas about each topic. I found the language and the jargon difficult and the reading was not that easy, having to read a chapter every week. One thing I did find difficult was having different lecturers. It meant that I had to adjust every week to a different way of presenting, a different way of speaking and I would have found it easier if the lecturer had been the same each week.

The seminars really helped me to see that it was not just me who found the topic difficult. Having the opportunity to discuss with others helped me to realise that if I could explain ideas to others, I would feel very proud of myself. The small research group was very difficult. I was quite unusual I think, as a Taiwanese woman, having had a lot of experience of working in groups and teams, and I believed that I understood how to ensure that a group was effective. In our group, we began well and there was a lot of harmony but then it became much more difficult because of the group's constituency. I felt that as Taiwanese women our background is to sit and listen, there is no need to say anything, that's the way we are taught in our culture. However, the men in our group were from cultures where it seemed that whatever a man says is considered to be important. I decided that I had to speak out and this was then difficult for them as I think they did not understand how a woman could speak like that. It was really difficult. I thought that I had learned how to work with all different kinds of people but in that group I saw my own limitations. I learned that I needed to find a way to speak out and I think the men learned that they too had to adjust. Because we had a task to focus on it enabled us all to recognise what we need to do in order to communicate in a multicultural group. People with cultural backgrounds similar to mine perhaps need to be a little bit more proactive and those from some other cultures, perhaps to sit tight and observe rather than always jumping in with opinions and questions. It was a really different experience and opened up to me just how difficult it is to really accept people who hold very different viewpoints'.

At Doctoral Level

In addition to the type of pedagogic approach, the material used is also important. Our doctoral-level research training courses, Understanding Educational Research, are designed to enable doctoral students to 'read' educational research critically and to ensure that they begin to develop their knowledge and understanding of different paradigmatic positions. Whereas, for many M.Ed. students discussed earlier, educational research is a very new activity, students come to doctoral research training with particular experiences and views about research garnered from experiences of Master's degrees. An activity that we have devised, designed to enable them to apply various classification taxonomies such as of Habermas (1972), is to select research articles that differ paradigmatically in addition to reflecting the constituency of the group, i.e. research into international higher education communities such as ours. Students work in culturally mixed groups, each with a selected research article to classify, summarise and evaluate the strengths and limitations. By choosing articles that reflect the constituency not only do they engage in conversations about strengths and limitations of the methodological approach but are also provided with opportunities to relate the research to their own experiences. Such activity leads to rich conversations and valuable feedback on the learning and teaching processes.

'When I came into the lecture room it seems like white people at the back, white people and then in the middle some like me yellow coloured people, and then at the front, black people. And when they divide groups, just like Malaysia students will go with Malaysia students. Muslim students would like to go with Muslim students. White people will get used to white people together.'

(Participant in HEA Perspectives on
Internationalising the Curriculum, 2008)

In another doctoral research training course, Advanced Qualitative Research, the group in 2008 consisted of students from Cyprus, China, Malaysia, Bulgaria, Oman and the United Kingdom, who reflected the statement above in their seating arrangements. I had given them a chapter to read as preparation for the session on narrative analysis. The chapter was written by a North American, Catherine Riessman, and included a series of exemplars of the dialogic/performance approach to narrative analysis. This method of analysis creates space for the 'audience', the reader of the research to form their own meanings about what is being retold. Riessman's (2008) claim is that sufficient information about the research context and the researcher needs to be provided to enable that process to occur. My rationale, shared with them, was to investigate the extent to which these exemplars, all from a North American context, enabled them to ascribe meanings, given that they were not North American. Were there questions they needed to ask? Was there sufficient information provided about the context and the researcher to enable judgements to be made about the analysis of the data? By ensuring that the groups engaging in this activity were culturally mixed, students were able to engage in intercultural conversations both to challenge and critique Riessman's assertions and to hear perspectives that differed not only from her exemplars but also from their own. Feedback from students on that activity attested to the value of being placed in intercultural groups for the discussion:

> 'It was really good that you put us into groups and mixed people up so that we were not all from the same culture. Being asked to discuss this chapter with people who were not from Malaysia was really valuable and made me think how we should do this more often.'

'Embarrassing Questions'

A lynchpin of professional counselling training in the United Kingdom is the importance of creating opportunities for trainees to challenge their own judgements and perceptions. I am not training people on the M.Ed. Counselling in Education Pathway to be professional counsellors but I am aiming to enable them to recognise that many of the stories that they will encounter in a 'counselling' or pastoral role in education will be outside their own experience. Providing students with opportunities to ask embarrassing questions (Palmer, 1999) can, therefore, be very fruitful. So often, students claim to value diversity and to welcome opportunities to learn from each other in the international classroom, but then someone will express a view that may not accord with the dominant one and is challenged, sometimes quite aggressively. It is important, therefore, to enable students to recognise perspectives and knowledge that may be particular to their own context and traditions.

An activity that can engage students on a deep level and engender rich and provocative conversations is to devise scenarios inviting them to express their views and to engage in a critical examination of their own values and beliefs in multicultural groups by asking them to focus on the question: 'What beliefs and values of your own might make it difficult for you to empathise with this particular person/situation?'

One such scenario is that of a student who was homosexual but did not want anyone in the group to know as, in his culture, homosexuality, while not illegal, was not welcomed. In setting this as a task in 2007, a student told me at the end of the session she could not understand why I had given this as a scenario – surely everyone now accepted homosexuality? I asked her to trust me and engage in the discussion. Sure enough, the following week when the small groups were discussing their vignettes in the larger group it emerged that for some of the students, homosexuality was indeed a problem because of their religion, their culture or because they themselves viewed it as inappropriate activity. This led to a rich discussion about not only how homosexuality is conceptualised in different cultures but the difficulties of being able to accept perspectives and viewpoints that really differ from our own. Subsequently, there came recognition that the activity was enabling us to do just that, to ask those 'embarrassing questions' of each other that we need to feel we have permission to ask in order to learn why we might hold different views.

'Critical Thinking' and Critical Pedagogy

A critical pedagogic approach seeks to dismantle the hierarchy that creates a power differential between academics and students (Ippolito, 2007) yet in an environment where there are multiple identities (ibid.) this can create a problem. In seeking to dismantle such hierarchies, we may overlook the different ways that people understand each other's behaviour and 'hierarchies'. 'Hierarchies' may be very familiar to many students who can feel threatened by apparent attempts to dismantle them. No matter how much we talk of shifting and fragmentary identities (Fox, 2006; Sarup, 1996) resisting essentialised notions of the latter, we *all* bring different understandings to the international classroom, including ways in which the relationship between learner and teacher is conceptualised (Salili, 2001). To what extent then, in seeking to dismantle this 'hierarchy' are we acting in ways that are at best counter-cultural for many people and at worst dismissive of their traditions? I have learned that, seeking to dismantle or dismiss the authority vested in me can be threatening for those students more familiar with positioning the academic as an authority figure. It is much more inclusive to accept the different conceptualisations of the teacher/student relationship, certainly at the beginning of that relationship, as this can lessen the anxiety of such students.

I have explored the cultural embeddedness of some other culturally inviolable Western academic traditions such as critical thinking and plagiarism elsewhere (see Trahar, 2006a, 2006b, 2007, 2008). Those such as Welikala (2008) engage in similar critiques. For instance, for Japanese learners, criticality is interwoven with their norms related to interpersonal relationships. Moreover, they do not relate verbal silence to intellectual passivity. Their argument is that critical learning also involves critical thinking, and hence, for them, arguing for a point of view itself is not an assurance of critical learning; those who talk too much during lessons may not be critically reflecting but 'shouting' since they have language fluency (Welikala, 2008, p. 166).

Such statements are a salutary reminder of the email I received from a Korean doctoral student following a seminar I had given where I had spoken of my developing learning of the ways in which learner and teacher are conceptualised in different cultures and how my own interpretations of students' silence as boredom, lack of understanding, lack of engagement and even disapproval, had been challenged:

'Some Korean students expect, sometimes demand, you to tell them about your expertise with authority. Most students are ready not to argue or discuss but to absorb your experience … Keeping quiet is seen as a virtue in Korea – meaning behaving well … A way of learning in Korea was traditionally reflecting, like Buddhist monks do … keeping on thinking with one clue until getting awareness.'

There is of course a more fundamental and perhaps more uncomfortable question to ask (Back, 2004) which is to what extent are we, certainly in the United Kingdom given our history as a coloniser, perpetuating imperialism by not opening up *all* of our higher education practices to scrutiny for their unacknowledged cultural entrenchment? 'Even the cultural hybridity permitted within an internationalised university is scripted by the neoliberal presumption that Western norms should prevail' (Sidhu, 2004, cited Haigh, 2007, p. 4).

Conclusions – Not Just a Bystander

In this chapter I have described some experiences of learning and teaching in the 'internationalised classroom' in the United Kingdom. I have striven to illustrate how, by developing understanding of ways in which learning and teaching are conceptualised in different cultures, it is possible to make adjustments to teaching to develop strategies that are inclusive of diversity – of cultural diversity as in this book, but I would argue of any diversity – that are evaluated positively by students. If learning and teaching is to be effective for all of us it needs careful preparation with a focus on the complexities of the constituency – a constituency that is not going to reduce in complexity. This chapter has very deliberately not focused on the economic priorities that drive universities because so much of the discourse is economic that there can be a feeling that there is little space to engage in any other (Koehne, 2005). I am, however, not so naïve that I do not recognise that these concerns will be those of many readers – as they are to me.

The Chinese have two symbols for the word 'change' – one means risk and the other opportunity. If we risk asking the question 'Has everybody seen a swan'? we create different opportunities not only for ways to determine whether all swans are white but also to explore people's differently situated knowledge about swans. Surely, in the troubled times in which we all coexist, that can only be a good thing for all of us, irrespective of whether we see ourselves as core players in the process or whether we prefer to stand on the sidelines of the 'internationalised classroom'? I argue that the latter is no longer possible, nor preferable nor ethical for, 'Before we can recognise the "Other", we have to know ourselves well. This requires a position of ethics, not just being bystanders of external developments' (Stromquist, 2002, p. 93).

References

Altbach, P., & Knight, J. (2007). The internationalization of higher education: Motivations and realities. *Journal of Studies in International Education, 11*(3/4), 290–305.

Appadurai, A. (Ed.). (2001). *Globalization.* Durham, NC: Duke University Press.

Back, L. (2004) Ivory towers? The academy and racism. In I. Law, D. Phillips & L. Turney (Eds.). *Institutional racism in higher education* (pp. 1–13). Stoke on Trent, UK: Trentham Books.

Crowther, P., Joris, M., Otten, M., Nilsson, B., Teekens, H., & Wächter, B. (2000). *Internationalisation at home: A position paper.* Amsterdam: European Association for International Education.

Devos, A. (2003). Academic standards, internationalisation and the discursive construction of 'the international student'. *Higher Education Research and Development, 22*(2), 155–166.

Fox, C. (2006). Stories within stories: Dissolving the boundaries in narrative research and analysis. In S. Trahar (Ed.), *Narrative research on learning: Comparative and international perspectives* (pp. 47–60). Oxford, UK: Symposium Books.

Habermas, J. (1972). *Knowledge and human interests.* Boston, MA: Beacon Press.

Haigh, M. (2007). Internationalisation, planetary citizenship and higher education. In *Compare.* Available from: http://dx.doi.org/10.1080/03057930701582731. [Accessed April 2009].

Ippolito, K. (2007). Promoting intercultural learning in a multicultural university: Ideals and realities. *Teaching in Higher Education, 12*(5), 749–763.

Koehne, N. (2005). (Re)construction: Ways international students talk about their identity. *Australian Journal of Education, 49*(1), 104-119.

Laungani, P. (1999). Culture and identity: Implications for counselling. In Palmer & Laungani (1999), pp. 35–70.

Minnich, E. K. (2005). *Transforming knowledge* (2nd ed.). Philadelphia: Temple University Press.

OECD (Organisation for Economic Co-operation and Development). (1999). *Quality and internationalisation in higher education.* Brussels: OECD.

OECD (2004). Internationalization of higher education: Policy brief. *OECD Observer.* Available from: http://www.oecd.org/dataoecd/33/60/33734276.pdf [Accessed June 2008].

Otten, M. (2000). Impacts of cultural diversity at home. In Crowther et al. (2000), pp. 15–20.

Otten, M. (2003). Intercultural learning and diversity in higher education. *Journal of Studies in International Education, 7*(1), 12–26.

Palmer, S. (1999). In search of effective counselling across cultures. In Palmer & Laungani (1999), pp. 153–173.

Palmer, S., & Laungani, P. (Eds.). (1999). *Counselling in a multicultural society.* London: Sage.

Riessman, C. K. (2008). *Narrative methods in the human sciences.* Thousand Oaks, CA: Sage.

Salili, F. (2001). Teacher–student interaction: Attributional implications and effectiveness of teachers' evaluative feedback. In D. A. Watkins & J. B. Biggs (Eds.), *Teaching the Chinese learner: Psychological and pedagogical perspectives* (pp. 77–98). Hong Kong: University of Hong Kong.

Sanderson, G. (2004). Existentialism, globalisation and the cultural other. *International Education Journal, 4*(4), 1–20.

Sanderson, G. (2007). A foundation for the internationalization of the academic self. *Journal of Studies in International Education.* Available from: http://jsi.sagepub.com/cgi/rapidpdf/1028315307299420v1

Sarup, M. (1996). *Identity, culture and the postmodern world.* Edinburgh: Edinburgh University Press.

Stenasker, B., Frolich, N., Gormitzka, A. & Maassen, P. (2008). Internationalisation of higher education: the gap between national policy-making and institutional needs. *Globalisation, Societies and Education, 6*(1), 1–11.

Stier, J. (2003). Internationalisation, ethnic diversity and the acquisition of intercultural competencies. *Intercultural Education, 14*(1), 77–91.

Stromquist, N. P. (2002). Globalization, the I, and the Other. *Current Issues in Comparative Education, 4*(2), 87–94.

Teekens, H. (2000). Teaching and learning in the international classroom. In Crowther et al. (2000), pp. 29–34.

Teekens, H. (2006). Internationalization at home: A background paper. In H. Teekens (Ed.), *Internationalization at home: A global perspective* (pp. 7–18). The Hague: Nuffic.

Trahar, S. (2006a). A part of the landscape: The practitioner researcher as narrative inquirer in an international higher education community. In S. Trahar (Ed.), *Narrative research on learning: Comparative and international perspectives* (pp. 201–219). Oxford, UK: Symposium.

Trahar, S. (2006b). Roads less travelled: Stories of learning and teaching in a multicultural higher education community. Unpublished PhD thesis, University of Bristol, UK.

Trahar, S. (2007). *Teaching and learning: The international higher education landscape – some theories and working practices*. Available from: http://escalate.ac.uk/3559.

Trahar, S. (2008). Close encounters of the cultural kind: reflections of a practitioner researcher in a UK higher education context. In M. Hellsten & A. Reid (Eds.), *Researching international pedagogies: Sustainable practice for teaching and learning in higher education* (pp. 45–64). New York: Springer.

Turner, Y., & Robson, S. (2008). *Internationalizing the university*. London: Continuum.

Volet, S. E., & Ang, G. (1998). Culturally mixed groups on international campuses: an opportunity for inter-cultural learning. *Higher Education Research & Development, 17*(1), 5–23.

Welikala, T. (2008). (Dis)empowering and (dis)locating: How learners from diverse cultures read the role of English language in UK higher education. *London Review of Education, 6*(2), 159–169.

12
Mutual Cultures
Engaging With Interculturalism in Higher Education

VIV THOM

Introduction

This chapter considers intercultural capacity as the key challenge which faces universities in responding to diversity and the relationship this might have to wider patterns of global economic and technological change.

Large numbers of students have chosen to study outside their country, providing a valuable source of revenue for universities in host countries, particularly where government regulates student numbers from the domestic market. Along with growth in transnational education, the trend indicates the growing importance of knowledge-based economies, and as universities widen their reach across their own societies and the world, it is unavoidable that the role of higher education will be redefined at this time of unprecedented and rapid changes. Countries which currently import skills and knowledge will soon not only meet domestic demand for higher education but also recruit internationally, increasing competition in education markets.

To remain globally successful, universities must demonstrate their responsiveness to their students' needs and guarantee the quality of the whole experience, not only in relation to learning and teaching, student success and employability. International students are often disappointed by the lack of opportunity to engage with home students, yet it remains an intractable challenge to create opportunities which promote intercultural relationships. The examples here illustrate simple ways to maximise the impact of connectivity and the potential of a focus to international students' voices to act as powerful tool for cultural change.

Internationalism and Interculturalism: Economic Change and the Politics of Inclusivity

Governments and educators are also alert to the potential of intercultural understanding. Progressive and liberal idealism linked to higher education is not new and both in the past and present, the inspiration has been to encourage harmony and enhance prosperity in the developing world or to build relationships of mutual benefit with the leaders of the future. The struggles of western economies to maintain their dominance are increasingly accompanied by considerations of global and national inequity, yet the only certainty for the future is that the balance of power will change.

Cross-cultural capability has become an urgent necessity for graduates as world leaders of all kinds call for egalitarian and ethical partnerships to resolve current unprecedented challenges. Employers claim that such skills are of the highest importance in graduate jobs (Fielden, 2007). Societies are characterised by greater plurality which demands higher levels of cross-cultural skill to manage cultural divisions (Modood, 2005; Phillips, 2005). No surprise that debate in the sector is focused on internationalism when there is such confluence in political and economic agendas. Internationalisation has become good business and good for business.

Whatever responses can be offered to these important issues, the evidence from students themselves suggests that the potential for the presence of international students to be a catalyst for a radical shift in university culture is not yet a reality.

Internationalism and Interculturalism in Higher Education

Universities deal with a widening degree of diversity. Ryan and Carroll use the analogy that international students are 'the canaries in the coalmine' in western universities (2005, p. 9); a powerful way to express an understanding that many educators have been quick to acknowledge; that being responsive to students is good practice and does not apply only to international students Brown and Jones (2007, p. 1). This has implications for pedagogy and for other aspects of student life.

De Vita and Case (2003, p. 388) define intercultural learning as 'the discovery and transcendence of difference through authentic experiences of cross-cultural interaction that involve real tasks and emotional as well as intellectual participation'. This entails exposure to others and a dialogue which enhances understanding of the differences between people as well as the elements which are shared. Such transformations take place when respect for, and tolerance of, difference is embedded in institutional culture, and where individuals are properly supported when required to act and think outside their comfort zone.

It is often assumed that a university is a diverse learning community, where students have space and time for personal growth through exposure to new and different ideas, people and lifestyles. As centres of academic freedom, genuinely international approaches to enquiry, research and exposure to interculturalism would be appropriate, but most students do not feel part of a community and may not seek one. If there is a community it does not seem to create opportunities for learning about diversity.

Internationalisation is often translated as 'integration', and universities have developed an impressive array of innovative ways to support international student integration on and off campus, but most of these are bolt-on and extra-curricular. Volet (2003) describes learning objectives and principles for designing internationalised curricula. She suggests the application of critical reflection in a multicultural context should be a core objective in university education actualised through learning tasks which require sensitivity to others, and opportunities for social debate. Despite the good intentions of internationalists, there is little evidence that such learning is taking place.

Students, Social and Technological Changes

In universities, as elsewhere in Western societies, possibilities for genuine engagement seem to be diminishing. In this context it is difficult to promote interculturalism. Western society encourages individualism, social and geographical movement and pluralism. The growth of mass higher education has led to greater diversity among students who no longer suspend other aspects of their lives, often maintaining strong connections to families, jobs and children. Communication between tutors and their students is more often mediated by technology and administrators. The context in which students communicate with teachers, with each other and with the world is different in quality and quantity and relationships which students have with each other can be transient and transactional. Teaching often takes place in large groups.

In a recent video published on YouTube (Wesch, 2007) presented by a group of anthropology students from Kansas State University, one student claims only 18 per cent of teachers knew her name; a common complaint from students in many countries. Social networking sites and free web links facilitate frequent and easy communication regardless of distance and are used to support learning. It is estimated that the average student spends around three and a half hours a day on-line. Students everywhere are telling us the same things about communications and intercultural relationships in universities. Classes can be almost entirely made up of international students, many are monocultural, and opportunities to meet home students are limited.

Students who study in another country must deal with cultural and linguistic adjustment, leaving less time to spend on social activities. Language skills, the high cost of living, the 'beer culture', each increase the likelihood of social isolation. Students are more likely to seek support from others with whom they feel 'cultural-emotional connectedness' (Volet & Ang, 1998). This is a common survival strategy when living abroad; such relationships reinforce shared ideas and values, which facilitate humour and feel comfortable. International students may develop relationships within their own national groups and with other international students. A critical network for many, it provides knowledge and support, especially at transition stages. The mere presence of international students on campus does not result in the internationalisation of higher education (De Vita, 2006; Leask, 2001; Wright & Lander, 2003). Smart, Volet and Ang (2000) noted that universities must actively intervene if they wish to promote intercultural interaction. They conclude that universities should establish projects which set out to break down the barriers to the development of intercultural communities.

Social networking sites may have a role here, although current research suggests it is used mainly to maintain existing connections as much as with fellow students and increases exclusivity rather than its opposite (Thom, 2008). Spontaneous, genuine, intercultural interaction between international students and their host community is unusual, and simply being exposed to people from different cultures does not lead to internationalisation any more than living in the same street creates a community.

Human beings are programmed to be wary of differences as a mechanism to avoid potential attack but this response is no more use to us now than a primitive desire to eat quantities of salt. Complex social and political relations require that we learn to overcome instinctive fears and develop a rational and intelligent tolerance to inform our behaviour. There are many threats to the hard-won liberties which have accompanied the advance of meritocratic and democratic processes. Without the intellectual skills and verbal capacity to defend tolerance of diversity, some people will gain liberty at the expense of others. The experience of strong intercultural communities in tertiary education may enhance awareness of our identity and a capacity for tolerance in place of violence and disengagement.

Capturing Student Voices

Methodological Issues

There is more than one student voice, and although research does acknowledge the diversity of most student populations, there is a tendency to assume that students are homogenous groups, especially if they are from other countries or continents.

Asking students about their experience may not produce reliable data. More dissatisfied students may respond more readily than the satisfied, and this will be true of focus groups, student experience surveys (commercial and small scale) and course-based research tools. Feedback requests may bring responses from students confident about giving their opinions, who seek attention, reward or simply to please. Universities sometimes offer incentives to students to participate. Other students, unfamiliar with being asked at all, may respond positively; to criticise would be impolite. Yet universities are increasingly aware that unrestrained criticisms of university facilities and teaching, which may misrepresent or decontextualise, can be instantly shared online and across the planet, with the potential to damage recruitment.

International Student Voices: A Challenge for Internationalisation

Despite these various limitations, some interesting quantitative and qualitative data has been collected by universities in recent years. All suggest that if interculturalism is measured by the degree of integration between home and international students, there is little evidence of willing or spontaneous engagement, creating disappointment among international students.

Broadening our Horizons (UKCOSA 2004), International Student Experience Report 2006 (UNITE & UKCOSA, 2006) and International Student Barometer (ISB) (International Graduate Insight Group, 2005–2007), are all surveys conducted among large numbers of international students studying in the United Kingdom. They consistently demonstrate that international students both value the opportunity to meet and make friends with host students and are more satisfied with their experience when this happens. Only 32 per cent of international students had a mixture of host and international student friends (Broadening our Horizons) and around 70 per cent were unhappy with their ability to develop host friends. Without such connections, social adjustment is more difficult, English skills can deteriorate and the international student experience is impoverished and widely quoted by international students as a cause of dissatisfaction. Sixty-two per cent said that meeting other students from overseas is a valuable part of the student experience, but only 35 per cent of UK students agreed. According to recent research (2006 ISB) UK universities were doing less well than comparative institutions elsewhere.

'Home' Student Voices on Difference

Various studies have revealed the reaction of domestic students to the presence of students from other countries. Harrison and Peacock's innovative research with undergraduates in two UK universities appears in this book and elsewhere (Harrison & Peacock, 2007). They found that British students complained that poor language skills slowed the pace and although there were some positive aspects, cultural differences were a barrier to wider interaction. International students were seen as sometimes rude or inappropriate, cliquey, shy and difficult to get to know. Sharing a joke and a drink were seen to make relationships easier and it is unlikely that many UK students will trouble to develop social relationships across different cultures. Some students acknowledged that understanding of another culture could be valuable and but these were more commonly recognised where students were studying courses with an international focus. Students often had difficulty identifying or articulating such benefits.

Language competence can be a major factor inhibiting communication and, in the context of learning and assessment, can lead to international students being perceived as less competent in their ability to understand ideas, or engage in analysis and discussion. UK students were sometimes surprised by the numbers of students from other countries they encountered at university and occasionally stated they felt intimidated by their linguistic skills, independence and resourcefulness. Teekens (2007) sees the development of language skills and competence in at least one other language as an essential part of an internationalised curriculum.

Dobson, Sharma and Calderon (1998) looked at the performance of all undergraduates in Australian universities in 1996, and Hacket and Nowak (1999) compared the academic performance of thousands of students, across all fields of study, at Curtin University. They found the only significant difference affecting performance was gender. Overall international students significantly outperformed Australian students in a range of subjects.

Research by Volet and Ang (1998) noted that the cultural diversity in universities provided opportunities for intercultural learning but both Australian and Asian students diminished their value, and after the first year, students preferred to remain harmoniously separate. Both groups explained their low rate of interaction in relation to perceptions about 'cultural bonding' and 'being on the same wavelength'. When students mixed through a shared activity, their perceptions of one another became more positive, although given the choice, they would still prefer to complete work in a group of the same cultural background. Wright and Lander (2003) in their study of group work interactions between Australian and south-east Asian overseas-born students found that culturally based assumptions led to different styles of interaction in groups and that cultural diversity affected the extent of interaction.

Other longitudinal research (Watson, Johnson & Zgourides, 2002; Watson, Johnson, Kumar & Critelli, 1998) was conducted with business students and showed that with early support in interpersonal and task leadership activities, diverse groups could, in a short time perform *better* in group projects and use their *diversity to their advantage*. Elsewhere in this book, Leask also describes similar results from early interventions, clearly offering scope for future research.

The Student Voice

Students Talking: Intercultural Conversations

The case studies presented here provide examples of intercultural activities where participants confronted cultural difference as the focus of a task and some transformations result.

One such project began as an investigation into international students' experiences of transition between academic cultures. Participants were nine international students, chosen to reflect a range of nationalities and disciplines. The students shared their recent experiences of managing such a transition, at a conference plenary session,[1] with several hundred education developers from many countries. The questions mainly dealt with learning, teaching and assessment, but listening to students explaining the different expectations in their previous courses, and their experiences of referencing and researching online, had a powerful impact on both students and educators.

> 'The presentation conference was an amazing experience and I not only enjoyed it at that moment, but I rejoice its memories even today. Speaking in front of such a big population was not a routine job for me, so it also opened me up to an extent.'

The students became connected to a community of staff and to each other, enhancing mutual understanding. Several also stressed the importance of being able to talk to class mates for advice and ideas about their work and how online communication helped them to resolve study problems together. At the same time students learned about each other; as one European student observed, 'some students find it difficult to openly speak about their difficulties in lectures and seminars with lots of other students'.

Students explained the importance of meeting the challenge of being open to new people, especially at the beginning. Cultural differences can also create temptations for students who have not been exposed to 'clubs, pubs, drinks, etc.': 'It would be easy to lose your motivation. I had to pull myself back'.

Equally, one Malaysian student gave advice on intercultural survival:

'My mother told me there was no need to worry about diminishing my own culture by opening myself up to another. I can learn about other ways of life without losing my beliefs. Although this will make me different, I shall always be the same with my family.'

A Chinese student described her experience of living with students from six other countries and how this had made her short stay a 'lifetime experience' as she had learnt much about different ways of living from her friendly housemates and hoped to travel to their cities and meet them in the future. All demonstrated the value of intercultural experiences for them, including improved language skills, despite negligible interaction with UK students and other people in the city.

The project generated visual and written resources which were quickly transferred to other contexts; giving advice to new students and for training programmes where home students were employed by the university, with the Students' Union, with volunteering projects, mentoring schemes and in staff development, particularly with new staff. Listening to the students leads audiences to recognise the diversity among international students and the dangers of generalisations and inaccurate stereotypes on our perceptions. Too often staff and students rely on assumptions which owe more to out-of-date misconceptions and fictional representations about life in other countries:

'I had so many wrong assumptions about what I used to call "foreigners" – I cringe when I think what weird ideas I used to have, you know and how much I have learned from my relationship with Yip.'

(Language student)

Using collections of student voices helps international students to develop confidence about managing life in the United Kingdom. Students' voices were captured by other students on film, podcasts, interactive forums and blogs and provide a dynamic basis for intercultural learning wherever they are used. Students take notice of each other and enjoy helping others, gaining new skills themselves. These activities led to further intercultural meetings.

The UKCISA training video (Barty & Lago, 2008), and the Hearing the Student Voice project (Campbell et al., 2007), are similar examples. When students can speak directly to educators, to fellow students, especially across cultures, the effect is tangible and direct. Their accounts led teachers to consider changing their practices.

Home students admit limited experience of any relationships with students from outside the United Kingdom but this can come about through students meeting accidentally, through a shared interest or activity such as a sport:

'I just went along to the club because I did a bit of judo at school and liked it. People were friendly and it was a laugh. They asked me if I wanted to dance in the dragon. I was flattered to tell you the truth. We go all over at Chinese New Year. I enjoy it more than Christmas now, its good fun and I've got so fit. Yes, I think I have a great respect for Chinese culture now, through this. It's awesome. They were writing and doing all this stuff thousands of years ago.'
(UK student in Chinese martial arts group)

Respect and admiration can also encourage self-reflection: 'This guy camped all over Scotland, on his own, with a back pack, on buses and trains – God knows I couldn't imagine doing that' (Student Union Executive member).

Watching the films provoked recollections of international students with whom the UK students had some personal contact and a new empathy and recognition developed: 'Reminded me what it was like when I was in Spain for a year'; 'Brought home all those little things you take for granted or never notice'.

These accounts reveal scope for personal development among students who feel they have benefited from widening their horizons, gain understanding and insight into the lives of others; among international students too, there are many archaic notions about English life and culture.

On-Course Cross-Cultural Communication

Opportunities for intercultural communication can be created as part of assessment. In one example, an undergraduate Events Management module, staff and students from different parts of India, the United Kingdom and across faculties, worked together to support an international award ceremony taking place in the city. They designed a week-long cultural awareness programme for key workers in hospitality, retail, transport and security services. They made a film, devised and presented activities, and organised events. Students shared personal experiences of living, visiting and working in other countries, with each other and with the audiences. Each gained greater insight and deeper understanding of each other's cultural traditions, history, beliefs and lifestyle:

'Working on this project has been so great because it meant I learnt such a lot about India and what's happening there. I got to know the guys really well over the week and, well, I would not have thought I would ever go there, but now I really want to.'
(Events management student working on Bollywood[2] project)

What also emerged was connection through similarity; students studying the same subject at different levels had similar interests and concerns. All became more aware of the rate of change affecting countries in South Asia and of the limitations of our cross-cultural understanding.

On Arrival

The meeting of international students together at the beginning of the year can be a unique opportunity to examine stereotypes and reduce insularity. Orientation sessions provide a warm welcome, assist transition and acknowledge respect and celebrate differences. There is much talk about global villages and borderless education, but few opportunities to experience it in action. It may not be unusual to be in a room with people from all over the world, but to meet face to face, be able to ask them questions, and get to know them a little is still quite rare. At International Orientation, students are invited to devise an activity for others to enjoy. We offer a few suggestions and resources and manage the event. Exchange Time is a rich festival of food snacks, dancing, writing, presentations and singing. Hundreds of students take part and share cultures and traditions, daring one another to eat hot chilli paste with sticky rice, tasting baked beans, croissants, Kheer and Tsatsiki for the first time. Gradually they share recipes and join in the singing and dancing.

Such events contribute to the support of international students, but is it leading to real integration and internationalisation? Fun it may be but does it merely focus on superficial manifestations of culture, and like other forms of multiculturalism, fail to address the continuing power differences in the cultural authority (Donald & Rattansi, 1992, pp. 4–5)? This could also be said for mentoring or volunteering schemes.

Many of the activities described here happen regularly and unremarkably in many UK universities, but what is striking about any occasion where people from different parts of the world meet and start to talk is the release of infectious energy. It seems to resemble the intentions of a 1960s performance art known as a Happening. Happenings involved improvisation and their spectators. They appeared primitive and amateurish but radical at the time as they were inclusive of the 'audiences' and their perspectives. However, Happenings were criticised as insular and compartmental (Kirkby, 1995), whereas the events described here were expansive and hard to contain. When they occurred in open spaces passers by watched curiously and some joined in. The positive benefits for students can be listed:

- Students are likely to at least recognise each other in the coming weeks, and may decide to meet in the future.
- Students have to use skills they will need in their studies and communicate in an intercultural context – usually testing out their English among peers.
- Students are able to see that their cultural differences are both of interest and value.
- Students are encouraged to reflect on their culture and identity, and on how differences might matter and how similar we are.
- Learning is cemented by fun and excitement.

What is unique about such opportunities is that they allow us to hear about life elsewhere from a real person, not a news reporter on screen, mediated by several news agencies. Unlike a posting on the internet it is possible to question and clarify, face to face; to establish the context and validity of what is being presented, especially if someone is there to facilitate and encourage dialogue. To participate may lead to the discovery that we share more than dances or ways with food. The trick is to get people to make the first move themselves. It may not be an example of an institution becoming international or multicultural but it is a genuine and simple way to start.

Conclusion

There is and has been much talk about a vision of an international university and what it might achieve in promoting interculturalism, along with graduate employability, genuine critical enquiry and the enhancement of the international student experience. There is no doubt that some university members, not least many home students, may find this challenging and uncomfortable.

What students' voices tell us is that although international students want more contact with host students, most people, including those students, will not choose to go outside of their cultural groups and these divisions reinforce negative perceptions of one another. When students are mixed together, they claim to learn new ways of interacting, perform better and see value in learning from each other. There is no adequate evidence that anyone loses out from such experiences and given the reluctance of many UK students to take up options for mobility, this is one way to ensure an international dimension.

It is proper that universities provide safe opportunities for genuine engagement with other academic cultures, styles and forms of knowledge, but this is increasingly rare both in universities and elsewhere in society. Genuine intercultural competence and learning is complex but all relationships, global or not, are and always have been challenging. Universities can adopt strategies to enable a real intercultural dialogue simply by listening to their students and finding creative ways for their presence to affect all activities both in formal and informal learning contexts.

Notes

1 ICED conference Sheffield Hallam University, June 2006.
2 The International Indian Film Academy (IIFA) Awards were held in Sheffield in June 2007.

References

Barty, A., & Lago, C. (2008). *Bridging the gap: A training DVD for working with international students*. London: UKCISA (UK Council for International Student Affairs).
Brown, S., & Jones, E. (2007). Introduction: Values, valuing and value in an internationalised higher education context. In Jones & Brown (2007), pp. 1–6.
Campbell, F. et al. (2007). Hearing the student voice. Available from: http://www2.napier.ac.uk/studentvoices/ [Accessed April 2009].
Carroll, J., & Ryan, J. (Eds.). (2005). *Teaching international students: Improving learning for all*. London: Routledge.
De Vita, G. (2006). Fostering intercultural learning through multicultural group work. In Carroll & Ryan (2005), pp. 75–83.

De Vita, G., & Case, P. (2003). Rethinking the internationalisation agenda in UK higher education. *Journal of Further and Higher Education, 27*(4), 383–398.

Dobson, I., Sharma, R., & Calderon, A. (1998). The comparative performance of overseas and Australian undergraduates. In *Outcomes of international education: Research findings.* Canberra: IDP Education Australia.

Donald, J., & Rattansi, A. (1992). *Race, culture and difference.* London: Sage.

Fielden, J. (2007). *Global horizons for UK students.* London: CIHE.

Hacket, J., & Nowak, R. (1999). Onshore and offshore delivery of higher education programs: A comparison of academic outcomes. In *International education: The professional edge*: a set of research papers presented at the 13th Australian International Education Conference, Fremantle 1999 edited by Dorothy Davis and Alan Olsen, pp. 3–13, 139. Deakin ACT: IDP Education Australia. Available from: http://www.idp.com/research/database_of_research/quick_search.aspx [Accessed 23 September 2009].

Harrison, N., & Peacock, N. (2007). Understanding the UK response to Internationalisation. *World Views, 23.* London: UKCISA.

International Graduate Insight Group (IG-I). (2005–2007). International student barometer (ISB) survey. Available from: http://www.i-graduate.org/services/student_insight–student_barometer.html [Accessed April 2009].

Jones, E., & Brown, S. (Eds.). (2007). *Internationalising higher education.* London: Routledge.

Kirkby, M. (1995). Introduction to M. R. Sandford (Ed.), *Happenings and other acts* (pp. 2–15). London: Routledge.

Leask, B. (2001). Bridging the gap: Internationalizing university curricula. *Journal of Studies in International Education, 5*(2), 100–115.

Modood, T. (2005). *Multicultural politics: Racism, ethnicity, and Muslims in Britain.* Minneapolis: University of Minnesota Press.

Phillips, T. (2005). After 7/7: Sleepwalking into segregation. Speech at Manchester town hall, 22 September. Available from: http://83.137.212.42/sitearchive/cre/Default.aspx.LocID-0hgnew07r.RefLocID-0hg00900c001001.Lang-EN.htm [Accessed April 2009].

Ryan, J., & Carroll, J. (2005). International students in Western universities. In Carroll & Ryan (2005), pp. 3–10.

Smart, D., Volet, S. E., & Ang, G. (2000). *Fostering social cohesion in a university: Bridging the cultural divide.* Canberra: Australia International Education.

Teekens, H. (2007). *Internationalisation at home: Ideas and ideals.* EAIE occasional paper 20.

Thom, V. (2008). Capturing student voices: Relationships, reliability and technology. Presentation at UKCISA conference, Lancaster University, UK, 9 July.

UKCOSA (2004). *Broadening our horizons: International students in UK universities and colleges.* London: UKCOSA.

UNITE, & UKCOSA (2006). International student experience report 2006. Available from: http://www.unitegroup.co.uk/data/Research/default.aspx [Accessed September 2008].

Volet, S. E. (2003). Challenges of internationalisation: Enhancing intercultural competence and skills for critical reflection on the situated and non-neutral nature of knowledge. In P. Zeegers & K. Deller-Evans (Eds.), *Language and academic skills in higher education* (Vol. 6, pp. 1–10). Available from: www.flinders.edu.au/SLC/Papers.pdf [Accessed September 2008].

Volet, S. E., & Ang, G. (1998). Culturally mixed groups on international campuses: An opportunity for inter-cultural learning. *Higher Education Research & Development, 17*(1), 5–23.

Watson, W. E., Johnson, L. Kumar, K., & Critelli, J. (1998). Process gain and process loss: Comparing interpersonal processes and performance of culturally diverse and non-diverse teams across time. *International Journal of Intercultural Relations, 22*(4), 409–430.

Watson, W. E., Johnson, L., & Zgourides, G. D. (2002). The influence of ethnic diversity on leadership, group process and performance: An examination of learning teams. *International Journal of Intercultural Relations, 26,* 1–16.

Wesch, M. (2007). A vision of students today. Kansas State University. Available from: http://www.youtube.com/watch?v=dGCJ46vyR9o [Accessed April 2009].

Wright, S., & Lander, D. (2003). Collaborative group interactions of students from two ethnic backgrounds. *Higher Education Research & Development, 22*(3), 237–252.

IV
Transnational Education and Support for International Students

13

The Internationalised Curriculum

(Dis)locating Students

VALERIE CLIFFORD

Introduction

One of the main current strategic priorities of many Western universities is 'internationalisation'. Whereas the meaning of this initiative is clear in many areas the concept of 'internationalising the curriculum' causes consternation. For some the presence of international students in the class constitutes internationalisation of the curriculum, for others adding overseas case studies or the like suffices, and others focus on the induction of international students into 'How the west is done' (De Vita, 2007; Doherty & Singh, 2005). However, few appear to address the notions of transformative pedagogy as presented in the theoretical literature (Giroux, 1992; Harman, 2005).

Resistance to internationalisation of the curriculum has been seen to come from some disciplines, from competing priorities, lack of resourcing, lack of resource materials for teaching, lack of staff competence and a potential loss of quality (Bond, 2003). For universities issues of quality assurance are frequently paramount, and one way to ensure the quality of degrees wherever they are delivered is to standardise. This involves the development of packaged courses delivered and assessed in the same way at all locations. This approach takes no account of the different backgrounds and previous educational experiences of students or the appropriateness of delivery methods for those students. It also does not focus curricula on local needs or make it relevant to students in different places. For local teachers it has the effect of de-professionalising and de-skilling them (Naidoo, 2007).

The large Australian university in this study has many onshore and offshore points of delivery, and has developed a packaged delivery model which was beginning to be questioned by staff (Schapper & Mayson, 2004). At the same time international student enrolment in Australia appeared to have plateaued and even to be declining due to increased competition from the West and the East, prompting the university to reconsider its approach to internationalisation. Interviews with staff and students explored the meaning of an internationalised curriculum to consider how the university could engage staff to move forward in this area.

This chapter introduces the voices of students studying at the same university but in three different countries. The students' voices focus on the interpersonal and intercultural and show contradictory, and regionally different, responses to academic issues. The chapter begins with an introduction to the study. It is followed by the questions raised by the voices of the students and then these questions are discussed in relation to the theoretical and practical literature.

The Study

The site of the study is a large university in Australia with eight campuses, including one in Malaysia and one in South Africa, and a myriad of other overseas 'delivery' arrangements in Hong Kong, Italy and other countries. Interviews were held with staff and students at all eight campuses to discover what an internationalised curriculum meant at the university and how staff could be engaged with internationalising the curriculum. Two Master's students were employed as research assistants at the Australian campuses. They used snowballing techniques to obtain a cross-faculty sample of students interviewed either in a focus group or individually. At the offshore campuses staff known to be interested in issues of internationalisation of the curriculum were approached to carry out interviews with staff and students, and were asked to select a variety of participants. The semi-structured interviews were audio-taped and the resulting transcripts categorised using the questions as a base and adding categories as required. The emerging analysis was negotiated between the author, student-researchers and staff who conducted the interviewers to ensure, not only that different voices were heard, but they were also understood in terms of context. Table 13.1 shows the demographic details of the students interviewed. There was a mixture of local and international students and a range of disciplines. Eight students were under 25 and seven between 25 and 34: six were female and nine male.

Students' voices are presented under the themes that emerged from the data.

Student Voices

Future Identities

The students all had similar and clear visions of their future selves. They wanted to be educated for futures living and working in multicultural environments. They wanted to be 'thinkers', to be open-minded, adaptable and continuously developing. They wanted to have the requisite knowledge and skills: generic communication skills; leadership skills; knowledge of and sensitivity to other cultures; creativity and perseverance. They expressed a sense of responsibility in how they interacted with others and in what they chose to do with their lives. One international student expressed the idea of living 'ethically' [Singapore, TA] and others of taking something back to their home societies 'acquire something that may be of benefit to someone else' [Serbia, TA].[1]

Table 13.1 Demographic Details of Students Interviewed

Campus	Country of Origin	First Language	Other Languages
Malaysia	Malaysia	Chinese	English, Malaysian
Malaysia	Malaysia	English	Malaysian
South Africa	Botswana	Tswana	English
South Africa	Botswana	Tswana	English
South Africa	Zimbabwe	Shona	English
South Africa	South Africa	Tsonga	English, Zulu, Sotho, Tswana
Australia	Poland	Polish	English
Australia	Australia	English	–
Australia	South Africa	English	–
Australia	Singapore	Malay-Tamil	English
Australia	Malaysia	Bahasa Malay	English
Australia	Serbia	Serbian	English
Australia	Australia	English	–
Australia	Australia	English	–
Australia	Brunei	Malay	English

An Internationalised (Intercultural) Curriculum

Responses to questions about an internationalised curriculum centred around ideas of interculturality. Students saw themselves as already living and studying in multicultural environments. Malaysia has three predominant ethnic groups living side-by-side (Ethnic Malays, Chinese and Indian) and South Africa has a variety of local ethnic groups plus those of colonial Dutch and English heritage. Even local Australian students often live in a different cultural environment in their homes to that of society at large. Australian society results from waves of immigration from all around the world imposed on, and largely submerging, the local indigenous society, and contributing to an emerging non-aboriginal Australian identity. At each campus international students made up over 20 per cent of the student body. One student described the pervasiveness of multiculturalism:

'In the real world people have to be aware, whatever you're doing you need to know that difference is going to impact on whatever you do, your relationships. I mean that's not just somebody who comes from overseas and has a different accent. I mean it's something that permeates every aspect of being an educated person.'

[Australia, TA]

Despite their strong desire to be sensitive multicultural persons there were also references at all campuses to the discomforts it brought. One student emphasised that intercultural communication can involve 'discomfort or misunderstandings or miscommunications'. She did not see this as something to be 'fixed' but something to be aware of, that we need to realise that we won't necessarily 'understand each other and we shouldn't pretend that we do, but we should find ways to acknowledge that' and that 'the discomfort should be valued as part of the learning process' [Australia, TA].

International students were aware they were out of their comfort zone in their roles and made friends with other international students but rarely fraternised with local students, 'we all feel like we're not really at home here, the one thing we have in common is that we are all foreigners in a strange land' [Serbia, TA]. One international student saw local Australian students as 'immature, seeing only the Australian culture and not trying to put themselves in the shoes of others' [Malaysian, TA]. This was acknowledged by some Australian students in stories they told of awkward moments with students whose first language was not English, one student saying that

'theoretically . . . I am really interested in people from China . . . but that doesn't mean I actually want to sit down and have a conversation with a person I find it hard to have a conversation with and don't have anything in common.'

[Australian, TA]

Similarly a South African student in Australia expressed his discomfort among fellow Asian students all talking their own language.

On the Malaysian campus the students described Asian people as being 'humble, they don't tell people things, they don't impose, while other cultures like to share their experiences. Asian people perceive this as arrogant/showing off, but then non-Asian people might think the Asian people are hiding things' [Malaysian, TM]. These students also talked about their peers who had been to a local American school and came to university with very different attitudes. Malaysian campus students also spoke of wanting to be confident enough to hold their own opinions and speak out 'politely'.

A Polish student in Australia talked about cultural shock and how difficult it is to describe the subtle things that make you feel uncomfortable. One international student in Australia described his shock at first of the physical contact between people (such as slapping each other on the back in greeting).

The disparities among students at the South African campus went beyond that of local–international student. While international students and local students from urban areas were often seen as well resourced in terms of 'educational capital' they brought to university (e.g. familiarity with computers) and greater financial resources, local students from rural areas often had little experience of educational resources including computers and few financial resources. One commented:

'it will be intimidating a little bit . . . I can't afford buying books and everything . . . at times I would like to be isolated from them, because they are like high class people and stuff and I'm not.'

[South Africa, TSA]

The South African campus students were also aware of the difficult histories and relationships between their peoples and spoke of misconceptions students from different countries brought to the campus and the playing out of rivalries. They saw how working together in small multiracial groups on tasks helped break down those barriers, to build understanding and confidence to cope in such groups.

However, despite difficulties of understanding and being comfortable with people from other cultures, students at all campuses saw the multicultural nature of the student body as a win-win situation for everybody. They felt they had had valuable experiences, had learnt a lot about other peoples and about themselves and had begun to value different points of view. 'It's a good place to study 'cos we're always trying to learn more about the world and it makes us not so we just see things from the end of our nose' [Australia, TA].

An Internationalised (Personalised) Curriculum

The other most salient factor the students dwelt on in discussing an internationalised curriculum was their relationship with staff. The students at all campuses saw the staff as crucial to the quality of their education. Without staff who, themselves, had global perspectives the students realised they could not receive an international education. They discussed the attributes staff needed in their role as well as the necessary knowledge and sensitivity to the backgrounds of the students. The students emphasised the need for staff to be open-minded, flexible, inclusive, enthusiastic and inspirational, and to have a good command of English. Some students saw a dominant cultural background in the people who wrote and delivered courses in their areas, 'good old Anglo-Australians' [Australia, TA], and a resistance to change. They saw one challenge of internationalisation as creating the 'openness and willingness' among staff to learn about other cultures and about teaching. A Zimbabwean student in South Africa suggested using inter-campus exchanges to 'give lecturers more exposure on different cultures'. The students also recognised that some staff were from overseas and others have immigrant ethnic backgrounds, and so already have experience of different cultures and different value systems. They saw the need to encourage the diverse teaching staff and students to share their perspectives.

Above all the students wanted lecturers to get to know them and be caring, approachable and understanding of students. They wanted staff to be sensitive and flexible, to respond appropriately to different needs and backgrounds, and be aware that students from some cultures have difficulty understanding the norms of the class and interacting within the class. They wanted assistance in adapting to the new classroom environment, especially contributing in class and asking questions. 'I'm the only black student in class, so sometimes just interrupting the lecturer as he delivers the material, I find difficult for me because I didn't learn that as part of my culture' [Botswana, TSA].

The students in Malaysia and South Africa especially talked about staff taking time to talk to students, to build relationships and be available outside class to discuss work. International students emphasised how lonely they felt and how 'just a five minute conversation would mean a lot to us sometimes' [Malaysia, TM]. They emphasised that students are motivated through 'two types of motivation. One is . . . because you are scared. And the other one of course is genuine interest . . . we realised that she actually cared for us and then we feel better . . . and we actually studied more to make sure we pass the exam.'

[Malaysia, TM]

South African campus-based students spoke of the usefulness of the shared student–staff eating facilities for meeting and getting to know staff. Students sometimes felt stereotyped as 'lazy' when they were in fact having problems understanding course content, 'the fact that we are failing to do the assignment is not because we are lazy, it is because we are struggling to understand' [Botswana, TSA].

Some students came from cultures that held teachers and elders in high esteem and behaviour towards them was always reverential. They found the way of relating to staff at the Australian university, and behaviours in the university classrooms, difficult to accept. Calling out answers to questions, the informality of addressing staff by first name and questioning staff were anathema to them.

Some students also experienced difficulty with expectations of participating in classroom activities and group work. The need to be tutored in skills for classroom participation was discussed. A number of students recognised the value of working in groups to aid intercultural understanding and build their confidence to work co-operatively, but acknowledged the lack of interaction between local and international students in and out of class.

'I think that's what the team aspect should really encourage . . . you have these people coming from different countries. They come with their own misconceptions of the countries. That's why you find there is sometimes rivalry between [ ] students and [ ] students . . . get them to work together and leave this place without those barriers anymore . . . I have seen it working.'

[Botswana, TSA]

'I think the students need to . . . develop more skills in group work . . . in a multicultural group you get to understand each other and get that confidence to know how to cope with that group. And that would develop them and equip them for their future and when they go to work.'

[Zimbabwe, TSA]

There was a plea that staff randomly assign students to racially mixed groups as it was very difficult for students to ask a group (of another race) if they could team up with them. They recognised that when

'you team up with friends, it is mostly like you are of the same kind and you have the same kind of experience, so it doesn't help much. So with us [mixed groups] it's like, okay, different things and different approaches to working together'.

[South Africa, TSA]

Internationalisation of the (Cognitive) Curriculum

Students' discussion of the intellectual component of their curricula was more limited than of the intercultural component. Generally the students were accepting of curriculum content and seemed to find it difficult to conceptualise changes beyond adding a case study or information about other cultures. The dissenting voices came from the South African campus. This is illustrated below.

The concept of the 'universality of knowledge' was frequently offered by students. Many started from the premise that the knowledge they were gaining was 'international', 'chemistry is chemistry, physics is physics' [Serbia, TA] and similarly for IT, engineering, biomedicine and music. However, as they continued to talk, students produced contradictory statements illustrating also the particularity of knowledge, without seeing their own contradiction. A music student said 'they've all got music . . . it's sort of good to bring everyone under the one understanding of this one language', but then went on to say 'but also last year I did a subject called [ ] musicology, in which we learnt about Indonesian, Indian and Japanese music . . . it is a whole different way of using it [this one language]' [Australia, TA].

Similarly students described the context in which theoretical principles were applied affecting the operation of and reaction to those principles, and saw that as rules, regulations, laws, practices and ethics are different in all countries the outcomes are, therefore, also different. 'The theory just does not apply in practice' [Malaysia, TA].

Imagining curriculum for an international education was perplexing for students, a number of the Australian-based students (both local and international) feeling that the curriculum did not need to be changed, that it was already international:

'[T]he [university] is already an internationalised university. . . a lot of people here are from all over the world, that the curriculum . . . seems to me to be fairly diverse and decentred . . . we have a globalised understanding of our place in the world.'

[Serbia, TA]

Another said, 'I'm not quite sure if the curriculum should be changed that much, I think it already accommodates everybody' [Australian, TA]. One student felt that what was done at present was quite adequate:

'In Education [there is] a lot of emphasis in teaching on understanding students needs and responding to students . . . most activities were designed to be inclusive for everyone to get an opportunity to speak and put across their opinion.'

[Australia, TA]

Students saw it was impossible to learn about all cultures in the world and one commented it would be impossible to meet everyone's needs, that the curriculum could end up diluted to the point of little value [Singapore, TA].

Despite claiming their curriculum was international, students did comment on its Australian focus, except for a few courses that used American textbooks and taught American theory. A number felt that the addition of texts from Asia, Africa and other places would be helpful. Others said that even though examples were used from other cultures, these were too small to offer cultural understanding as such and they were not learning in a multicultural way.

However, despite apparent satisfaction with the curriculum of Australian-based students, students in Malaysia and South Africa were less content. They expressed more concern over curriculum relevance for their context. They found it difficult to relate to Australian examples used, a student from landlocked Botswana particularly describing her frustration at studying coastal geography when she had never seen the sea or coastal vegetation. Students from the South African campus argued strongly that using examples from and dealing with issues for developing countries was critical to future work environments of the African students and that anything less would constitute colonial education. This theme was picked up strongly by staff at the offshore campuses.

An Internationalised (Transformative) Curriculum

This data presented from students at one university but differently positioned in terms of cultural, educational and political backgrounds raises a number of questions about the education being offered by Western universities to their diverse student bodies, the impact that education has on the development of students' identities and the effect of resistance being offered, in this case, by staff and students at the campus in South Africa.

First, we need to set students' perceptions within the literature on internationalising the curriculum. The aim of internationalisation of the curriculum is to prepare students to live and work in a multicultural world and as global citizens to develop attitudes and values of responsibility towards issues such as sustainability and justice (Clifford & Joseph, 2005; Morey, 2000; Nilsson, 2003). While definitions abound, what this means for curricula has been differentially explored by universities (Nilsson, 2003). Internationalisation of the curriculum developments have been seen as moving through different phases and can be illustrated through Banks' (2005) four categories: the contributions approach (where cultural events are celebrated), the additive approach (where content is added to the curriculum without changing its structure), the transformative approach (where a constructivist approach informs the structure to view the discipline knowledge from diverse perspectives), and the action approach (where students take action on important problems and help to solve them).

The additive or integrative/infusion approach is that most familiar to staff in higher education and offers a 'low risk' approach as it does not disturb the fundamental ontology or epistemology of the discipline. However, this is also its disadvantage in that the curriculum retains its western philosophy and 'adding bits' can interfere with the cohesion of the course. De Vita and Case (2003) also argue that this approach offers a monocultural model of internationalisation and that the focus on knowledge elements can lead to neglect of intercultural learning.

Universities appear to find moving from the additive to the transformative approach difficult. Banks (2005, pp. 256–257) writes that in the transformative approach 'the basic goals, structure and nature of the curriculum are changed to enable students to view concepts, events, issues, problems and themes from the perspectives of diverse cultural, ethnic and racial groups'. Giroux (1992) urges teachers to become 'border crossers' and to provide a safe space and a border pedagogy (that challenges existing ways of thinking), through which students can explore the situated nature of their own identity and that of others. Gough (1998, 1999) believes that knowledge is actively produced within specific locations and views universities as places where learning can be a process where different knowledges are critiqued and many kinds of knowledge are valued. Similarly Mohanty (2003, p. 239) argues that we should move from 'academic-as-tourist' where we see everything through the Eurocentric gaze to an Academic Solidarity Model where, through comparative studies, we explore how power works to create knowledge and values.

In this study students state that their grasp of internationalisation of the curriculum is dependent on that of their teachers, and the struggle of staff with transformative ideas is reflected in the students seeing internationalisation of the curriculum as about intercultural learning and additive curricula. It is probably unfair to expect students to have a deeper understanding of internationalisation of the curriculum than their teachers. However, many students have experienced living and studying in other cultures and have the possibility of reflecting on their own culture. One question arising is why international students in Australia appear to accept their 'western' education as 'international', why students in Malaysia do not publicly question knowledge and behaviours which are anathema to their religion and culture, but why students in South Africa do question what they are exposed to.

The recent history of South Africa is fairly unique in the world with the defeat of apartheid leading to desegregation of university campuses. Current students are fully aware of South African politics and know their experience of a multiracial campus is new in South Africa. They are also part of the future of a developing country, with differential access to resources, the university staff being very clear they are educating future leaders of Africa. In such an overtly political environment it is perhaps unsurprising that students express the need for an education relevant to a developing country tackling issues of poverty and unemployment.

Not only is the curriculum of concern to students in South Africa, but also the mode of delivery. Some students described difficulty with independent study and reading. They came from an oral culture where learning involved an idea being discussed in a group until it was understood before the group considered the next idea. Given a book to read and study alone, some did not know what to do. One lecturer described going through the course textbook idea by idea and spending hours out of class debating with students as he realised they would not move on until an idea was grasped fully through discussion. The small classes and dedication of this lecturer allowed the curriculum to be covered but in most classes not enough would be covered to cope with centrally administered examinations. The South African students have the advantage of proactive lecturers unwilling to accept the status quo of the transnational education offered, who are producing their own courses and obtaining accreditation for them through the Australian host university.

At the Malaysian campus students were predominantly Malaysian Chinese and well aware of their need to pay for a foreign higher education due to the Malaysian government university quota system. In Malaysia priority is given to ethnic Malays, even unfilled quota places being denied to qualified students from other ethnic groups. However, even within this political context, while staff were questioning the transnational curricula, students were more reluctant to do so. The blend of a predominantly Muslim-based culture mixed with a Confucian heritage (Phuong-Mai, Cees & Pilot, 2006) brings students with behaviours based on concepts of respect and beliefs in maintaining harmony, and with a colonial history, into a western style classroom, where familiarity with and questioning of the teacher is the norm. While transnational education privileges western pedagogy, research is beginning to document the discomfort of students from non-western educational systems with these teaching methods and the possible detrimental effects on their learning (Dunn & Wallace, 2004; Krause, 2006; Novera, 2004; Pyvis & Chapman, 2004). These students have already entered a borderland but it does not appear to be one in which they feel safe or are yet guided by Giroux's (1992) 'transformative intellectuals'.

The positioning of international students in Australia also is interesting. These students come from all over the world but are predominantly ethnic Chinese. However, students in this study included one from Serbia, one from South Africa and a recent immigrant from Poland. These students have other points of reference yet appear to see their Australian education as international. This raises the question whether the Australian campus offers a different perspective from their home country enabling them to reflect on this in their studies or privately, or whether the Australian campus environment is not conducive to critique. Arguments that students travel to Western countries to receive a Western education are prevalent in Australia and the United Kingdom and international students may be predisposed to accept what they find, but they also need something useful to take back to their own countries, whether skills and knowledge or values and attitudes.

The orientation of local Australian students offers little surprise as most 'have yet to learn to think of themselves as Others' (Singh, 2005, p. 16) and to move beyond local, monolingual contexts.

Students' general lack of knowledge about knowledge creation is interesting in that higher education is supposed to develop skills of inquiry and analysis. However, such questioning appears to be heavily contextualised within disciplines and does not stretch to critiquing the discipline per se. While 'soft' subjects (Becher & Trowler, 2001) will take on epistemological challenges, 'hard' subjects do not prioritise such questions, seeing them as pedagogically unimportant (Martinez, Aleman & Salkever, 2004; Mestenhauser & Ellingboe, 1998). Caruana and Spurling (2007) question the extent to which skills of analysis and critical thinking are taught in modern universities. These skills are seen as an essential part of curriculum internationalisation (Giroux, 1992; Rizvi, 2002) but the issue is perhaps a more generic question about higher education and disciplinary approaches, rather than just about internationalisation of the curriculum.

Conclusion

This chapter has raised many questions about the status of the internationalisation of curriculum in western universities. It has looked at these from the point of view of students undertaking transnational education at different locations. It reveals that Eurocentrism is alive and well in terms of content and pedagogy, despite the discomfort it can cause in delivery. Students do not appear to have the conceptual knowledge or skills to question their education despite a clear idea of what they wish to achieve. The only students who do question their education are those in the midst of political change in South Africa. Perhaps a first step in moving towards transformative international education is to 'politicise' students by enhancing critical thinking skills and introducing them to differing theories of knowledge.

Note

1 Quotes from interview transcripts are coded with the country of origin of the student and the campus, e.g. [Russia, TSA]. The campuses are shown as: TA = Australia, TM = Malaysia, TSA = South Africa.

References

Banks, J. A. (2005). Approaches to multicultural curriculum reform. In J. A. Banks & C. A. McGee Banks (Eds.), *Multicultural education. Issues and perspectives* (5th ed., pp. 242–264). New York: John Wiley.

Becher, T., & Trowler, P. R. (2001). *Academic tribes and territories* (2nd ed.). Buckingham, UK: Society for Research into Higher Education and Open University Press.

Bond, S. L. (2003). *Untapped resources: Internationalization of the curriculum and classroom experience: a selected literature review.* Ottawa: Canadian Bureau for International Education.

Caruana, V., & Spurling, N. (2007). The internationalisation of UK Higher education: A review of selected material. Available from: http://www.heacademy.ac.uk/assets/York/documents/ourwork/tla/lit_review_internationalisation_of_uk_he.pdf [Accessed April 2009].

Clifford, V., & Joseph, C. (2005). Report of internationalisation of the curriculum project. Monash University.

De Vita, G. (2007). Taking stock: An appraisal of the literature on internationalising higher education learning. In E. Jones & S. Brown (Eds.), *Internationalising higher education* (pp. 154–174). London: Routledge.

De Vita, G., & Case, P. (2003). Rethinking the internationalisation agenda in UK higher education. *Journal of Further and Higher Education, 27*(4), 383–398.

Doherty, C., & Singh, P. (2005). How the west is done: Simulating western pedagogy in a curriculum for Asian international students. In Ninnes & Hellstén (2005), pp. 53–74.

Dunn, L., & Wallace, M. (2004). Australian academics teaching in Singapore: Striving for cultural empathy. *Innovations in Education and Teaching International*, *41*(3), 291–304.

Giroux, H. (1992). *Border crossings: Cultural workers and the politics of education.* New York: Routledge.

Gough, N. (1998). Transnational imaginaries in curriculum inquiry: Performances and representations. Paper presented at the Australian Association for Research in Education, Adelaide.

Gough, N. (1999). Globalization and school curriculum change: Locating a transnational imaginary. *Journal of Education Policy*, *14*(1), 73–84.

Harman, G. (2005). Internationalisation of Australian higher education: Critical review of literature. In Ninnes & Hellstén (2005), p. 119.

Krause, K. L. D. (2006). *Student voices in borderless higher education: The Australian experience.* London: The Observatory on Borderless Higher Education. Available from: http://www.obhe.ac.uk/ cgi-bin/swish.pl?si=0&si=1&query=krause [Accessed September 2008].

Martinez Aleman, A. M., & Salkever, K. (2004). Multiculturalism and the American liberal arts college: Faculty perceptions of the role of pedagogy. *Studies in Higher Education*, *29*(1), 39–58.

Mestenhauser, J., & Ellingboe, B. (1998). *Reforming higher education curriculum: Internationalizing the campus.* Phoenix, AZ: American Council on Education.

Mohanty, C. (2003). *Feminism without borders: Decolonising theory, practicing solidarity.* London: Duke University Press.

Morey, A. I. (2000). Changing higher education curricula for a global and multicultural world. *Higher Education in Europe*, *XXV*(1), 25–39.

Naidoo, R. (2007). *Higher education as a global commodity: The perils and promises for developing countries.* The Observatory on Borderless Higher Education. Available from: http://www. obhe.ac.uk/documents/view_details?id=13 [Accessed April 2009].

Nilsson, B. (2003). Internationalisation at Home from a Swedish perspective: The case of Malmo. *Journal of Studies in International Education*, *7*(1), 27–40.

Ninnes, P., & Hellstén, M. (Eds.). (2005). *Internationalizing higher education: Critical explorations of pedagogy and policy.* Dordrecht, The Netherlands: Springer.

Novera, I. A. (2004). Indonesian postgraduate students studying in Australia: An examination of their academic, social and cultural experiences. *International Education Journal*, *5*(4), 475–487.

Phuong-Mai, N., Cees, T., & Pilot, A. (2006). Culturally appropriate pedagogy: The case of group learning in a Confucian heritage culture context. *Intercultural Education*, *17*(1), 1–19.

Pyvis, D., & Chapman, A. (2004). *Student experiences of offshore higher education: Issues for quality.* Melbourne: Australian Universities Quality Agency.

Rizvi, F. (2002). Internationalisation of the curriculum. Available from: http://mams.rmit.edu.au/ ioc/sf012iqo4uzn.pdf [Accessed September 2008].

Schapper, J., & Mayson, S. E. (2004). Internationalisation of curricula: an alternative to the Taylorism of academic work. *Journal of Higher Education Policy and Management*, *26*(2), 189–205.

Singh, M. G. (2005). Enabling transnational learning communities: Policies, pedagogies and politics of educational power. In Ninnes & Hellstén (2005), pp. 9–36.

14
International Students and Academic Acculturation
The Role of Relationships in the Doctoral Process

MICHAELA BORG, RACHEL MAUNDER, XIAOLI JIANG,
ELAINE WALSH, HEATHER FRY AND ROBERTO DI NAPOLI

Introduction

Until relatively recently, it was often assumed that doctoral study was training for an academic career; the student worked as apprentice for a more experienced academic, learning about research techniques and procedures, and was assisted in their entry into the academic and disciplinary communities (Harland & Plangger, 2004). The successful doctoral student would subsequently take up an academic teaching post. However, the recent increase in fields outside academia where advanced postgraduate training is expected has meant that students are undertaking doctoral degrees for a variety of reasons. The result is that doctoral students now form a diverse group, with different motivations for study.

Of significance in this more diverse group are international postgraduates who may have come from academic and pedagogic cultures quite different from those of the host country. They may foresee careers in academic or non-academic environments – either returning home or remaining in the host country (Deem & Brehony, 2000). Because of their international status, they may conceive of academic practice as distinctly different from domestic counterparts.

This chapter discusses the results of an investigation of a group of international doctoral students studying science and engineering in the United Kingdom at the Universities of Warwick and Imperial College London. Our focus was on the experiences and expectations of international students as they become acculturated into the practices of their department and discipline. According to Berry (2005, p. 699) 'acculturation is a process of cultural and psychological changes that involve various forms of mutual accommodation'. In our study we focused on changes the individual students experienced in this process. Relationships emerged as a central concern to the students we spoke to, for example with supervisors and fellow students.

Our research was undertaken through an online questionnaire eliciting background information, following which 18 students were interviewed about their experiences, expectations and career aspirations. All students were from science and engineering disciplines, the specialised focus of one of the research partners. We also hoped that focusing on two disciplinary areas would facilitate the emergence of more meaningful patterns that might be lost if we looked at students across disciplines with very different research and supervision practices. We also focused on two groups of students: those from China, chosen due to their numbers in UK higher education; and students from Central and South America. We wanted to avoid countries that might be more similar to UK models by virtue of a British colonial past. Students were chosen from across all years of the Ph.D. programme.

What the Students Said

During interview, students were asked about a range of issues including their reasons for undertaking doctoral study; how they became interested in the discipline; what made them choose to come to the United Kingdom to study; how they found it on arrival; what they found surprising and what difficult; the important early experiences and how involved they felt in their department, discipline and university life. Analysis showed that the relationships students developed with individuals and/or groups during early stages of their Ph.D. programme were significant to their experience. Students who reported positive relationships even with only a few key individuals appeared to have a more positive experience overall.

The most frequently mentioned and seemingly most important relationship was with the supervisor. Students also spoke of relationships with other Ph.D. students and postdoctoral students they were working closely with; relationships with their research group; links with the department and university as a whole, and also relationships with their discipline. The following sections will examine each in turn describing how students experienced relationships and their importance in making students feel part of the culture in which they were studying.

Supervisor

The supervisor was central in the students' relationships. One interviewee emphasised the important role that the supervisor played generally:

> '[Y]ou really have to know your supervisor very well, whether he is a good person, both academically and reputation. And also in terms of personality, how much he is giving help to you. If he is not helping, there is no way you are going to finish your Ph.D., you may have trouble.'

In many cases students chose their supervisor and hence the institution they applied to based on knowledge of their work and reputation. When asked why he came to the United Kingdom to study, one participant responded by referring to his supervisor, saying that, 'his name is big name in this field. I am interested in his project'.

A major aspect of the supervisor–student relationship emerging from interviews was the various roles supervisors play. The most frequently mentioned aspect was academic support. The second area, though mentioned much less frequently, was personal support.

A number of students mentioned the importance of the supervisor in helping them to choose their topic and guiding them on the direction of their study. One student related how he had 'met my supervisor the first day, we talked about what I could do, he already had some points in mind … actually I liked one of them very much, that's what I am doing'. Another interviewee emphasised the personal choice involved in this negotiation: 'when supervisor provided those topics … I can decide what I will do, I can do this part not that part. And the supervisor, he respect my opinion'. Sometimes students arrived with their idea formed but more often the supervisor recommended reading and in some cases workshops to attend. Several students also mentioned that supervisors were responsible for the schedule of work: 'my supervisor gave me some paper and say ok spend one or two week and read through'. Supervisors seemed also to be centrally important in recommending contacts to students who needed to develop expertise, for example, in the use of particular equipment or knowledge of an area new to them: 'if you have any problem, your supervisor will tell you who to ask, to learn the new technique'. Supervisors were often mentioned in connection with bringing together groups of students for meetings or to participate in seminars in which students would take turns to present their work: 'same supervisor from different labs, we have the meeting all together'. Other areas of help included giving advice and feedback on writing abstracts and preparing papers for conferences: 'when you write an abstract or maybe poster, your supervisor will check it for you before you apply'.

One area bridging academic and personal support was the role supervisors took in helping students get paid work, either laboratory demonstrating or in one case working on projects for companies. This helped financially in addition to supporting career development: 'my supervisor knew the money I had from Mexico is not enough so he asked me to do demonstrating to undergraduates'. A small number of students also mentioned care in a more personal sense with one supervisor even meeting his/her student at the airport and helping them settle in to their accommodation and another student reporting that her supervisor 'supports his student quite well. He understand that we are far away from home … he always asked if I found the project interesting or if I had problems in accommodation, money'. Supervisors also helped students socialise with others in their research group. One participant, for example, explained that their supervisor regularly took the research group out for dinner.

One clear theme emerging from the interview was the surprise students felt at having more freedom and much less guidance than expected from their supervisor. One student said, 'I expected more supervision from my supervisor but I am more or less on my own. That's a surprise I guess'. Similarly, another student commented, 'It's quite free because my supervisor … didn't … .come to my office every day and asked what I am doing … I just meet him maybe once a week'. In many cases students attributed this to the nature of working at Ph.D. level; in other cases they mentioned their supervisor was so busy it was difficult to see them. In a small number of cases difficulties between student and supervisor were significant and students spoke of feeling 'isolated' and of feeling their work was not valued: 'If you failed, it won't do any harm to him.' In these problematic cases, the breakdown in the relationship seemed to have an impact on the whole Ph.D. experience. For example, one student reported feeling unsure of what to do because his supervisor was away: 'communicating with my boss, he is not here, I can't talk with him about my research areas'. Another student summed up the importance of a good supervisory relationship: 'without relationship … you will have a tough time in the university'.

The experience of doing a Ph.D. and the relationship with a supervisor was seen by many to be quite different to their earlier experiences on taught programmes:

> '[Y]ou have your own office, your own laptop. I mean you just work everyday, the relationship between you and your supervisor is more like colleague. You will have meeting every week, you discuss or maybe even argue. It's quite different. And also it's your responsibility to find what you need. It's you who decide what you need for this research.'

In contrast to the idea of the supervisor as colleague, others were clear that for them the supervisor was in charge and students expected to be told what to do. This was particularly clear in the case of two who continually referred to their supervisors as 'the boss', explaining, 'because when we think supervisor, he is the boss'.

Postdoctoral Researchers and Other Ph.D. Students

After supervisors, postdoctoral researchers appeared to be the most important contact for many Ph.D. students with six out of eighteen interviewees explicitly referring to the essential role of a postdoc in their research process. Ph.D. students felt they had benefited from relationships with postdocs in three ways: learning practical skills and experimental techniques, knowledge transmission and experience sharing.

Ph.D. students in science and engineering disciplines often carry out experiments and tests in laboratories using various techniques and pieces of equipment. In the interviews, students reported a common practice of being taught how to use equipment/machinery by postdocs. In some cases these were through referral from their supervisor and in others students were simply helped out by the postdoc. One explained, 'I want to do chemistry experiment. I can't do it in our department … the English postdoctor there … because it's my first time to use the equipment, he is very patient and trained me'. This support was crucial in resolving difficulties: 'sometimes if I don't understand something, I will come to him, ask him, so its kind of luck to know this people'. This is particularly the case if the supervisor is unavailable: 'If you have a question like where something is or how to do something you never go to your boss and ask and he is busy in other thing. You ask your lab mate [a postdoc].'

In many cases postdocs also helped Ph.D. students broaden their knowledge of their field and become acquainted with areas outside their main research domain. Postdocs, as mentors, helped Ph.D. students fill knowledge gaps: 'I didn't have any background in biology … [I] got help from a postdoc.'

Finally, in a few cases there was a social element to these relationships. As people who had successfully completed a Ph.D., postdocs were in a good position to help Ph.D. students cope with settling into their studies. One interviewee emphasised this supportive role: 'they are very cool very relaxed, help you settled down very quickly … and also since they've been here for a few years, they also help you things with research'.

It is worth noting, however, that Ph.D. students were not the only beneficiaries in the relationships with postdocs. One interviewee described his relationship with a postdoc as being on a more equal academic footing, 'Once a week I talked with this postdoc … Because we have similar interests … we are reading books together'.

Students also spoke about the relationships formed with other Ph.D. students – often their peers they shared an office with. When asked who was important to them in the early days, one student specifically mentioned other Ph.D. students: 'my supervisors and Ph.D. students … they gave me advice, they were very helpful'. Many students commented on these relationships, for example 'we are very close friends, we started at the same time, we are in the same office, sat back to back, it's nice to have someone sharing'. Being in the same office seemed significant in helping relationships with fellow Ph.D. students to develop:

'I think the atmosphere in our office becoming better, becoming more relaxing … At the beginning, we are too polite to each other. We don't want to disturb each other during office hour, so we simply didn't talk to each other. But now … maybe begin to know more about each other, sometimes we just say some jokes to each other.'

One student spoke about not being able to get to know other students because he was in a different office: 'I tended to segregated from other Ph.D. students. Because others are 8 to 10 in an office … they probably know each other better.' Having contact with fellow research students provided an important opportunity to share experiences and discuss areas of common concern:

'Very good in office, we have nearly 20 guys, all this guys are not from one supervisors so we share different disciplines. In that case, I think interaction with them are quite good, because we share the same worry about our supervisor [laugh] that's something connect us.'

Research Group

Another important relationship emerging from the data is the link with their research group. In principle, they become members of a group after enrolment. The majority of students indicated a positive influence on both their academic and personal life: 'in our group we know each other very well, we know each other's project, we talked a lot'.

Students' major concern was to attain the Ph.D. degree whether academia was their preferred trajectory in the future or not. Therefore, most were keen on participation in formal research group activities such as presentations, seminars, and workshops. These provided a sound platform for both opinion exchange and information sharing: 'our group is very good, the relationship is very good ... we have seminar regularly ... everyone presents their own research ... then others will ask questions'. Another interviewee explained, 'if you want to do something good, especially for research study, you have to discuss with others all the time, whether this idea is proper'. For her, the research group discussion formalised a process of incorporating other perspectives, thus validating the research and eventually improving research standards. In addition, for some interviewees, research group activities helped broaden their vision through information sharing: 'every week we have seminar. I tried to attend as many as possible and I think I learned a lot'; 'you learn a lot of different techniques, and also you got different idea from different people in your group'. Engagement with research group activity had another function – it maintained continuity of research when supervisors were extremely busy. Two interviewees mentioned their supervisors were often unable to make individual face-to-face tutorials and they used regular research group meetings instead to seek answers to queries and exchange opinions on their work: 'now supervisor is encouraging us to talk with each other, so we may have some ideas. Now in the group meeting sometimes without supervisor'.

Besides opportunities for academic engagement, students also mentioned social activities organized by the research group: for example the 'teatime chat', eating out, playing sports, or taking short trips. According to these interviewees, such social activities are often initiated by a few active organisers but may be facilitated or even paid for by the department.

Students' sense of belonging to their research group was clearly indicated through regular use of terms like 'our group' or 'my group', and several referred to their 'colleagues'. As one student commented, 'everything I am talking about is about my little group ... like pretty much everything I said. I don't know anybody else from the other group'.

Department

The sheer size of departments was seen to be a barrier for some in forming relationships beyond their immediate research group. One student commented, 'I feel part of my research group more than part of the department. Because engineering is a huge department people usually work in the group rather than in the department'. However, organised events and activities assisted integration into departments, this included involvement in teaching, demonstrating or invigilation.

Departmental seminars with invited speakers were mentioned by many as a good opportunity to learn more about their subject and meet others: 'In our department, there is seminar every week. The department will invite professors, research fellows, and maybe employers from outside the college.' Seminars were often followed by a social gathering giving the chance to meet other people and speak about their work. One interviewee made this connection clear:

'[E]very one month or two months, there is a department seminar together. We all talk to each other, maybe some people you want to talk to related to your project, and can have some food, some drink at that time.'

In addition to post-seminar social events, some referred to department-organised social events such as a Christmas party and a cricket match or 'something like picnic or bowling or going to football or playing Frisbees'. A common room for eating lunch and socializing was also seen as important by some.

A key role for the department was ensuring circulation of information about events and activities: 'the secretary gave us the information … every week … so we can choose'. Students who did not receive such information about the department felt isolated, 'when I came here for three months I haven't received any email from the department … so I missed a lot of things. So it's very difficult for me to continue to be involved'.

University

In a similar way to departmental involvement, students expressed being part of university life as having access to events and activities, often organised by the respective Graduate Schools. One student referred to courses such as 'how to start a Ph.D., how to communicate with supervisor, I think they are good' and another student listed a range of events:

'Lots of presentations, lots of seminars, talks for us. Like for Ph.D., first year, there are sets of courses for engineering postgraduates. You can choose, for example … how to present poster … your personality type and how to network … I would say both academic related or both broad or general knowledge.'

Students living in university accommodation appeared to have more access to organised social activities: 'I lived in the residence hall for postgraduate, part of the committee there so we always organize things to other students, we organize to visit places, or parties. And also we have football team.' Although some referred to taking part in sports or joining Student Union societies and going to pubs with other students, these purely social activities were mentioned less frequently than work-related socialising.

Interestingly, one student felt that the nature of Ph.D. study made it more difficult to form relationships with people in the wider university environment, 'we are in research group, not like undergraduate, we are not having lots of chance to lecture, we don't know many people, we only know people in our group'. However, in general, university life did not seem to be very important to those we spoke to: 'the university life, I haven't seen that'. Almost half described a lack of engagement or saw it merely as the academic environment supporting their research activity. One student stated baldly, 'well, university to me is just a place to learn to get my degree, nothing more than that'. Their motivation was purely for study, 'except for library, nothing much in other parts, our main task is to do experiment', and activities outside that intense focus were peripheral.

Students were asked how they settled into life in the United Kingdom and a couple mentioned language difficulties, transportation and city living, etc., but most examples related to the university environment. It should be noted that some students mentioned the support they received from partners or family.

Discipline

About half the students appeared confused when asked about involvement with their discipline and many asked for clarification about what was meant. Most interpreted the discipline in very vague terms, thinking of a body of knowledge, rather than a community of scholars bound together by customs, conventions and paradigms (Becher & Trowler, 2001). Several students described a progressive entry into the discipline but invariably considered themselves just at the beginning stage, 'I think just a normal Ph.D. level just beginner ... Ph.D. is not enough, if you really want to specialize an academic career, you really have to know more, to do a postdoc, to accumulate more experience'. Even a final-year Ph.D. student commented, 'I think although my final year in my field, I only kind of start, starter, there is many many more to be learned'.

Relationships with(in) the discipline appear to be built principally via dissemination of the students' own work. When asked if they felt part of their discipline, one student said, 'not yet ... one has to accumulated lots of knowledge before contributing ... so I didn't write papers or give presentations in conference. So not yet' and another student commented, 'If you publish more work, you will ... feel part of the group . . . this kind of ... very strong belonging'.

Attending conferences and forming professional relationships was an important aspect of acculturation into their discipline. Opportunities to meet leaders in the field were particularly prized. Describing a recent conference one student commented, 'I've met the top scientist there, that's the most important thing ... most important activity last year'. Being part of seminars with international visitors organised by the home department was also seen as important, 'in other situation I couldn't have chance to sit down and have a drink with top scientists. And I did. So it's quite ... precious'.

The supervisor appears to play a key role in the progress of these broader relationships, 'sometimes they have conferences ... they can tell the supervisor to apply for the fund, so we can attend the conference'. In some cases the supervisor did not prioritise the submission of articles or papers, 'he said you know the most important thing is to get your Ph.D., you can submit papers afterwards'.

It was interesting that a negative experience can have a damaging impact on the sense of belonging to a discipline. One student describing a conference presentation said, 'I felt many people didn't know what we are doing ... Most of the people didn't understand' and he felt little was gained by the experience. Only one student mentioned broader aspects of disciplinary connection such as involvement with employers (through taking part in the supervisor's consultancy work) and attendance at events organised by relevant professional institutions.

Discussion

What is apparent is the central role that a few individuals have had on their experience. Some relationships have developed via informal means but their role was crucial. In many cases students' relationships with supervisors seemed of central importance and therefore critical. The fact that in many cases students came to study specifically with their supervisor is indicative of this. Gardner (2007) found that the research group was the central element of chemistry research students' experience, with the supervisor working as a 'boss' to this group of students. She contrasts this with history students for whom the supervisor relationship was far more central. She also found that peer support was crucial for doctoral students although higher importance was given to the social support these relationships provided than is indicated in our study.

In our study, students appeared to look to their supervisor for direction, and when not provided there was often confusion and uncertainty. Many students we spoke to expected more guidance and found it surprising being left to work alone. It is difficult to say whether this is due to the nature of doctoral study or to cultural influences and expectations about roles and relationships. However, it should be noted that a number of students contrasted this aspect of their study with an earlier taught course:

'Ph.D. is a larger commitment, you have to work for three years on project, when you do Master, you have classmates, you support each other. But for Ph.D. student you have to … work on our own. No one can do the work for you, no one can really help you. You have to work out by yourself … I think you will have more student life when you are doing a Master because like Ph.D. student you don't have to stay in college for many hours. So you can make more friends.'

This would indicate that the surprising level of independence was not necessarily culturally framed and therefore, whilst our results only relate the experiences of the international students we spoke to, they may not be unique to this group.

In this respect, the role of other Ph.D. students and postdoctoral students became very important for advice and support. It is interesting that postdocs in particular emerged in many cases as 'informal mentors' to the students – helping with practical aspects of projects in the absence of their supervisor. Hasrati (2005), who investigated the experiences of Ph.D. students in engineering and social sciences/humanities, found that engineering senior students informally supported less advanced students and this was encouraged by supervisors. In contrast, social science/humanities students worked much more closely with supervisors, but otherwise alone. They met their peer group largely through participation in more formal learning experiences such as department seminars and workshops. Deem and Brehony (2000) also contrast the team work in science subjects with the lone researcher life of the non-science student.

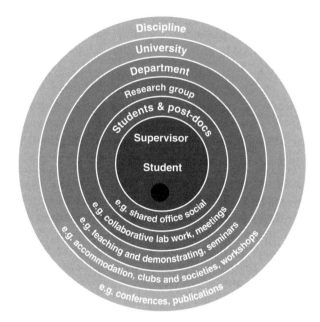

Figure 14.1 Circles of Support and Influence

Figure 14.1 illustrates the relative closeness or distance of relationships reported by students in our study.[1] The student is at the centre, and the inner rings represent the people that are closest and most significant to them. The lighter shading as the rings expand indicates the lessening importance of the relationships to the students' experience.

A striking feature of responses was students' intense focus on their Ph.D. study, almost to the exclusion of everything else. This may seem unsurprising given the goal of doctoral study, but interestingly this appeared to impact on the nature of relationships with others. Relationships were strategic to the extent they helped students advance their research projects. Those we spoke to did not often refer to purely social relationships. For example, when asked about participation in university life, they often responded by emphasising they were here to get their Ph.D. The fact that many students came to the university to work with a particular academic indicates their clear focus, with university life and associated social aspects peripheral for the majority we spoke to.

Deem and Brehony, who looked at non-science students, report that access to research cultures may not be equal for all students, with international students less likely to feel included in seminars, events and other aspects of department life. They ascribe this to various factors including 'language barriers, cultural differences, not understanding how the UK system of higher education works, [and] variations in expectations about what doctoral study involves' (2000, p. 158). Our study found differences in experiences and levels of engagement with departmental life *within* the international student group.

Doctoral study by its nature involves students working much more closely alongside staff members in the department than at undergraduate or Master's level, for example by attending departmental seminars and contributing to teaching activities. Therefore the experience of being a Ph.D. student may parallel the employee in the workplace rather than a student at university. It may be unsurprising therefore that those we spoke to were not as involved with social aspects of university life. It was regarded as their place of work, hence relationships developed were collegial.

As outlined, students we spoke to were from China or Central/South America but we did not attempt to make comparisons between reported experiences based on nationality as this was not a focus of the study. International students form a diverse group with different experiences and we would be reluctant to attribute these differences purely to cultural background, particularly without more extensive research. Importantly, having focused on international students, we cannot assume findings would be comparable for home students. However, we would anticipate that the quality of relationships with supervisors and significant others would be important for the experience of all doctoral students, both international and domestic. For example, Gardner's (2007) study, based on interviews with domestic doctoral students in America, noted the importance of peer support, good faculty relationships and challenges surrounding the independent nature of doctoral study, showing distinct overlaps with our findings. Of course, given that domestic students are more familiar with the cultural environment in which they are studying and typically have a stronger network of relationships outside the immediate academic environment, the way in which these relationships develop, and the purposes they serve may differ. For example, the Deem and Brehony (2000) study noted differences between the accessibility of peer cultures for home and international students. A larger-scale study comparing home and international students would provide more insight into these issues.

Implications

Although focused on Chinese and Central/South American students studying science and engineering, the experiences described by these postgraduate research students suggest a number of areas where appropriate support or provision could help enhance students' acculturation into doctoral study. We feel these suggestions reflect good practice for *all* doctoral students and are not limited to supporting international students.

Clearly supervisors have a role in nurturing informal relationships between Ph.D. students, fellow doctoral students, research groups and/or laboratory groups. Taking the initiative to organise meetings, introduce people and create appropriate networking opportunities for their Ph.D. students helps these important relationships develop. Hasrati (2005) pointed out that research-funding bodies tend to place particular importance on formal learning opportunities for doctoral students, for example research workshops and training, whilst more informal learning through interaction and collaboration does not receive as much attention. Development activities for new or experienced supervisors should emphasise the important role such informal relationships have for Ph.D. students and suggest how supervisors could have a key role in initiating and developing them. Institutions might consider providing support for postdoctoral students who find themselves assuming an unofficial mentoring role. This support may include optional workshops or one-to-one advice. Where formal provision is taking place (for example, Graduate School courses for Ph.D. students), organisers may consider facilitating networking/social time for students around the event. Induction activities for Ph.D. students should also take this into account.

In terms of dealing with expectations of the doctoral process and supervisory relationship, the induction process for new Ph.D. students might include a discussion on the nature of Ph.D. study highlighting the contrast between undergraduate and other taught programmes in level of independence expected. For international students in particular, showing awareness of possible cultural differences in educational systems and the role and responsibilities of students between home and host countries may be helpful. Further, a learning agreement between supervisors and Ph.D. students could be discussed and agreed at the outset so that differing expectations of roles and responsibilities are identified and resolved early.

It is acknowledged that many institutions are already engaged in such work, although this is generally focused on providing support and development for new supervisors and workshops for Ph.D. students on topics such as managing their time and working independently. However, in light of the findings of this study, it would seem important that these activities are reviewed and that more thought is given to supporting the development of relationships beyond that of student–supervisor.

Acknowledgements

The project was funded by the Centre for Excellence in Teaching and Learning in 'Preparing for Academic Practice' at The University of Oxford.

Note

1 This figure also appears on the website of the Oxford Centre for Excellence in Preparing for Academic Practice, part of the Learning Institute, University of Oxford. The Centre is funded by HEFCE as a Centre for Excellence in Teaching and Learning (CETL): http://www.learning.ox.ac.uk/cetl.php?page=54

References

Becher, T., & Trowler, P. R. (2001). *Academic tribes and territories* (2nd ed.). Buckingham, UK: Society for Research into Higher Education and Open University Press.

Berry, J. W. (2005). Acculturation: Living successfully in two cultures. *International Journal of Intercultural Relations, 29,* 697–712.

Deem, R., & Brehony, K. J. (2000). 'Doctoral students' access to research cultures – are some more equal than others?' *Studies in Higher Education, 25*(2), 149–165.

Gardner, S. K. (2007). "I heard it through the grapevine": Doctoral student socialization in chemistry and history. *Higher Education, 54*(5), 723–740.

Harland, T., & Plangger, G. (2004). The postgraduate chameleon: Changing roles in doctoral education. *Active Learning in Higher Education, 5*(1), 73–86.

Hasrati, M. (2005). Legitimate peripheral participation and supervising Ph.D. students. *Studies in Higher Education, 30*(5), 557–570.

15
Refugees
Home Students With International Needs

JACQUELINE STEVENSON AND JOHN WILLOTT

Introduction

This chapter details the experiences of six refugees[1] all currently or recently studying in a UK university. It outlines the barriers they have faced in attempting to integrate into the university and the practical approaches we suggest for meeting their needs. Quotes from other refugees who have studied at our own university are also included to illustrate the barriers faced by many refugees in attempting to study at UK universities.

By the end of 2007, the total population of concern to the UNHCR[2] was estimated at 31.7 million people, including 11.4 million refugees forced to leave their homes by conflict or persecution (UNHCR, 2008a). Afghans and Iraqis accounted for nearly half, with Colombians, Sudanese and Somalis also fleeing in large numbers (UNHCR, 2008b). The majority of refugees, up to 90 per cent, are hosted by some of the world's poorest countries including Pakistan, Syria and Iran, and only a relatively small number are living in industrialised countries, such as the United States, Germany and France (UNHCR, 2008b). The United Kingdom ranks just 16th in the league table of industrialised countries for the number of asylum applications per head of population and hosts less than 2 per cent of the world's total refugee population (UNHCR, 2008a, 2008b).

Those seeking asylum have immediate needs for safety and security, shelter, clothing, food and, where possible, education for their children. Many will also have survived torture, abuse, rape and bereavement and may have substantial physical and mental health needs. As asylum seekers they face uncertainty over their right to remain and will look to gain refugee status, as quickly as possible. If asylum is granted, longer-term goals may include learning new languages and finding permanent accommodation, undertaking training and, particularly, gaining employment (UNHCR, 2007). In the main, refugees are highly motivated, resilient people who want to work and to contribute to the country that has given them refuge.

'What is important isn't the choice of job and what you choose. It's the principle of working, of being able to contribute to the country, to support yourself. It's so humiliating. People think you're just happy to have money from the government and not work. But it's not so. You need to contribute something. You want to pay back somehow. We aren't even allowed to do unpaid jobs as asylum seekers. I felt reduced to nothing.'

(Female Iraqi refugee)

Once they have refugee status, however, many refugees find that their qualifications are not transferable to the United Kingdom (such as lawyers trained under the French legal system or doctors trained overseas). Others whose qualifications are potentially transferable may struggle to re-gain former professional status through a lack of English language skills:

'I taught Arabic and German and I was a translator. I need to get my English improved and get a secure job. I'm a decorator's labourer at the moment. I want a better, secure job.'

(Male Iraqi refugee, UK)

In 2004, the European Council adopted the Common Basic Principles (CBP) on Immigrant Integration with CBP 5 stating that 'efforts in education are critical to preparing immigrants, and particularly their descendents, to be more successful and more active participants in society' (European Council, 2004, p. 1). However, few countries consider *higher* education as a route to integration. For example, the current UK Refugee Integration Strategy (Home Office, 2005) states that refugees 'should be regarded respectfully as new residents and new communities who are a resource and not a liability' (p. 41) and that solutions to help refugees meet their full potential, contribute to communities and access requisite services 'lie in the provision of opportunities for language training [and] ... retraining and re-accreditation where necessary' (p. 6) but the document makes no reference to higher education. In contrast, in an attempt to re-establish lives torn apart by displacement, bereavement and trauma, refugees often regard higher education as a 'fast track' route to high-level employment, (re)-gaining self-esteem and professional standing and integrating into their new communities (Stevenson & Willott, 2006a).

Refugees in UK Higher Education

The rights of refugees to tertiary education was recognised in the Geneva Convention, established to deal with the 'temporary' problem of refugees following the Second World War. The contracting states were urged to

accord to refugees treatment as favourable as possible ... [in] respect to education other than elementary education and, in particular, as regards access to studies, the recognition of foreign school certificates, diplomas and degrees, the remission of fees and charges and the award of scholarships.

(United Nations 1951, Article 22)

However, little progress appears to have been made in ensuring that refugees are supported in their efforts to access university. Accurate statistics on the number, educational background and entry into university of refugees are notoriously difficult to determine since their qualifications are not collated. In addition, in the United Kingdom, as with many other countries, refugees are classed as domestic students, with the same rights and entitlements to university as native citizens. As a consequence there is no means of calculating the number of current or former refugees in UK universities. However, evidence indicates the barriers faced by refugees in attempting to gain access are numerous and, consequently, refugees are under-represented in UK universities (Stevenson & Willott 2006a, 2006b, 2008).

Aside from considerations of social justice or inclusion, the number of well-educated refugees settling in the United Kingdom each year (even if relatively low) means there is a strong business case for universities to help them be admitted. However, few UK universities undertake activities to increase the number of refugees studying with them, failing to recognise them as a specific 'widening participation'[3] target group unlike, for example students with disabilities, Looked After children,[4] or specific ethnic minority groups. In addition, leave to remain in the United Kingdom is now only granted for five years, after which the refugee can apply for indefinite leave but this is not guaranteed. This lack of long-term security means refugees may be less likely to consider university education until they are certain of being able to stay. In common with other international applicants, refugees often have difficulty understanding the differing and numerous universities and courses available and the often complex application process (Stevenson & Willott, 2006b). Refugees are also amongst the poorest members of society and may be unwilling to take the financial risk of undertaking a degree course (Willott & Stevenson, 2008). For some these barriers are, or are considered to be, insurmountable.

'I'm dreaming of continuing to have a university education. I would like to improve my qualifications here. My husband is a teacher. We respect education very much. We like our child to study well and to prepare for classes. It's important to us. But for now we must work.'

(Female Sudanese refugee)

Despite these barriers a small number of refugees do manage to make the transition to university. Once there, however, they find they have the same social, psychological and practical support needs as international students but, as refugees, are classed as domestic students. Thus they do not have access to the extensive support mechanisms put in place for other international students.

Pastoral Care

Under the UN Geneva Convention (1951) a refugee is a person who is likely to have experienced, or been in fear of experiencing, persecution including torture, abuse and/or imprisonment. These experiences are made worse by the trauma and upheaval experienced in fleeing one country and the isolation and confusion of attempting to settle in another. It is unsurprising that mental health problems are widespread, including suicide and post-traumatic stress disorder, anxiety and depression (Johnson et al., 1997). Whilst many refugees are resilient and resourceful, refusing to see themselves as victims, they may still need substantial and longer-term pastoral and emotional care. Clearly the experiences of refugees are shared by others: experience of trauma, violence or threat (victims of abuse), interrupted education (Looked After and Traveller children), culture shock and language difficulties (economic migrants and international students) and poverty (those from low socio-economic households) (Stevenson & Willott, 2006b). However, the difference is that unlike other students, refugees may have encountered *all* of these. Most UK universities have structures in place to support those from the kind of backgrounds referred to above. For example, Looked After children can have accommodation for the full 52-week year, rather than just during semesters; there are support mechanisms for students with disabilities, and flexible programmes for those who have responsibilities as carers. The needs of international students, as new arrivals to the country, are also specifically catered for. However, interventions targeted at refugees have been primarily limited to aspiration raising and helping them to enter higher education. There is little evidence of support for refugees once they become students. This is exemplified by Dominique, a 29-year-old Cameroonian refugee who, following a violent attack was forced to flee her homeland without her two young children. Dominique found studying highly difficult as she was suffering from both post-traumatic stress disorder and depression. Support was very much dependent on individual tutors and there was a lack of consistent and sufficient care and support:

> 'I was proper sick and depressed when I came here. I couldn't cope. I didn't get my assignments in on time but tutors gave me lots of support. One particularly understood what I was going through. He told them at the meeting they had about me that I was sick and not just lazy. I didn't want to speak because I didn't want to talk about my private life.'

In the end Dominique found asking for help so often so difficult that she dropped out part way through her first year.

Social Networks

Peer support and friendship networks are important components of the student experience, but refugees may find it harder to socialise than others. Trauma may have affected self-esteem and confidence, making it harder to form relationships. Most are also older students. Consequently they may find it difficult integrating either into domestic student society or engaging with international students even, or perhaps especially, those from their home country. In addition, because of their circumstances, refugees may have less experience of participating in volunteering, sporting or other extra-curricular activities, so have fewer avenues through which to integrate with others. Equally, they are more likely to be in paid employment (often supporting family members in the United Kingdom and sending money back to other relatives in their home countries) and living at home rather than in student accommodation (although of course this is not truly 'home', with its implications of security, stability and lifelong family and friendship networks): 'I was asked where I wanted to go. I didn't know anywhere in England so when they suggested Leeds I just said OK. It'll do' (male Syrian refugee).

This is the situation faced by Mada, a 27-year-old woman from the Sudan who arrived in the United Kingdom 5 years ago with her husband. Mada had previously experienced higher education in her home country where she had formed a close group of women friends and benefited greatly from studying and socialising with her peers. Since entering university in the United Kingdom, despite her high expectations, Mada has found it difficult to form friendships. Her course has few international students and they socialise closely with each other, having met at events for international students on arrival. Mada also works part time and runs a home which makes it difficult to join clubs or societies. She is keenly aware her experiences of higher education are different from most students. As she explained, whilst she is *attending* she is not *participating*: 'For me it is different. I go to my classes but then I come home. The next day I go to my classes and then I come home. It is just not the same for me as for others.'

Difficulties socialising may be shared with other groups of students, specifically those living at home (Holdsworth, 2006) or those who work (Moreau & Leathwood, 2006), but many refugees may not have established social or familial networks outside university. They have invariably moved into the region to settle and may have undergone frequent moves during their application for refugee status resulting in looser networks than other students. International students have also moved away from their support networks, but there are often considerable numbers of students from one country or region who can offer peer support. In addition, other international students rely increasingly on email and telephone to keep in touch with family and friends overseas, strategies which assist acculturation (Cemalcilar, Falbo & Stapleton, 2005). However, refugees may no longer have friends or family overseas (or are not aware of their whereabouts) or contacting them might expose them to risk if the authorities intercepted communications.

Academic Practice

As with other international students, refugees can find academic practice in UK universities unfamiliar. They may have previous experience of higher education but may not have the requisite study and communication skills to enable them to be successful in other countries.

Similarly, refugees may have language difficulties which can create problems in the learning process. International students admitted to university have to demonstrate a sufficiently high level of English language. However, along with other non-native speakers of English domiciled in the United Kingdom, the assumption is made that refugees are domestic students, so the test of English ability is at a much lower level. Although this makes entry to university easier, it may leave refugees less able to communicate *academically* and without the language support which is made available to international students: 'Sometimes I sit there in class and really I understand almost nothing. I listen but don't understand' (male Syrian refugee).

This lower level of academic communication skills, alongside unfamiliarity with study methods (for example, understanding of plagiarism, effective essay and report writing) means that some refugees are considerably underprepared for the study environment. International students generally receive the option for support in these areas but this may not be open to refugees as 'domestic' students. These were some of the difficulties faced by Hamid when he recently undertook a University Certificate in Personal and Professional Skills. Hamid is a 42-year-old man from Iraq. He left his home country for political reasons, moving to the United Kingdom without his family. Aside from English, he speaks three languages fluently and has gained a GCSE in English. He is a bright, articulate man who worked in a professional capacity in his homeland. His earliest university experiences were of struggle, failure and disappointment. As Hamid explained: 'I thought I was ready. I thought I could do this but I knew nothing. Nothing I'd learned before was of any use.'

Hamid found that, initially, his written English was insufficiently robust to cope with the academic demands of the course. He struggled to produce essays of a high enough academic standard, finding referencing and the avoidance of plagiarism particularly difficult. He also found it demoralising that everything he wrote appeared to be 'lacking' but that other students in his group appeared to be coping, making him feel further alienated. This was compounded when the class was split into smaller groups and asked to work on activities which would be assessed as a group. Hamid felt he had little to offer and that his contribution would be inadequate. Fortunately his tutor was willing to provide him with extensive one to one support, spending time teaching the skills needed to be successful as well as building his confidence. With support he struggled through his first module (unit of study) and by his fourth and final module was approaching academic tasks with much greater confidence.

Hidden assumptions can also cause considerable problems for refugees. This was the case for Mary, a 35-year-old woman from Iran. On arrival in the United Kingdom Mary did not speak English, but has subsequently learned the language. She now holds a UK passport and has started her second year studying for a science-based diploma. Mary struggled during the first few months of studies, partly because of a lack of study skills after several years away from education, but also because of limited academic and scientific English (although she was able to work in a customer-facing environment, this required different skills). As an example, she was set a mathematical problem and was given the formula for the surface area of a sphere, given as $4\pi r^2$, but the symbols were not explained, it being assumed that a UK science student would know them already. While international students are eligible for, and signposted to, free academic English and study skills courses at the university, being classified as a home student meant that Mary did not automatically receive this.

A final aspect which can be very difficult for refugee students is reflective practice. Over the last decade reflective learning has made increasing inroads into the university curriculum. All UK universities are required to offer progress files to students. These include records of learning and achievement and personal development planning, a structured process undertaken by each student to reflect upon their own learning, performance and achievement. Today reflection is considered one of the essential principles underlying good teaching practice. Whilst much of the literature suggests that learners are happy to engage in reflective learning and find it enjoyable, other research has shown that there are barriers to learning which must be overcome, including a lack of self-worth and anxiety and previous negative educational experience amongst others. In addition, many students do not value personal knowledge and their own role in the construction of expert knowledge. Our research with international students (including refugees and asylum seekers) as well as those from non-traditional UK backgrounds has indicated (Stevenson & Willott, 2006a, 2006b, 2008; Willott & Stevenson, 2006, 2008) that those who engage most successfully with reflective practice have cultural values most closely aligned to the dominant culture of the academy (Becher & Trowler, 2001). In contrast, those who face the greatest obstacles to engaging with reflective practice are those whose cultural values are dissimilar, even contradictory. This not only creates tensions for students but may further alienate those who are already marginalised or at risk of dropping out. Consequently, as with other international students, refugees can find the process of reflection difficult. In addition, reflecting on current learning can also trigger remembrance of past events. And for many refugees remembering the past is a deeply uncomfortable, and often painful, experience. This is true for Sahin, a 43-year-old Iraqi Kurd.

Previously a teacher in Iraq, Sahin recently undertook a short course in Personal and Professional Skills, designed to help improve her study and employability skills and evidence her ability to undertake university study. Part of the course involved an element of reflection on learning. For Sahin, reflecting on her current learning was difficult as she found it hard to think about this without thinking about her previous study and thus the successful life, the friends and the two children she had left behind which was extremely painful for her. As she explained:

'When I think back it is with sadness. I had so much, my life, my job, my friends. But coming here I lost everything. I had to start again from nothing. I do not think about my past. I need to think about my future.'

Sahin found separating out reflection on her learning from reflection on her past history highly problematic and this greatly affected her ability to produce the required reflective portfolio.

Placements

In the United Kingdom a number of courses require students to undertake long-term work experience placement or internship and most students welcome the opportunity to travel abroad for a year or gain a year's industry experience. For refugees international placements are often impossible to undertake. The majority do not have national passports, but even if they do they may be fearful of leaving their country of asylum. Even placements in the United Kingdom may be difficult as most refugee students are living at home, may have caring responsibilities or be working alongside their studies. For these reasons most refugees will steer away from courses which have a compulsory year abroad, such as languages, or vocational courses which require students to undertake a one-year internship. However, increasingly other courses require students to find shorter-term placements, or undertake work-based learning or voluntary work. They are then faced with a situation which might be challenging for other non-traditional students but can be overwhelming for refugees.

To have to find and then be successful in a placement is not beyond the abilities of student refugees. However, it is important that universities recognise that they may need significantly more support to find placements than most other students as is evidenced by Aaliyah's experiences. Aaliyah is a 22-year-old African woman who fled her native country in 2003 after her family was murdered. She has full refugee status with indefinite leave to remain. When she arrived in the United Kingdom Aaliyah spoke no English (her native language is French). She is now undertaking her second year of an honours degree having been supported by a mentor from the university's refugee mentoring scheme. At the end of her first year, Aaliyah phoned her mentor for support explaining that she needed to find a placement for 90 days. Her course leader had explained that, as independent adults, they needed to try and arrange this placement for themselves, but as Aaliyah told her mentor:

> 'I don't even know where to start. I don't know what I want to do and so I don't know who I should phone. And is it ok to just phone people up and ask if they will help? They don't know me.'

Aaliyah had no experience of voluntary work and the concept of a work-based placement was unfamiliar to her. For Aaliyah finding a placement was a daunting prospect and she immediately started to grow anxious that if she could not find an appropriate placement she would fail her course. Through her contacts the mentor was eventually able to secure a placement for Aaliyah but for other refugee students the outcome might not be so successful.

Provision of Support

We have identified key areas of support needed by refugees. Clearly many of those referred to in this chapter may have faced difficulties in succeeding at university whether they were a refugee or not. Some of the issues highlighted are equally true for international students, for those who enter higher education as mature students, those who live at home or who work part time. The difference is that for most refugees all of these factors come into play at once and refugees may not be identified by universities as falling into any of the categories which would trigger automatic support.

Many refugees do not wish to identify themselves as such, either through fear of stigma or because they want to move on from their past traumas (Kaprielian-Churchill, 1996; Hannah, 1999). This makes targeted intervention difficult even though universities may be willing to help. Refugees themselves may be unaware of the extensive range of support services offered, and consequently do not take advantage of them unless they specifically ask for help, which many are reluctant to do. In particular programmes of language support, study skills, induction and development which are widely provided for international students are often not open to domestic students so refugees miss out on just the kind of services which might help them to succeed.

Suggestions

As we have shown, refugees are often highly desirous of accessing higher education. However, rather than being accorded 'treatment as favourable as possible' (UN, 1951) many refugees are struggling to achieve parity with other students in entering higher education and in being successful in their studies. Whilst there are difficulties in providing support, from our experience, some measures that universities could take include:

- Raising awareness of refugee issues through community events and, for example in the United Kingdom, participation in Refugee Week. These can celebrate the contribution of refugees to society and the university.
- Offering staff development courses and workshops on working with refugees and asylum seekers, focusing on their rights, entitlements and support needs. Refugee support organisations often have outreach workers (frequently refugees themselves) who are able to talk to groups, and can provide an enriching experience.
- Ensuring there are several staff with expert knowledge of complex refugee and asylum issues to whom other staff can refer for advice and support.
- Automatically making those additional support measures for international students available for refugees.
- Using information systems to identify refugees who have not self-declared. Appropriately sensitive contact could then be made to highlight some of the support measures available.
- Embedding these commitments through incorporation of refugees and asylum seekers as groups with specific needs in relevant policies.

Notes

1 Names changed to protect anonymity.
2 United Nations High Commissioner for Refugees.
3 Activities undertaken by universities to target groups that have been identified as under-represented in Higher Education.
4 A child or young person in the care of a local authority or a ward of the state.

References

Becher, T., & Trowler, P. R. (2001). *Academic tribes and territories* (2nd ed.). Buckingham, UK: Society for Research into Higher Education and Open University Press.

Cemalcilar, Z., Falbo, T., & Stapleton, L. (2005). Cyber communication: A new opportunity for international students' adaptation? *International Journal of Intercultural Relations, 29*(1), 91–110.

European Council (2004). Council conclusions, immigrant integration policy in the European Union, 14615/04 of 19 November 2004. Available from: http://www.enaro.eu/dsip/download/eu-Common-Basic-Principles.pdf [Accessed January 2009].

Hannah, J. (1999). Refugee students at college and university: Improving access and support. *International Review of Education, 45*(2), 153–166.

Holdsworth, C. (2006). 'Don't you think you're missing out, living at home?' Student experiences and residential transitions. *Sociological Review, 54*(3), 495–519.

Home Office (2005). *Integration matters: A national strategy for refugee integration.* Croydon, UK: IND Communications Team and Home Office Communications Directorate.

Johnson, S., Ramsay, R., Thornicroft, G., Brooks, E., Lelliot, P., Peck, E., Smith, H., Chisholm, D., Audini, B., Knapp, M., & Goldberg, D. (1997). (Eds.), *London's mental health: The report to the King's Fund Commission.* London: King's Fund Publishing.

Kaprielian-Churchill, I. (1996). Refugees and education in Canadian schools. *International Review of Education, 42*(4), 349–365.

Moreau, M-P., & Leathwood, C. (2006), Balancing paid work and studies: Working(-class) students in higher education. *Studies in Higher Education, 31*(1), 23–42.

Stevenson, J., & Willott, J. (2006a). Overcoming multiple barriers to accessing learning. In T. Hudson, M. Abramson, T. Acland, J. Braham, M. Hill, A. Lines, M. McLinden, D. Saunders & J. Storan (Eds.), *Towards a global understanding of lifelong learning: Making a difference* (pp. 252–259). London: Forum for Access and Continuing Education.

Stevenson, J., & Willott, J. (2006b). The aspiration and access to higher education of teenage refugees in the UK. *Compare, 37*(5), 671–687.

Stevenson, J., & Willott, J. (2008). The role of cultural capital theory in explaining the absence from UK higher education of refugees and other non-traditional students. In J. Crowther, V. Edwards, V. Galloway, M. Shaw & L. Tett (Eds.), *Whither adult education in the learning paradigm?* (pp. 484–492). Edinburgh, UK: SCUTREA.

UNHCR (2007). Note on the integration of refugees in the European Union. Available from: http://www.unhcr.org/protect/PROTECTION/463b462c4.pdf [Accessed January 2009].

UNHCR (2008a). Statistical yearbook 2007, trends in displacement, protection and solutions. Available from: http://www.unhcr.org/cgibin/texis/vtx/home/opendoc.pdf?id=4981c4812&tbl=STATISTICS [Accessed January 2009].

UNHCR (2008b). Asylum levels and trends in industrialized countries. Available from: http://www.unhcr.org/statistics/STATISTICS/48f742792.pdf [Accessed January 2009].

United Nations (1951). Convention relating to the status of refugees. Available from: http://www.unhchr.ch/html/menu3/b/o_c_ref.htm [Accessed December 2008].

Willott, S. J., & Stevenson, J. (2006). An analysis of gendered attitudes and responses to employability training. *Journal of Vocational Education & Training, 58*, 441–453.

Willott, J., & Stevenson, J. (2008). Refugees: Home students with international needs. Paper presented at the annual conference of the British Association for International and Comparative Education, Glasgow, UK, 4–6 September.

Index